OXFORD ENGLISH MONOGRAPHS

General Editors

HELEN BARR   DAVID BRADSHAW   PAULINA KEWES
HERMIONE LEE   LAURA MARCUS   DAVID NORBROOK
FIONA STAFFORD

Acknowledgements

This book began as an Oxford D.Phil. thesis supervised by Helen Barr, and it would not have been possible without the support I received from the Arts and Humanities Research Council's Doctoral Award Scheme. I am also particularly grateful to my examiners, Thorlac Turville-Petre and Charlotte Brewer, for giving me a new sense of purpose and a wealth of suggestions. Both have since been enormously generous in offering help. More recently, the two anonymous readers for Oxford University Press have stimulated further improvements with their provision of copious, sympathetic commentary. Ariane Petit at the Press has been most helpful and efficient. I owe special thanks, too, to the original publishers of earlier versions of materials in Chapters 3, 4, and 6 for permission to publish these materials in revised form, and to Emily Steiner, Malcolm Godden, and Nicholas Rogers for providing me with opportunities to present my work in progress.

Many others have helped to guide me along the wikkede wey. Vincent Gillespie survived the supervision of my M.St. dissertation and was kind enough to take on a further term of supervisory duty in Michaelmas 2006. Anne Hudson responded generously to my requests for assistance. Andrew Cole's meticulous reading of an earlier version of Chapter 3 for publication in *The Yearbook of Langland Studies* not only benefited that material, but helped me to improve my whole dissertation. I also especially thank the dedicated staff of all the Oxford libraries that I have been fortunate to use.

Ralph Hanna's Oxford M.St. tutorials on *Piers Plowman* (co-taught with his legendary canine sidekick, Cruiser) first inspired me to work on this poem, and without his ongoing encouragement I would never have completed the project. My late friend and my fellow student in those M.St. tutorials on *Piers*, Debbie Marcum, was cruelly deprived by illness of the opportunity to bring her own projects to fruition. The research proposal which eventually turned into this work was written while I stayed at her home during Christmas 2004, and she remains an inspiration and example.

Most of all, I am grateful to have my wonderful family. I am confident that this book will inspire none of them to read *Piers Plowman*.

UNIVERSITY PRESS

Great Clarendon Street, Oxford OX2 6DP,
United Kingdom

Oxford University Press is a department of the University of Oxford.
It furthers the University's objective of excellence in research, scholarship,
and education by publishing worldwide. Oxford is a registered trade mark of
Oxford University Press in the UK and in certain other countries

© Sarah Wood 2012

The moral rights of the author have been asserted

First edition 2012

Impression: 1

All rights reserved. No part of this publication may be reproduced, stored in
a retrieval system, or transmitted, in any form or by any means, without the
prior permission in writing of Oxford University Press, or as expressly permitted
by law, by licence or under terms agreed with the appropriate reprographics
rights organization. Enquiries concerning reproduction outside the scope of the
above should be sent to the Rights Department, Oxford University Press, at the
address above

You must not circulate this work in any other form
and you must impose this same condition on any acquirer

British Library Cataloguing in Publication Data

Data available

Library of Congress Cataloging in Publication Data

Data available

Printed in Great Britain
on acid-free paper by
MPG Books Group, Bodmin and King's Lynn

ISBN 978–0–19–965376–8

Conscience and the Composition of *Piers Plowman*

SARAH WOOD

Contents

Acknowledgements	v
List of Abbreviations	ix
Note on the Text	xi
Introduction: Conscience and Personification in *Piers Plowman*	1
1. 'Who May Scape þe Sclaundre': Scandal, Complaint, and Invective in B 3–4	20
2. Penitential Texts and Vernacular Conscience in B 13–14	45
3. 'Ecce Rex': Conscience and Homiletic Discourse in B 19	70
4. 'To a Lord for a Lettre Leue to Haue': Lordly Conscience and the Friars in B 20	87
5. New Modes in the C Text: Clerical 'Suffraunce' and Vernacular Counsel	107
6. Conscience in the Versions of *Piers Plowman*	134
Conclusion: Conscience and the Composition of *Piers Plowman*	160
Bibliography	167
Index	181

List of Abbreviations

BIHR	*Bulletin of the Institute of Historical Research*
BRUC	Emden, A. B., *A Biographical Register of the University of Cambridge to 1500*. Cambridge: Cambridge University Press, 1963.
BRUO	Emden, A. B., *A Biographical Register of the University of Oxford to A.D. 1500,* 3 vols. Oxford: Clarendon, 1957–59.
CCSL	Corpus Christianorum Series Latina
EETS	Early English Text Society: e. s. Extra Series; o. s. Original Series; s. s. Supplementary Series
EHR	*English Historical Review*
ELH	*English Literary History*
ELN	*English Language Notes*
ES	*English Studies*
EWW	*The English Works of Wyclif Hitherto Unprinted*, ed. F. D. Matthew, EETS o. s. 74. London: Trübner, 1880.
JEGP	*Journal of English and Germanic Philology*
MED	*Middle English Dictionary*, ed. Hans Kurath et al., 13 vols. Ann Arbor, MI: University of Michigan Press, 1952–2001.
MP	*Modern Philology*
NM	*Neuphilologische Mitteilungen*
NQ	*Notes and Queries*
PL	*Patrologiae Cursus Completus... Series Latina,* ed. J.-P. Migne, 221 vols. Paris: Migne, 1844–64.
PMLA	*Publications of the Modern Language Association of America*
PQ	*Philological Quarterly*
PROME	*The Parliament Rolls of Medieval England,* ed. and trans. Chris Given-Wilson, Paul Brand, Anne Curry, Rosemary Horrox, Geoffrey Martin, Mark Ormrod, and Seymour Phillips, internet edition (www.sd-editions.com/PROME/home.html). Leicester: Scholarly Digital Editions and The National Archives, 2005.
RES	*Review of English Studies*
SB	*Studies in Bibliography*
SEWW	*Select English Works of John Wyclif,* ed. Thomas Arnold, 3 vols. Oxford: Clarendon, 1869–71.
SP	*Studies in Philology*

SPCK	Society for Promoting Christian Knowledge
TRHS	*Transactions of the Royal Historical Society*
YLS	*The Yearbook of Langland Studies*

Note on the Text

Any study that attempts, as this does, to deal with the implications of *Piers Plowman*'s existence as a series of versions inevitably faces certain methodological issues, not least of which is the choice of an edition. Because it is the only edition to present the full corpus of variants, I have adopted the Athlone *Piers Plowman*, and in general I have assumed the accuracy of its representation of what Langland wrote (though I also note some possible objections where these occur).[1] Of course, any critical edition must be but one interpretation of the manuscript evidence, and any conclusions about Langland's processes of composition and revision based upon it must therefore be provisional. But since the Athlone edition has proved especially controversial, some of the particular difficulties associated with its use should be indicated briefly here.

The Athlone B text is especially problematic, because George Kane and Talbot Donaldson's belief that the B archetype is seriously corrupted led them to extensive emendation by comparison with the other versions of the poem. Kane had not admitted the testimony of the parallel readings in the other versions when editing A, but by the time Kane and Donaldson came to edit B they assessed, and frequently felt able to emend, its archetypal readings against the parallel readings of A and C. Whilst in theory an unobjectionable procedure, its practical consequence, as Robert Adams shows, was that Kane and Donaldson were led to displace 'many strongly attested B manuscript readings'.[2] Kane and Donaldson assumed that agreement between A and C against B 'sets up a presumption that no revision occurred at that point'.[3] But as Adams and others have pointed out, the possibility cannot be entirely excluded that Langland changed his mind when revising from A to B only to change it back again when revising B into C.[4] As Thorlac Turville-Petre suggested in his review of the Athlone B text, nor are all of B's unique readings demonstrably inferior to

---

[1] *Piers Plowman: The A Version*, ed. George Kane (London: Athlone Press, 1960); *Piers Plowman: The B Version*, ed. George Kane and E. Talbot Donaldson (London: Athlone Press, 1975); *Piers Plowman: The C Version,* ed. George Russell and George Kane (London: Athlone Press; Berkeley: University of California Press, 1997). Unless otherwise stated, all references to *Piers Plowman* are to these editions. All translations from the Vulgate bible are from the Douay Rheims Version, revised Bishop Richard Challoner (Rockford, IL: Tan Books, 1989). Unless another source is given, all other translations are my own.
[2] Adams (1992; 31).
[3] *The B Version*, p. 76.
[4] Adams (1992; 54) and cf. Brewer (1996; 390).

those of AC.[5] In cases where Kane and Donaldson emend on the evidence of A alone, their B text is especially problematic. In numerous instances where a reading rejected as scribal in Kane's A text turned out also to be the reading of the B archetype (and sometimes of C as well), Kane and Donaldson emended in favour of the reading selected by Kane in editing A, giving the Athlone B text the unfortunate appearance of having been emended to protect Kane's edition of A.[6]

The Athlone B text, in particular, is therefore not an unproblematic choice as the basis of an investigation into the versions of *Piers Plowman*. Kane and Donaldson's belief that they could correct the presumptively corrupt B archetype by collation against the A and C versions means that their edition of B most likely under-represents the frequency of small-scale revision between the versions where the three texts run in parallel. However, this remains, I hope, a largely hypothetical problem here, since my own argument tends in any case to focus on larger configurations of character and action rather than the individual lection.

It should also be acknowledged here that the central hypothesis upon which the Athlone *Piers Plowman* is based—that there are but three versions, composed in the order A, B, C by a single poet—commands majority but not universal support. This traditional view of the number and sequence of the versions I share with the Athlone editors, but I discuss some of the opposing arguments as these arise.

[5] Turville-Petre (1977).
[6] See Adams (1992; 49–50) and Brewer (1996; 394–404).

Introduction

Conscience and Personification in Piers Plowman

Conscience has long attracted critical attention as one of the most interesting figures in *Piers Plowman*. He plays a central role in some of the most memorable scenes in the poem, from his debate with Meed in passus 3, to his banquet with Patience and the corpulent Doctor of Divinity in passus 13, all the way to the poem's final scene in which he presides over the collapse of Unity. He thus occupies an important position in Langland's exploration of major themes such as the relation of labour and reward, the value of academic versus more pragmatic forms of knowledge, the sacrament of penance and its contemporary abuses, and the role and responsibilities of the secular and ecclesiastical powers. He also engages interest in terms of the poem's formal design. Like other figures always perceived as central, Will and Piers, but unlike most of the poem's other personified figures, Conscience appears across passus and vision boundaries; like Piers, he seems to transform as his role is developed and refined during the course of the poem, from the accuser of Meed to the guardian of Unity. Moreover (unlike Piers), Conscience's role expands not only during the course of the narrative of the poem, but also during the course of Langland's revisions. Langland gives Conscience a prominent place in several of his new poetic initiatives in the C text, including his interpolation of the 'autobiographical' episode in C 5 and the new passages on Hophni and Phineas in the Prologue and on grammar in passus 3. In C especially, as Andrew Galloway has observed, Conscience commands 'a wide range of languages and levels of style, perhaps... the widest of any figure in the poem'.[1]

Yet the very diversity of his appearances that makes Conscience such an intriguing figure also manifests in particularly acute form the difficulties attending any interpretation of Langland's personified figures, and the

[1] Galloway (2006; 127).

critical problems—and possibilities—Conscience presents have not been fully answered in the literature. Many readers have sought to explain Conscience's place in the poem as an allegory for the operation of 'conscience' as defined by scholastic moral/faculty psychology. But such readings typically confine themselves to the first vision of the poem and encounter difficulties in responding to what seems to be the rather different presentation of Conscience in later parts of *Piers Plowman*. On the other hand, some readers have abandoned 'personification allegory' altogether as a useful mode of investigation, insisting that Conscience is no different from any other kind of character, and indeed that he undergoes a process of education or character development during the course of the poem.[2] This approach, however, raises obstacles of its own. As David Lawton observes in his study of the first-person 'subject' (dreamer/narrator/Will) of *Piers Plowman*, it in fact makes little difference whether one sees a faculty (in Will's case, *voluntas*) or a person whose psychological development is traced through the text. Both approaches seek in the poem's figures a unity and continuity that is at odds with the common critical perception of the work's diversity and discontinuity.[3]

The outlines of the 'faculty psychology' approach to Conscience in *Piers Plowman* were established in the 1930s by Greta Hort and T. P. Dunning, and although some details have been modified by subsequent criticism, the underlying assumptions have remained the same.[4] Medieval thinking on conscience inherited from Jerome's *Commentary on Ezekiel* a distinction between 'synderesis' and 'conscientia'. Bonaventure and other Franciscan writers defined conscience as an act of judgement directed towards behaviour, synderesis as a bias of the will towards the good. In the Dominican camp, Aquinas described synderesis as a disposition of the practical reason by which theoretical principles are known, and conscience as an actualisation, the application of knowledge of principles to particular cases.[5] Critics who have argued for the relevance to *Piers Plowman* of these scholastic discussions have not always agreed on whether or not Langland intends to maintain a distinction between synderesis and conscience. Nevertheless, a general consensus may be observed. According to this consensus, Langland's personifications fit, as Gerald Morgan puts it, 'within the bounds of scholastic orthodoxy',[6] and they reflect specifically the Dominican view of Aquinas rather than the Franciscan tradition exemplified by Bonaventure.

---

[2] Mary Carruthers (Schroeder)'s well-known essay manages to combine both approaches. See Schroeder (1970).
[3] Lawton (1987; 1–2).
[4] Hort (1938); Dunning (1980). Dunning's first edition was published in 1937.
[5] See Potts (1980; 1–60).   [6] Morgan (1987; 351).

So Hort argues, for instance, that Langland aligns himself with Aquinas's discussion in that 'Conscience does not teach of itself, it is guided by Reason'; hence Reason, not Conscience, preaches before the confessions of the seven deadly sins in the second vision (although this particular argument will not of course hold for A, where Conscience is the preacher).[7] More recently, Morgan has offered various modifications to the earlier discussions, but Langland's Conscience remains in his account 'the application of knowledge to act...distinguished by Aquinas from synderesis'.[8]

One might raise some objections to this broad consensus, however, and some indeed have been lodged in the past. Britton Harwood, for instance, points out that the claim that Conscience represents an act of the practical reason seems hardly borne out by the action of the poem itself: in the C-text version of the banquet scene in passus 15, Conscience continues to act even when Reason disappears.[9] One might also argue that since Langland never uses the term 'synderesis' or a readily recognizable translation, it is difficult to support the confidence with which Hort asserts that the poem reflects 'the Dominican view of synderesis, which makes it the highest principle of the cognitive part of the soul', as opposed to the Franciscan, which placed synderesis in the affective part of the soul, the will.[10] As David Aers suggested in his earlier work on *Piers Plowman*, Langland perhaps had in mind at the end of the poem a discussion of conscience such as that of Aquinas, in which conscience is both fallible and yet nevertheless binding.[11] Still, one must consider seriously the possibility that scholastic moral psychology is entirely irrelevant to the depiction of Conscience and Reason in passus 3–4 (that part of the poem most typically read in the light of scholastic discussions), and perhaps more generally as well. John Alford's authoritative account of Reason demonstrates that Conscience's partner in the first vision denotes eternal law rather than the *faculty* of reason or intellect (for which, according to Alford, Langland prefers the term 'wit' or 'kind wit').[12] Galloway's recent discussion of

---

[7] Hort (1938; 81–5). Dunning (1980; 24–7, 73) shares essentially the same view as Hort. Morton Bloomfield (1962; 167–9) also argued that Langland's Conscience was consistent with scholastic discussions of the faculty, although he suggested that in the later parts of the poem Langland turned to an older, monastic conception of Conscience.
[8] Morgan (1987; 353–6).
[9] Harwood (1992; 198, n. 3).
[10] Hort (1938; 72, 82). For the suggestion that Langland in fact adopts the *Franciscan* view of the faculty, see Clopper (1997; 187). I cite Bonaventure's view of conscience in connection with B 13 in Chapter 2, although without suggesting that Langland had necessarily read or intended to allegorize it.
[11] Aers (1980; 203–4, n. 69) and cf. Potts (1980; 54–60). In his more recent work, Aers has retracted his reading of Conscience in the 1980 title as a 'mistakenly individualist account of this power', but Aquinas remains central to his reading of the figure. See Aers (2004; 230, n. 138).   [12] Alford (1988b; 205).

Conscience likewise implies that the concepts of 'reason' and 'conscience' in legal discourse are probably more relevant to the first vision than Dominican moral psychology.[13] Indeed, I shall argue in Chapter 1 that in passus 3–4 Langland interrogates the meaning of 'conscience' as a legalism.

But while one might want to question some of the particulars of the Dominican 'faculty psychology' reading of Conscience, the assumptions that lie behind such accounts present a more significant difficulty. One might consider, to begin with, the only definitive discussion Langland offers of the faculty of conscience. This discussion is the well-known catalogue of the various parts of the soul provided by Anima in B passus 15, closely based on either Isidore of Seville's *Etymologies* or the pseudo-Augustinian *Liber de spiritu et anima,* and Englished as follows:[14]

> And whan I deme domes and do as truþe techeþ
> Thanne is *Racio* my riȝte name, reson on englissh;
> ...
> And whan I chalange or chalange noȝt, chepe or refuse,
> Thanne am I Conscience ycalled, goddes clerk and his Notarie.
>
> (B.15.27–28, 31–32)

Typically, this passage has been cited in support of the view that Langland intends, as elsewhere in the poem, to allegorize Dominican scholastic psychology.[15] But one must insist, first of all, upon the seemingly ad hoc nature of this account of Conscience. As Joseph Wittig points out, Langland himself adds to the material he would have found in Isidore and the *De Spiritu* the descriptions of Amor and Conscientia.[16] More importantly, one should also notice that the language in which Langland couches the English version of his (apparently improvised) Latin *'dum negat vel consentit'* (B.15.39*a*) is not the technical terminology of 'habitus' and 'potentiality' and 'disposition' found in a scholastic discussion such as that of Aquinas. 'Chepe' is merchant-talk, 'To engage in bargaining (either as buyer or seller)'.[17] 'Chalange' is a legalism, 'To accuse (sb), bring charges against' (a sense which chimes with the traditional view of Conscience as a legal witness or accuser) or 'To claim (sth.) as one's right, due, privilege, or property'.[18] Both words, in fact, return to the teeming picture of

---

[13] Galloway (2006; 103–4, 378).
[14] See Wittig, J. (1972; 212–13). Walter Skeat first made the identification with the passage from Isidore: see Skeat, *Parallel Text*, II, 215, n. 201.
[15] See Dunning (1980; 73–74) and Morgan (1987; 351).
[16] Wittig, J. (1972; 213, n. 9).
[17] *MED*, s.v. 'chepen', 1. Cf. Haukin's description of the activity at B.13.379.
[18] Alford (1988a, s.v. 'chalangen'). For Conscience as legal witness or accuser, see Alford (1988a, s.v. 'conscience').

contemporary life in the Prologue of the poem, and indeed 'challenging' associates Conscience, God's clerk, rather embarrassingly, with those clerks who have gone off to the bright lights to serve the king, 'and his siluer tellen,/In Cheker and in Chauncelrie chalangen hise dettes' (B.Prol.92–93).[19]

To seek in Langland's poem merely an English translation of Latin terminology from scholastic discussions of moral faculties is to lose, then, much of the texture of the poem, and therefore much of its meaning. Anima's discussion of Conscience provides a notable instance of the continuities Stephen Justice finds in Langland's diction 'between clerical vocabularies and social experience'; this is a poet who 'conferred on empirical language a conceptual utility and a public force'.[20] But in examining Langland's Conscience one ought to beware of putting the conceptual cart before the empirical horse. The case of Anima illustrates that Langland grounds his representation of Conscience as much in 'social experience', in institutional practices (such as law), as in scholastic philosophy. Ignoring the particular languages in which Langland composes Conscience (which do not, in my view, in fact include scholastic discussions of the faculty) estranges the poem from the historical and social situation that rendered those languages mutually intelligible to Langland and his audience.

My purpose here, then, is not to supply alternative sources or analogues for Langland's understanding of 'conscience' so much as to challenge the mode of reading that the accounts discussed above adopt. Arguments based upon faculty psychology tend to flatten the texture of *Piers Plowman* by assuming that pre-existing medieval discourse determines its meaning. These readings assume that Langland composes the poem to illustrate an already-extant proposition and that he revises to bring it more thoroughly into line with this prior formulation.[21] Such a procedure has received powerful critiques from readers such as Aers and David Lawton.[22] Nevertheless, this approach to reading Langland's personifications still regularly resurfaces, even where the unity and coherence it would seek seem belied by what one might otherwise observe about the form of the poem and the way personifications appear in it.

---

[19] 'Deme domes' in the description of Conscience's companion in the first vision, Reason (*Ratio*), is another legalism; see Alford (1988a, s.v. 'demen'), 'To preside over a court... to judge'.

[20] Justice (1996; 132, 137).

[21] See Whitworth (1972; 4). Whitworth argues that Langland revised the three versions of his poem to reflect his 'increasing knowledge of and attention to theological distinctions'.

[22] Aers (1975; 78 and *passim*); Lawton (1987).

Similar assumptions about personifications underlie, for instance, Nicolette Zeeman's recent discussion of Will's serial encounters with personifications in the poem's third vision. Personifications in Zeeman's account are paraphrasable—and by implication stable—units of meaning. Clergy and Scripture, for instance, 'refer primarily to "Christian teaching and its texts"'; Thought 'represents the preliminary cogitative functions of the soul'; Wit 'is reason and represents the proper development of *thou3t*'. Zeeman's method is one of concordance, collating analogues, often references to Latin cognate terms ('studium' for Dame Study, for instance). Her procedure implies that Langland's personifications derive their meaning primarily from their prior existence in other texts. The 'eclecticism' of Langland's portrayal of 'will', volition/affect, for instance, is 'underpinned by an instability in the medieval distinction between the rational will and less rational appetites and passions'.[23]

Robert Frank's essay 'The Art of Reading Medieval Personification-Allegory' articulates more explicitly the approach that Zeeman has recently adopted.[24] In *Piers Plowman*, Frank argues, personifications are 'abstractions' and 'have only one meaning'.[25] Personifications therefore 'mean what their names say they mean'; 'a personification cannot stand for a concept or quality other than that expressed by the name of the personification'; 'The names of the characters are all-important, for it is through them that the allegorist states a good part of his meaning. The reader must therefore understand what a character's name means, for that will be the key to his speeches and actions'.[26] Studies of the personifications in *Piers Plowman* have, implicitly, followed Frank's lead by proposing ever more numerous alternative 'meanings' for the 'names', without in general challenging these basic assumptions about reading personification.[27]

---

[23] Zeeman (2006; 132, 103, 105, 65–6). Compare also the approach of Harwood (1990) and (1992; 91–2).

[24] Frank (1953).

[25] Frank (1953; 237).

[26] Frank (1953; 243, 244, n. 23, 245). A more sophisticated account of the names and naming of personifications may be found in Paxson (1994). While Frank is confident that personifications 'have only one meaning', Paxson shows that *Piers Plowman* 'explores ways in which the name of a personification figure can work to represent a being that may be more than a monolithic concept' (1994; 131–3).

[27] For notable exceptions see Griffiths (1985), esp. p. 59, and, more recently, Scanlon (2007). Scanlon critiques the conventional view of allegory in which it 'becomes the stable signifier par excellence' (p. 3). In *Piers Plowman,* he argues, 'the allegorical and the mimetic constantly converge, and the trope which most characteristically effects that convergence is personification' (p. 22). The figures in the poem are often personifications and characters at the same time (p. 24)—not simply the allegorical 'name' which Frank emphasizes.

As Lawton has noted in his discussion of the first-person subject of the poem, the approach Frank represents—an approach that Lawton rejects as an 'economy of one voice per name'—tends inevitably to discover unity and continuity even where readers are in other ways sensitive to the poem's apparent discontinuities.[28] So Zeeman, for instance, emphatically rejects the idea of 'development' in *Piers Plowman* as conventionally understood. She favours a kind of *via negativa* of failure and loss. Yet she nevertheless finds 'a real sense of development and sequence as *thou3t* leads to *wit*, the rational power that will preside over the exploration of *studie*, *clergie* and *kynde*'.[29] The shape of Langland's poem conforms, in her argument, to a prior ontological reality.

Zeeman seems not to notice, though, that the sense of progression that she identifies can only be projected onto the text retrospectively. Her argument about 'development' belies the disarming impression readers receive at many points in the poem that Langland is somehow making it up as he goes along. One might cite, for example, the abrupt appearance, at the beginning of a new passus, of Dame Study: 'Þanne hadde wyt a wyf þat hatte dame studie' (A.11.1). This moment typifies many other similarly abrupt arrivals, such as the unannounced appearance, head-first, of Peace with the petition that turns the debate of passus 3 into the trial scene of passus 4, or the first entrance of the poem's title figure: '"Petir," quaþ a plou3man and putte forþ his hed' (A.6.25). Whatever the actual degree of Langland's forward planning at the transition of A passus 10–11, 'þanne' as a connective introducing the next personification presents cognitive 'development' or progression as mere narrative happenstance. One might compare Langland's use of 'Thanne kam' as the introduction of the newly-inserted account of the 'founding of the commonwealth' in the B-text Prologue (B.Prol.112). Commenting on Langland's use of this phrase, Galloway argues that it 'suggests both a perpetual condition of surprising arrivals or unpredictable changes of topic, and a continuous processional movement to the whole... It is a form of dramatic parataxis, requiring the reader to supply the syntax of interpretation, association and connection to other moments in the poem'.[30] As the introduction of a new personification, the phrase as used at A.11.1 suggests that the process of composition itself with its 'continuous processional movement' and 'unpredictable changes of topic' is as important to Langland's personifications as any ontological reality. It implies that Langland's personifications can be understood only as the outcomes of the compositional process that creates them, rather than by reference to any prior external formulation.

[28] Lawton (1987; 2, 10).   [29] Zeeman (2006; 84).
[30] Galloway (2006; 115).

Of course, in one sense Zeeman and others are right to emphasize the essentially static nature of personifications as compared with other kinds of 'characterization'. Personification represents the ultimate development of a perspective in which human 'character' is felt to express unchanging moral characteristics. Warren Ginsberg points out that where in antiquity a person 'was identified by his ruling passion, in the Middle Ages the disposition itself came to be depicted'.[31] In some fundamental way, personification precludes character 'development' in any real sense; a personification can only be an exemplification, as Frank argues, of its name.

However, such a wholly static view of Langland's personifications seems at odds with that radical instability readers encounter when reading personifications in the poem. As Lavinia Griffiths shows, Langland's personifications have a 'disconcerting habit of appearing in different guises'; 'even once a proper name has been established, there can be no confidence that it will continue to refer to the same person'.[32] It is difficult to reconcile a conventional understanding of personification allegory with the impression that Conscience's multiple appearances in the poem unsettle the stability that such an understanding would presuppose. Unsurprisingly, then, a number of readings eschew 'personification allegory' altogether, or at least in part, as a valid mode for describing Conscience and his role in the poem. These readings look for continuity not in the abstract concept to which the name of a personification refers, but in a unified self or subject, a 'character' who undergoes development or education in the poem. Traugott Lawler, for instance, treats Conscience's progress in the poem as if it were fully naturalistic 'development' or education. His behaviour in the final scenes of the poem, in this reading, is explained as his having learned Christian tolerance and openness from Patience in B passus 13–14.[33]

But possible objections to such readings again emerge, perhaps most conspicuously in Elton Higgs's essay on Conscience and Piers. Like Lawler, Higgs draws upon the language of spiritual or moral/psychological 'development', describing a 'spiritualization of his character', 'amazing developments' in the characters, the 'lesson' that both Conscience and the Dreamer must learn, and even Conscience's behind-the-scenes education by Patience, which happens somewhere between B 14 and his reappearance in B 19.[34] I shall return to this last point below in order to show how

---

[31] Ginsberg (1983; 78); cf. the discussion in Aers (1975; 50).
[32] Griffiths (1985; 22, 6).
[33] Lawler (1995; 100, n. 23): 'what Conscience learns from Patience sticks'. Cf. also Schroeder (1970; 19–20).   [34] Higgs (1993; 124, 145, 134).

Langland's narrative and compositional process tempts Higgs to read the text in this way. But first one may notice from Higgs's essay that the notion that Langland's characters undergo any *actual* development or 'human education' begins to founder when one tries to locate precisely where or when in the poem's narrative such a development could have occurred. As Anne Middleton argues, 'it is difficult to reconcile the single event, which often ends with a rupture or abrupt shift of ground, with a plot which is said to record a progression'.[35] Tellingly, Higgs must locate Conscience's 'education' or transformation precisely in the non-narrated/able, the 'behind-the-scenes' between appearances: 'Although we see nothing more of Conscience in this section, it is clear that he is under instruction from Patience, and when he reappears in passus XIX... he is ready to accept... the more radical spiritual approach to establishing God's order that is spoken of by Patience here'.[36] Our sense of the characters' 'development' seems to be predicated precisely on something that doesn't actually happen in the narrative.

The most obvious example, of course, is the 'spiritualization', to use Higgs's term, of Piers's character after he tears the pardon and resolves to reduce his labour. The scene signals the beginning of the poem's consistent heightening of Piers's symbolic significance, but this 'development' seems to necessitate precisely the virtual disappearance of Piers as a 'real person'. His decision to exchange his literal plough for a metaphorical one is never converted into any subsequent narrative development;[37] it seems, indeed, to preclude it. As Middleton observes, 'a gain in figurative coherence is purchased at a marked and lamented loss to narrative continuity'.[38] Likewise, none of the 'developments' that befall Conscience at the level of story give rise to further narrative which would encourage one to believe that the *action* of one vision produces any real effect on that of the next. Except in the C text, where he appears at the head of passus 5 in the judicial role to which he was promoted in passus 4, Conscience's promotion to royal service at the end of passus 4 is apparently non-narratable. Conscience's decision to embark on pilgrimage with Patience in B 13 does initiate further narrative, in which the pilgrimage is indeed undertaken. But this apparently dramatic transformation produces the *narrative*'s development, not Conscience's own. Langland almost immediately relegates Conscience to the periphery of the scene as Patience takes centre stage. The dream issues not in Conscience's further development (he disappears silently somewhere in passus 14), but in another of the poem's reiterations: at the end of the passus, Haukin collapses into tears, recalling both

[35] Middleton (1982a; 92).
[36] Higgs (1993; 134).
[37] Cf. Burrow (1993; 11–12).
[38] Middleton (1982a; 108).

Conscience's own penitential gesture and the originary one made by Piers in B 7. The inconclusive or unresolved episode, which Middleton suggests is the poem's basic narrative unit, frustrates narrative progress and with it the possibility of any real character 'development'. The poem is 'not quite a story, nor a collection of shorter ones'.[39]

We read, then, the development of the *poem*, not of 'characters',[40] and here *Piers Plowman* is typical of much medieval characterization. Critics such as A. C. Spearing have recently argued powerfully that the representation of subjectivity within medieval narratives need not imply a coherent 'subject consciousness' or character of whom psychological or moral development might be expected.[41] As Ginsberg points out, the speeches and actions of medieval characters 'define not only themselves but central themes or principles of structure or signification as well'.[42] One might feel, then, that those aspects of *Piers Plowman* that readers such as Higgs have described in terms of realistic character development would be better explained as the effects of a particular mode of composition than as the reflection of single, consistent 'selves' within the poem. *Piers Plowman* might thus be taken as representative of Spearing's 'textual subjectivity', in which formal properties of the text 'encode' subjectivity but nevertheless do not require a consistent centre of self or a singular subject/character.

Ginsberg's discussion of medieval narrative provides further insight into those formal properties that might 'encode' subjectivity in the way that Spearing describes. Ginsberg highlights two related narrative techniques: 'parataxis' and 'literary typology'. Parataxis customarily refers to the juxtaposition of clauses, often without conjunctions, but Ginsberg employs the term to describe the element of 'disjunctiveness' in medieval works, even those that present a continuous narrative.[43] Langland's unique formal innovation, composition by an accretive series of discrete dreams rather than a single dream, constitutes a special form of parataxis. As Galloway notes, parataxis demands that the reader discern the connections between different parts of the poem.[44] Narration via discrete dreams, as a disjunctive, paratactic mode, frustrates the narrative continuity of which actual character 'development' might be predicated. Nevertheless, it invites the reader to supply connections between the serial appearances of a particular character, to read, retrospectively, a process of character 'development' such as Higgs finds between Conscience's appearances in

---

[39] Middleton (1982a; 92).
[40] Higgs (1993; 123) is much closer to the mark when he says at the beginning of his essay that 'the alternating appearances of Conscience and Piers and their interaction with the Dreamer focus our attention in various ways on major themes of the poem'.
[41] Spearing (2005; 15 and *passim*). [42] Ginsberg (1983; 5).
[43] Ginsberg (1983; 83–4, 90). [44] Galloway (2006; 115), quoted above.

B 13–14 and B 19–20. Ginsberg's analysis helps explain why we read the 'development' of the poem's characters as taking place 'behind the scenes' (as in the case of Conscience's supposed education by Patience between B 14 and B 19). As he argues concerning the related technique of 'literary typology', parataxis is an 'essentially dramatic' mode: it resembles the 'before and after' pictures presented in successive scenes in Shakespeare's plays, the way the characters seem to 'undergo development offstage'.[45]

The second narrative device that Ginsberg describes—'literary typology'—also helps shed light on some aspects of the narrative of *Piers Plowman* that have seemed typically 'Langlandian'. If, in the medieval study of the bible, typology seeks correspondences between actual events in history, 'literary typology' converts this understanding of history into a narrative structure in which the prefigurations and foreshadowings that the exegetes found in the events of the Old Testament are rechannelled into the use of type scenes, repeated actions in which one character's experiences reflect those of another, and/or which develop thematic correspondences between scenes and actions.[46] Readers of *Piers Plowman* invariably notice its tendency towards reiteration, such as the way B 19 revisits, in a different key, the ploughing of the half-acre of the second vision. In B 19, too, Conscience presents a discussion of the life of Christ as 'knight, king and conqueror' that translates into the realm of the divine law the themes of his earlier debate with Meed in passus 3. Similarly, the action of which Conscience is the centre in B 13 both recapitulates Piers's penitential gesture in B 7 and foreshadows the conclusion of the poem where Conscience will once again embark on pilgrimage. Here one might also usefully recall Middleton's argument for *Piers Plowman*'s affinity to romance narration.[47] Middle English romances frequently baffle readers seeking 'realistic' character-driven motivations for events, because the narrative is driven not 'internally' by the characters' motivations, so much as 'externally' by the pre-existing narrative forms of the genre. Type-scenes, repeated configurations of character and action, reinforce certain central, underlying themes: love and marriage, exile and return, and so on.[48] Repetition, as Middleton shows, also constitutes Langland's basic compositional method; by this means, he transforms the short *chanson d'aventure* form into a long episodic narrative composed of multiple adventures, each at an abrupt angle to the previous one.[49] Conscience's importance

---

[45] Ginsberg (1983; 97).   [46] Ginsberg (1983; 96).
[47] Middleton (1982b; 114–18).
[48] See Benson (1976; 73–80) and Wittig, S. (1978; *passim*).
[49] Middleton (1982b; 114–18). Zeeman (2008) has recently discussed the parallels between *Piers Plowman* and Grail romances, which have a similarly 'recursive' narrative form.

to *Piers Plowman,* then, lies not in his taking part in exemplary action that glosses his own name. Rather, he contributes to the development of the poem's themes and structure through repeated type-scenes. His various appearances do not display actual character development: the themes of knighthood and kingship, for instance, are 'spiritualized' in B 19, not Conscience himself (as Higgs implies).[50] The poem's argument develops, not the character.[51]

Ginsberg's analysis of parataxis and literary typology helps to show, then, that specific aspects of the poem's narrative and mode of composition 'encode' subjectivity, to use the term recently employed by Spearing, without implying a single subject or consciousness of whom a moral or psychological development might properly be predicated. The effect of character 'development' in *Piers Plowman* is produced by the poem's accretive, repetitive narrative, its ceaseless transformation of repeated themes, its ongoing shifts of argument and of discursive mode.

Similar arguments have been proposed before in connection with the figure of Piers and the first-person narrator of the poem. Aers has pointed out that Piers is much less 'out there' as a character than has often been suggested. Rather, the successive appearances of Piers provide the focus for the development of the poem itself (or, in Aers's reading, Will's own development). And, of course, Aers recognized that these observations about Piers could be extended to other figures in the poem, arguing that

> It is not enough merely to say with Frank that the 'names' of personifications are necessarily 'all-important'. The writer may be much more concerned with context and shades of meaning than such a generalisation allows.[52]

Lawton puts forward a similar argument, drawing on modern French theories of the subject. He goes one further than Aers in denying even to the poem's narrator that actual *development* that Piers projects. As grammatical subject, Will

> responds differently in different discourses, according to the semantic role offered by whichever is the dominant context at a given time: as dreamer when the conditions of the dream-vision prevail, as prospective penitent when the discourse of penance is strong, as a scholar in scholarly contexts, and so on.[53]

---

[50] Higgs (1993; 140) says that Conscience speaks with 'newly acquired spiritual wisdom' in B 19.
[51] On the narrative structure of the poem and its relationship to typology, see also Kirk (1972; 181–2) and more recently Tolmie (2006; 124–5).
[52] Aers (1975; 119–20 and see p. 79).
[53] Lawton (1987; 14).

Much the same thing can be said about Conscience, and by extension any other character who appears more than once in the poem.[54] As I discuss in Chapters 1 and 2, Conscience appears differently, for instance, in B 13–14, which is dominated by penitential discourse, than he does in the first vision of the poem, which I shall argue is inflected by literary modes used in contemporary discussions of court controversy. In the chapters that follow, then, I will be suggesting that effects that others have mistaken for character 'development' actually result from Conscience's re-presentation within a series of different discourses in the course of the poem's composition. By attending to the variety of contemporary discourses within which Conscience is composed, I hope to restore a sense of the embeddedness of the figure and of the poem in a particular social and historical context that made these discourses intelligible to Langland and his audience. This historical context has often been overlooked in accounts of the personifications exclusively interested in academic theology.

The series of discourses that I will be discussing in this book do not only indicate Conscience's embeddedness in particular social and historical contexts, however. They also represent, as I have been implying, a series of stages in a compositional process, in the 'history' of the poem. Langland initially conceived Conscience within what may have begun as a rather limited project, a single-vision satire in the manner of alliterative precursors like *Wynnere and Wastoure*.[55] Conscience 'develops' as a figure within a series of new contexts as one discourse gives way to another in the progress of the poem's developing argument and expanding design. But of course, the compositional process that effects Conscience's transformation extends beyond a single version of *Piers Plowman*. Conscience changes not only during the composition of the series of different episodes in various modes that makes up the single version, but also during the composition of the poem as a series of versions. The versions of *Piers Plowman* form a single continuous narrative, with each version in dialogue with the previous one. In this ongoing argument, extending through the versions as well as through the single version, a figure like Conscience undergoes a continuous 'development'. If Conscience appears to transform in the course of the single version as the poem's themes are developed within a variety of different discourses, so too he appears to change

---

[54] Tolmie (2006; 134–7) offers provocative suggestions in this direction in her brief discussion of Conscience. As she points out, Conscience's own speech on Christ as knight, king and conqueror in B 19 suggests that the same person might appear differently in different contexts.

[55] For the suggestion that the poem began as a single-vision satire in this mode, see Hanna (1996; 232).

with the development of these themes through the course of the composition of the versions of the poem.

In one sense, then, although his argument for actual 'development' or 'education' in the characters seems doubtful, Higgs doesn't take his observation that the 'cumulative experiences' of Conscience and Piers 'provide a basic structure for the poem'[56] quite far enough. In Langland's reiterative, accretive mode of composition, the themes and arguments within which a character is presented become a cumulative set of 'experiences' upon which their subsequent appearances, *in the later versions* as well as in later episodes within the single version, are predicated. The revisions to Conscience's role in the versions of *Piers Plowman* make best sense if these versions are read, like the episodes of the single version, in sequence and from end to end—rather than, as typically, simply in parallel-text.

In the following chapters, then, I shall be tracing Conscience's 'development' within the compositional process of *Piers Plowman*: firstly, within the composition of the B text (as the first long version of the poem) from a variety of different discourses and secondly as the figure is subsequently transformed during Langland's composition of C. In the first four chapters, I discuss how Conscience is transformed during the course of B by means of his re-presentation within a range of discourses: debate, slander, and invective (Chapter 1), vernacular penitential discourse (Chapter 2), sermons (Chapter 3), and antimendicant polemic (Chapter 4). In Chapter 5, I examine the new discourses, including Latin grammar, that Langland introduces in his presentation of Conscience in C, and explore the effect these have upon the character. In Chapter 6, I show how these revisions to Conscience's role in C continue the 'development' of Conscience within a process of composition begun in B. I demonstrate how the changes to Conscience in the C text can be explained in terms of the compositional 'history' of the poem—that is, in terms of the earlier developments to Conscience's role during the composition of B. The Conclusion offers some reflections on the variety of Conscience's roles in the poem in all versions and on the significance of the particular combination of contemporary discourses with which Langland composes this figure.

The chapters that follow begin with B, as the first full presentation of Conscience. But as a prequel to the argument of subsequent chapters, the one appearance of Conscience in the A text that does not also appear in B first deserves a closer look. In A, as in both the subsequent versions of the poem, Conscience makes his initial appearance in the first vision. But in A, unlike in B, he also appears briefly in passus 5, preaching

[56] Higgs (1993; 145).

before the confessions of the seven deadly sins. In this fleeting second appearance, Conscience morphs from courtly character to preacher as Langland expands the poem by the addition of a second vision in an entirely different mode from the first. Langland excises Conscience from passus 5 when he revises this part of the poem in the B text. Nevertheless, Conscience's appearance in A 5 remains part of his cumulative textual 'experience' within the composition of the poem. His compositionally later appearances in B 19 and C5, as I will demonstrate, implicitly respond to his earlier presentation in A 5. The three scenes and Conscience's development within them, then, may be traced as a single compositional sequence, beginning with A.

Conscience's role in the A text is confined virtually to a single episode: the debate with Meed in passus 3 and 4. Langland creates him, initially, within the context of a single-vision poem in the mould of *Piers Plowman*'s alliterative progenitors, such as *Wynnere and Wastoure*. As I discuss in more detail in the next chapter, Conscience's first appearance in the poem is shaped by the generic conventions that this part of *Piers Plowman* shares with 'topical' debate poems like *Wynnere*. The A text, however, is not, of course, a single-vision poem. Although A is that version most closely resembling earlier alliterative social satire, its third vision, beginning Will's spiritual quest for Dowel, marks a decisive break with such earlier works. Yet in a sense the most dramatic break with literary precedent occurs earlier, at the beginning of A passus 5. Here, with Will waking from a tentative harmony (as the king and his knights head for church, A.5.1–2), Langland takes the first step towards his unique enterprise of the multi-vision poem. For Will awakes only to fall almost immediately asleep again (A.5.8), and thus initiates the process that will extend the first vision of A into a multi-vision and multi-version poetic enterprise.

That upon falling asleep Will should see not only the field of folk of the Prologue that began his first vision, but also Conscience, one of its protagonists, here carrying a cross and preaching a sermon (A.5.11), is thus highly significant. If the third vision of A represents a fragmentary effort at recasting the poem in an entirely new and much more ambitious mode, the reappearance of Conscience here represents a brief (it lasts only approximately thirty lines) but significant effort in sustaining a character across the boundaries between visions in a multi-vision sequence. Conscience here escapes not only from the boundaries of visions but also from the courtly context in which he appeared in the preceding vision. His companions in the first vision, the king and his knights, cross the passus but not the vision boundary. Nevertheless, their activity at the beginning of the new passus, as they head for mass, also refigures Conscience when he reappears in the subsequent vision. Conscience's transformation here from knightly to ecclesiastical garb is effected by a shift of context as the political discourses of the first vision make way for the sermon and confession sequence of the second.

Conscience's role in this second vision is highly circumscribed. He is superseded by Repentance at line 43, and he will not appear in the A text again, except as dimly reflected, as an ordinary common noun, at the frustrated end of its third vision (A.11.309). In the B text Reason, not Conscience, preaches the sermon in passus 5. The change is perhaps appropriate: not because of any presumed hierarchy between the two figures as psychological faculties, but because Reason, not Conscience, has carried the day and won the approval of the king.[57]

Conscience, then, is written out of passus 5 in the revision from A to B. But as I will show in subsequent chapters on B and C, each version of the poem, like each vision, provides the basis for further development in the next, and this excision does not represent an utter elimination from the ongoing poetic creation. Although Langland revises A.5.1–42 in B so as to exclude Conscience, he apparently recalls and develops this scene when Conscience reappears much later in the B version. In the B text, Conscience's appearance in A 5, preaching 'wiþ a cros' before the assembled people, is displaced into a much later part of the poem, the episode that begins B passus 19 and the poem's seventh vision. Here *Piers* appears 'wiþ a cros bifore þe comune peple' (B.19.7); Conscience, at Will's request, provides instruction on the significance of the spectacle, including the icon that links the two scenes, the cross (B.19.199). Both sequences represent the dream-displacement of collective and individual acts of worship. In A passus 5, where Conscience preaches before all the people with the bishop's cross, the dream sermon both picks up where the previous dream left off (the king and court going to mass) and grows out of the prayers Will mutters (in imitation?) as he falls asleep. In B passus 19, Conscience's instruction, which ends in an act of collective worship (the masses venerate the appearance of the holy spirit with him at the end of the 'sermon'), functions as the substitute for the church service through which Will is sleeping. In both sequences, too, a speech by Conscience is ultimately followed by a ploughing scene.

The new episode in B passus 19 is also related to other changes in the B text. These revisions reinforce the probable connection of the scene to A passus 5. They involve the expansion of the sermon and confession sequence in the B version of passus 5. The revision of this sequence is

---

[57] Lawler (1996; 153) points out that the preacher should be Reason, since the sermon in passus 5 develops his *impossibilia* speech in passus 4.

accomplished, as Alford has shown, largely by the expansion of the organizing role of Repentance.[58] Particularly significant in this context is the newly elaborated climax to the confession sequence. In the A version, the sequence ends with the doubtful fate of Robert the Robber, to whose contrite tears are joined the 'Wepynge & weylyng' (A.5.252) of the assembled folk, collectively crying for grace; Robert appeals to the thief who was crucified with Christ. This rather muted conclusion is developed in B to a much more impressive climax. Repentance's expanded role in bringing the confessions to their proper conclusion means that the sequence ends not with the doubtful fate of Robert and the cry of the people, but with a collective prayer, offered by Repentance on behalf of all the assembled. Langland expands upon Robert's brief allusion to the crucifixion, providing an account of the crucifixion, resurrection, and harrowing of hell. The sequence ends in joyful clamour, with the horn of hope sounding *Beati quorum remisse sunt iniquitates* (B.5.507) to link the penitential gesture of the people with the central event of Christian history, which has procured the forgiveness of their sins.

The obvious parallels between the two scenes suggest that the composition of the new episode in passus 19 is closely connected to the revision of passus 5 in the B version. One might cite, in particular, the climax of Conscience's 'sermon'. Here, he urges Will to kneel and sing:

> Thanne song I þat song; so dide manye hundred,
> And cride wiþ Conscience, 'help vs, crist, of grace!'
> (B.19.211–12)

Repentance, too, had urged all to kneel (B.5.477), and had related the events of Easter, which have been dramatized in passus 18. The conclusion of the sequence in passus 5 is more or less the same in both A and B texts:

> A þousand of men þo þrungen togideres,
> Cride vpward to Crist and to his clene moder
> To haue grace to go to truþe.
> (B.5.510–12; cf. A.5.251–54)

But the parallel between the sequence in passus 5 and the episode in passus 19 is much clearer in the revised B version, where the song of the saints that mingles with the cry of the people in passus 5 echoes in the Easter bells from which Will awakes in the transition from passus 18 to 19. The original lines in A 5, that is, have provided the basis for both the B-text revision of the same episode, and the recapitulation of it at a point

---

[58] Alford (1993).

far removed in the narrative, B 19.[59] Conscience's instruction to Will in passus 19 has its origin in that part of the A text which, although revised in B so as to exclude him, nevertheless provides the original precedent for his role as preacher/teacher, his first figuration in the terms of homiletic discourse.

Equally, the materials in B 19 themselves provide the basis for subsequent revision in the first two visions of the C text. The beginning of B 19, in which for the first time Conscience provides Will with direct instruction, along with the corresponding direct encounter with Reason in B passus 11, provides, perhaps, the precedent for the appearance of the two figures as Will's interlocutors at the beginning of C passus 5.[60] The roles Conscience and Reason perform in B 19 and 11, respectively, motivate, at least in part, Langland's rectification of an omission in the AB versions of the second vision: the lack of any direct encounter with an 'authoritative' figure.

These three related episodes in A 5, B 19 and C 5 may serve as a preliminary illustration of my argument that Conscience only appears to 'develop' within the compositional process of the poem. In them, one may trace Conscience's 'development', both within the composition of the single version from a series of different discourses, and during the writing of *Piers Plowman* as a series of versions that form a single cumulative composition.

Within the first two visions of A, as I have shown, Conscience appears to transform as he moves from the knightly royal counsellor of the first vision to the preacher of the second. But Conscience 'develops' only in so far as his role is here extended to straddle the two different discourses of the two first visions. Just so, as I show in the following chapters, his more extensive 'development' in the course of the B text is the effect of his re-presentation within a wide variety of contemporary modes of writing.

If Conscience appears to change as he is re-presented within different discourses during the composition of the first two visions of the A version, so he also seems to develop during the course of the serial versions,

---

[59] For the parallel between the prayer which closes Conscience's speech in B passus 19 and the concluding prayer in B.5.510–12 and A.5.251–54, see also Barney (2006; 133). Lawler (1996; 167, n. 20 and 178) argues that Repentance's prayer in B 5 was written only after Langland had at least drafted passus 19–20. For the suggestion that Langland first wrote the B continuation (passus 11–20) and only afterwards returned to revise the existing A portion, see Gwynn (1943) and Hanna (1993; 12–13).

[60] Although the encounter with Reason and Conscience in C 5 also develops another moment elsewhere in the previous version, Will's own discussion of the sinful Christian as a runaway 'cherl' pursued and brought to account by Reason and Conscience (B.11.127–36). Both the manorial allegory and the theme of penitence in this sequence reappear in the interrogation in C 5.

as Langland continues to rework the themes and dramatic settings within which he presented the figure. Conscience's appearance as a preacher in B 19 logically follows upon his similar role in A 5, while his position as Will's direct interlocutor in C 5 in turn develops his original appearance as the Dreamer's instructor in B 19. Each version is just one more re-vision added to the cumulative sequence of dreams of the single version. The versions form a single narrative or dialogue, in which Conscience appears to undergo a continuous transformation within the development of the poem's argument.

The revisions thus reveal a logic that remains invisible if they are read only in relation to the immediately parallel passages in earlier versions. The versions of *Piers Plowman* must also be read in sequence, from end to end. As I have argued, Langland apparently recalled Conscience's appearance early in the A text when composing B 19, a passage which lacks any direct parallel in A. The continuities that I have traced between Conscience's turns in A 5, B 19, and C 5 imply that Langland revised with *all* this figure's previous appearances in mind, not just the directly parallel passages in earlier iterations of the poem. When I return to the subject of versions in the final chapter of this book, I will show that just as B 19 draws upon the earlier representation of Conscience as a preacher in A 5, so, too, changes to the way Conscience appears in the C version draw on the cumulative logic of *all* his previous appearances in the B text, the later version in dialogue with the earlier. Elizabeth Kirk has suggested that 'The key to almost every enigma of *Piers Plowman* is a sense of its sequence'.[61] One needs to take seriously this claim both when reading any single version of the poem (and the role of the characters within it), and also by approaching the serial versions as an intelligible sequence. With this sense of sequence in mind, the first chapter now turns to Conscience's first appearance in *Piers Plowman* B.

---

[61] Kirk (1972; 11).

1
'Who May Scape þe Sclaundre': Scandal, Complaint, and Invective in B 3–4

In the A and B texts of *Piers Plowman,* Conscience is originally summoned into being by the king as his own knight, 'cam late fro biyonde' (B.3.110). The local and 'topical' flavour of that introduction ('cam late') resists easy assimilation to the terms of scholastic discourse (what 'conscience' might mean in medieval moral psychology). Academic discourse is not, in fact, the dominant mode of the first vision (it presides over the third and the beginning of the fourth, to which I turn in the next chapter). To reduce Conscience to the categories of scholastic faculty discussions is to overlook Langland's decision to present him, at least initially, within a courtly and judicial setting as part of the poem's interrogation of Meed's effects on the contemporary realm.

On the other hand, the apparently topical reference of much of the debate between Conscience and Meed in passus 3 has stimulated many readings that interpret the first vision as a more or less straightforward fictionalization of particular historical events. Walter Skeat first suggested (although with some hesitation) that Meed might represent Alice Perrers, the notorious mistress of Edward III.[1] Subsequent efforts at dating the versions of the poem typically assumed that the debate between Conscience and Meed is a form of political allegory, the actants of which should be identified with specific historical individuals. Oscar Cargill took up Skeat's suggestion about Alice Perrers in emphasizing what he called the 'historical side of the poet's allegory'. Arguing that Conscience represents the Black Prince and Meed Alice Perrers, Cargill urged readers to use the account of the Good Parliament of 1376 in Thomas Walsingham's *Chronicon Angliae* 'as a key to the poem, for passage after passage of the chronicle tears the shroud from the verse'.[2] Ber-

---

[1] Skeat, *Parallel Text,* II, 31, n. 9. Skeat suggested that although the A-text pre-dated Alice's rise to notoriety, Langland may have perceived the resemblance between Perrers and Meed when he came to revise his poem in the B version, amplifying the description of Meed's extravagant dress accordingly.   [2] Cargill (1932; 357, 362).

nard Huppé, attempting to demonstrate that the A text was written in 1370–76, claimed that the description of Meed at Westminster in the first vision 'has significant points of contact with the story of Alice's rise to power as it is related in the "scandalous" chronicles'. It is, he asserted, 'clear that Langland had Alice Perrers in mind when creating Lady Meed'. Huppé suggested that during the course of the debate, Meed tries to identify Conscience with 'his worldly representative, John of Gaunt': 'Conscience is the executive virtue, the virtue of statesmen... John was the active head of the English government after 1370'.[3] J. A. W. Bennett subsequently demolished much of Huppé's evidence for a later dating of the A version of the poem. But he accepted the identification of Meed and Perrers. Bennett argued that the existence of records pointing towards a relationship between the king and Alice as early as 1364 supported an earlier dating of the A version.[4] More recently, John Selzer has revived the view that the poem was composed 'in the context of the Good Parliament of 1376'. Although he rejects Huppé's identification of Conscience with John of Gaunt, Selzer maintains the emphasis on topical allusion by arguing that Conscience represents Edmund Mortimer, the Earl of March, whose steward Peter de la Mare led the Commons' attack on the court in 1376.[5]

Recent scholars tend to show more circumspection than earlier readers when it comes to suggesting that Langland might have written such thinly veiled 'topical allegory'. Nevertheless, possible allusions in the first vision to historical events of the 1360s and 1370s, and particularly to Alice Perrers, still exert a strong hold on the critical imagination. Stephanie Trigg, for instance, has found in Perrers 'a well-documented life that reveals a complex dialectic with the story of Meed', arguing that both Perrers and Meed demonstrate a powerful female agency in their manipulation of the courts for their own ends.[6] Clare Lees implicitly makes the same connection between Meed and Perrers, even as she argues that 'as "woman"... Meed would have little power to represent her legal interests' in the way that Langland implies. In Lees's presentation, Perrers becomes an exceptional rather than a representative figure.[7] Some of the most recent work on this part of the poem continues to read the debate between Conscience and Meed in similarly 'topical' terms. Kathleen Kennedy, for instance, draws parallels between Perrers and Meed in order

---

[3] Huppé (1939; 51, 49, 61, and n. 46).
[4] Bennett (1943a; 566 and n. 1). Bennett asserts that 'there can be little doubt that Lady Meed embodies certain aspects of the character of Alice Perrers'.
[5] Selzer (1980). Selzer rejects Huppé's earlier identification of Conscience with John of Gaunt on the basis that Gaunt was the enemy of the Commons, not its champion.
[6] Trigg (1998; 11, 22).   [7] Lees (1994; 115).

to analyse the medieval practice of maintenance.[8] Likewise, although ultimately retreating from any suggestion that the action of passus 3–4 might directly represent historical events around 1376, Matthew Giancarlo nevertheless makes much of the 'striking' parallels between Perrers and Meed as women of uncertain parentage and marital status who enjoy connections and influence at court: 'In the biased chronicle accounts of Perrers' activities, a more compelling real-life figure of "Meed" could scarcely have been found.'[9]

Of course, Langland's contemporaries may well have been inclined to read the first vision of the poem in topical terms themselves, and comparisons between Langland's personified figures and particular historical persons certainly do not lack interest and value. As Anna Baldwin points out, Langland presents in Meed not only a personification of reward but also 'a lifelike example of the kind of person who used such reward in order to sustain and protect an unscrupulous retinue'.[10] As a conspicuous contemporary instance of just such a person, Perrers offers a useful point of comparison for the activities of Meed, and for the responses such activities elicit in both Perrers's/Langland's contemporaries and in critics of *Piers Plowman*.[11] Nevertheless, efforts to link Conscience and Meed with specific historical events or people inhibit a more nuanced reading of the first vision in much the same way as attempts to identify Langland's personifications with fixed terms borrowed from scholastic discourse. Conscience (like Meed) is first and foremost a literary creation, and the very proliferation of alternative names put forward as his 'real-life' referent provides eloquent testimony to the difficulties inherent in the attempt to identify him with any particular historical individual.

Specific allusion to particular events or people such as the Good Parliament and Alice Perrers is not, in fact, what makes the first vision of *Piers Plowman* seem 'topical'. Nor does Langland merely share with Thomas Walsingham's account of the Good Parliament in the *St Alban's Chronicle*, and with parliaments more generally, an interest in 'representation' ('who gets to speak, both in and for a community'), as in Giancarlo's account.[12]

---

[8] Kennedy, K.E. (2006) and (2009; 65–76). I quote from the slightly fuller presentation of the material in the earlier article.

[9] Giancarlo (2003). This article appeared in revised form as Giancarlo (2007; 179–208 (p. 184)). References are to Giancarlo (2007) except where there are substantive differences in the earlier version.

[10] Baldwin (1981; 27).

[11] The feminist readings by Lees (1994) and Trigg (1998) offer a compelling account of the mesmerising effect of the symbolic equation of woman/money in both Perrers and Meed.

[12] Giancarlo (2003; 137). Cf. Giancarlo (2007; 199), where the author says that using a parliamentary setting in passus 3–4 allowed Langland 'to find a speaking voice through the *poetical* representation of *political* representation'.

Rather, Langland shares with Walsingham's history, and with other histories, particular *modes* of representation. In composing the debate between Conscience and Meed in passus 3, Langland draws on a set of closely related literary and textual modes: debate, invective, slander, and complaint. These modes are also used to analyse court controversies in contemporary histories (including Thomas Walsingham's account of the Good Parliament), as well as in a variety of other texts, including petitions, parliamentary documents, and debate poems. Langland's presentation of Conscience and Meed strikes the reader as 'historical' or 'topical' because he employs the same literary modes that historians like Walsingham incorporated into their own narratives about contemporary events. Indeed, as I will demonstrate, the *forms* or modes used by the speakers themselves become one of the explicit subjects of the debate between Conscience and Meed.

DEBATE AND INVECTIVE

As Ralph Hanna has recently argued, the exchange between Conscience and Meed in passus 3 should be read 'against its alliterative background, as a debate'. The conventions of debate poetry govern this passage throughout, as they do many others within the poem.[13] In debate poems, opponents are typically evenly matched and equally self-interested, their arguments proceeding from particular biases or personal animosities. Thomas Reed shows that in the Middle English debate poem most proximate to *Piers Plowman*, *Wynnere and Wastoure*, Winner's extended attack on Waster's feasting reveals in its accumulation of lavish detail 'as much envy as righteous indignation'.[14] Similarly, as Hanna has suggested, one might see Conscience's attack on Meed as motivated by enmity,[15] perhaps by an envy much like Winner's. Meed, at least, suggests as much when she points out that Conscience has himself enjoyed meed in the past:

---

[13] Hanna (2005; 262). For the ubiquity of the debate mode in *Piers Plowman* and for Langland's knowledge of the conventions of particular sub-genres, such as Wit and Will debates, see Bowers (1986; 176–80). Both Hanna and Bowers point out that several manuscripts give the title of the work as 'Dialogus Petri Plowman', which suggests that some readers, at least, identified debate as the most prominent literary mode in the poem.

[14] Reed, Jr (1990; 282). For the description of the feasting, see *Wynnere and Wastoure*, in *Alliterative Poetry*, ll. 330–65.

[15] Hanna (2005; 265). Hanna explains this animosity within the specific context of the Good Parliament of 1376. But even if Langland had particular historical events in mind, Conscience's enmity towards Meed is pre-determined by the generic conventions of the debate mode.

> Wel þow woost, Conscience, but if þow wolt lie,
> Thow hast hanged on myn half elleuene tymes,
> And ek griped my gold and gyue it where þee liked.
> Whi þow wraþest þee now wonder me þynkeþ.
>
> (B.3.180–83)

The French wars in which Conscience has apparently participated as a knight (cf. B.3.189–208) undoubtedly would have required 'meed' in order to motivate and reward the king's armies. Meed seems to imply that Conscience has dispersed 'meed' among his own retinue during his military ventures. Her implication of Conscience in 'meedish' behaviour should serve to qualify, as Hanna has argued, the conventional reading of this scene, in which Conscience is viewed as an 'unerring' speaker, one immune from Langland's critique.[16] In *Piers Plowman*, as typically in the debate form, neither speaker may be assumed 'unerring'. Each is shown to be limited by his or her individual bias.

Throughout the exchange, Meed cunningly manipulates Conscience's arguments to serve her own cause in a way that is also typical of debate poetry. In *The Owl and the Nightingale*, for instance, the Nightingale seizes upon the Owl's claim that she has only one talent, singing, and turns it to her own advantage by claiming that this one skill is better than anything the Owl can do: 'Betere is min on þan alle þine'.[17] Similarly, Meed turns Conscience's argument that she is 'commune as þe Cartwey to knaue and to alle' (B.3.132)—that reward attaches itself to all men without regard to their individual worth—into a claim for her universal utility. Meed can right wrongs as well as cause them (B.3.177, 'Ther þat meschief is most Mede may helpe') and, as Meed goes on to argue in the lines I quoted above, Conscience himself has apparently relied upon her in the past.

Meed's effort to implicate Conscience in the same abuses that she practises herself follows another pattern typical of debate poetry. According to this pattern, two apparently opposing principles or speakers are eventually revealed to be mutually dependent. In *Wynnere and Wastoure*, the two debaters finally emerge as complementary principles, each apparently equally vindicated by the judgement of the king. In the final ruling offered by the king in *Wynnere*, wartime pillaging in France (to be practised in the future by Winner) and conspicuous consumption at home (to which the king despatches Waster) emerge as two sides of the same

---

[16] Simpson (2007; 39) calls Conscience 'an unerring lexicographer, whose concern is to define and fix the senses of words according to moral criteria'; contrast Hanna (2005; 265). The conventional view, in which the debate between Conscience and Meed represents relatively uncomplicated venality satire, was established by Yunck (1963).

[17] *The Owl and the Nightingale*, l. 712.

economy: 'Þe more þou wastis þi wele, þe better þe Wynner lykes'.[18] Likewise in *Piers Plowman,* Meed suggests that Conscience is merely Winner to her Waster, acquiring by pillage ('winning') in France what Meed will 'waste' in 'gifts' to her retinue:

> Wiþouten pite, Pilour, pouere men þow robbedest
> And bere hire bras at þi bak to Caleis to selle
> ...
> Hadde I ben Marchal of his men, by Marie of heuene!
> I dorste haue leyd my lif and no lasse wedde
> He sholde haue be lord of þat lond in lengþe and in brede,
> And ek kyng of þat kiþ his kyn for to helpe,
> The leeste brol of his blood a Barones piere.
>
> (B.3.195–205)

In Meed's presentation, Conscience has simply failed adequately to perform the Winner-like role appropriate to his status as king's knight: to generate the income that, dispersed as 'meed'/gifts, supports and binds the retinue. As typically in the debate mode, clear moral distinctions between the speakers persistently threaten to collapse.

The exchange between Conscience and Meed thus becomes what Andrew Galloway calls 'a war of mutual redefinition'.[19] In *Wynnere and Wastoure,* as both Reed and Britton Harwood have noted, the identities of the two speakers are redefined during the course of the poem, so that each comes to mean something quite different from that which their allegorical names and their initial presentations imply. At the end of the poem, Winner, who earlier condemned Waster's lavish feasting, is sent to grow fat at the papal court. Conversely, Waster, who formerly lavished his goods on others (cf. his 'rowte wele rychely attyrede', l. 270) will now live it up in London at others' expense.[20] During the progress of the poem, as well, each of the debaters attacks the basis of the allegorical identity of their opponent. Waster hints that Wanhope is Winner's brother (l. 309), arguing that his obsessive anxiety over his worldly goods and his lack of enjoyment of life tends towards despair.

Similarly, as Galloway indicates, in the debate between Meed and Conscience, 'the very basis of their allegorical personification is an issue throughout'.[21] All readers notice, of course, that Conscience aims to redefine 'Meed' during the course of their debate. Theology had earlier objected that Meed denotes good as well as bad reward, since Amends was her mother (B.2.115–33). Conscience similarly distinguishes two kinds

---

[18] *Wynnere and Wastoure,* in *Alliterative Poetry,* l. 495.   [19] Galloway (2006; 288).
[20] Harwood (2004; 170). Harwood's essay was revised as Harwood (2006). Cf. Reed (1990; 285).   [21] Galloway (2006; 288).

of reward, one licit and one illicit. But he restricts the meaning of the personification 'Meed' to the latter, the 'Mede mesurelees þat maistres desireþ' (B.3.246). In Conscience's presentation, Meed becomes not a personification of reward in its potential for both good and evil, but the embodiment of reward put to bad use.[22]

But Conscience's own signification, as well as Meed's, is also questioned and complicated during the course of the debate. In its most basic sense, 'conscience' derives from 'con-scire', to 'know with'. It denotes knowing something along with someone else, and thus being able to bear witness to it.[23] Conscience as a legal witness or accuser has a venerable history that goes back to the Bible.[24] Quite in contrast to those readings that insist on Langland's interest in the distinctions of academic theology, Langland could have found Conscience acting in the capacity of a legal accuser (here at the last judgement) in, for example, the popular English poem for 'lewed' folk, *The Prick of Conscience*.[25] Langland may, however, also have had more specific contemporary legal developments in mind. In the later fourteenth century, the court of Chancery, which would come to be known as a 'court of conscience', was beginning to hear cases in which either a remedy was unavailable at common law or where the usual common-law remedy could not be obtained because of circumstances such as maintenance or the poverty of the petitioner.[26] Langland may be thinking of this emerging 'court of conscience' when he has Conscience complain that Meed's practice of maintenance prevents the poor receiving a fair hearing at law: 'For pouere men may haue no power to pleyne þou3 hem smerte' (B.3.168).[27] Perhaps equally pregnantly for this part of *Piers Plowman*, 'conscience' also occurs in legal discourse in the 1346 Ordinance for the Justices, where it appears as the special property of the king:

> Because that, by divers Complaints made to Us, We have perceived that the Law of the Land, which We by our Oath are bound to maintain, is the less well kept and the Execution of the same disturbed many times by Maintenance and Procurement, as well in the Court as in the Country; We, greatly moved of Conscience in this matter [Nous meuz grandement de

---

[22] See the useful discussion in Stokes (1984; 121–7). [23] Potts (1980; 2).
[24] For which, see Alford (1988a; s.v. 'conscience').
[25] *The Pricke of Conscience*, ll. 5440–53.
[26] See Avery (1969); Baldwin (1981; 22–3); Hanna (2005; 272); and Galloway (2006; 103).
[27] Although the fact that Langland makes Reason, not Conscience, Chancellor at the end of passus 4 in the C text might make one hesitate over any definite association of Conscience with the court of Chancery. As Kennedy points out, too, most historical research into the development of Chancery relies on fifteenth-century documents, so that 'any discussion of the fourteenth-century Court of Chancery...must remain speculative'. See Kennedy, K.E. (2003; 180 n. 9).

conscience]... have ordained these things following... We have commanded and utterly defended, That none... shall... take in hand Quarrels other than their own, nor the same maintain by them nor by other, privily nor apertly, for Gift, Promise, Amity, Favour, Doubt, nor Fear.[28]

This ordinance, of course, addresses the issue central to the action of passus 4. In this part of the poem, Langland explores the problem of 'maintenance', taking in hand legal actions not properly one's own. In order to protect her retainer Wrong from proper legal penalty, Meed attempts to intervene in the case of Peace v. Wrong, by offering Peace a 'Gift' or 'present' (cf. B.4.95). As Hanna indicates, the language of the ordinance provides at least one of the personages of the first vision, the 'Dread' (or 'Fear') who warns False and his companions to flee at the end of passus 2. This ordinance possibly also suggested to Langland the figure of Conscience as an opponent of Meed's maintenance as well.[29]

The basic identity that Conscience assumes in this part of the poem, then, is that of (legal) witness or accuser. Nevertheless, his meaning, as well as Meed's, is contested during the course of the debate. Meed, as Galloway shows, attacks Conscience on the basis of his figuration as a king's knight, and therefore as a representative of failed royal policy. One might note especially her comments on the king's abandonment of his claim to France, B.3.206–7: 'Cowardly þow, Conscience, conseiledest hym þennes/ To leuen his lordshipe for a litel siluer'.[30] Meed's attack implies an attempt to redefine 'cowardly' Conscience as mere pusillanimity—perhaps even something like the 'conscience and tendre herte' of Chaucer's Prioress.[31] Langland's use of the debate form makes his allegory in this part of the poem particularly complex and unstable. One cannot securely fix Conscience as any single historical figure, or as a psychological faculty, or even as a term within legal discourse, because Langland is working within the conventions of a genre in which the allegorical significances of the debaters' names are under continual reassessment.

Nor are the difficulties and objections raised by the two speakers conclusively resolved by their debate. Langland here again follows the

---

[28] *Statutes of the Realm*, I, 20 Edward III, cc. 1–4, 303–4.
[29] Hanna (2005; 301, n. 26). As William Dunham indicates, 'maintenance' was one of the chief responsibilities expected of the lord by his retinue, and as the support of the retainer in his 'right' was not unlawful. However, as is apparent from Meed's intervention in the case of Wrong (and cf. B.2.196, 3.167, 3.247), 'maintenance' became synonymous with the protection of one's retinue at the expense of the legal rights of others, and in 1346 maintenance as the 'taking in hand' of 'Quarrels other than [one's] own' was outlawed. See Lewis (1945); Dunham, Jr (1955; 50, 67); and McFarlane (1981). For discussion of 'maintenance' in *Piers Plowman*, see Baldwin (1981; 24–31); Alford (1988a; s.v. 'maintenaunce', 'maintenen'); Hanna (2005; 264–7); and Kennedy, K.E. (2006).
[30] Galloway (2006; 286–8, 308).   [31] Chaucer, *The Riverside Chaucer*, I. 150.

conventional contours of debate poetry with its 'aesthetics of irresolution', as Reed describes it. Judgement, in such poems, is invariably deferred to some future time outside the boundaries of the text. In *The Owl and the Nightingale*, the debate concludes with the avian protagonists agreeing to seek the judgement of Master Nicholas of Guildford, but this judgement remains unpassed as the poem ends. In *Wynnere and Wastoure*, the king delivers a whimsical provisional judgement on the two debaters that avoids making any actual choice between them. The serious matter of the king's wars, and his future recalling of Winner and Waster to wartime service, is postponed to some future date.[32] Similarly in *Piers Plowman*, Langland's king impatiently calls time on the dispute at the beginning of passus 4, but refuses to choose between the debaters: 'Ye shul sauȝtne, forsoþe, and serue me boþe' (B.4.2). Langland's king tends to confirm Meed's argument for the mutual dependence of the two speakers, and resolution is deferred until the end of passus 4. Here, where the debate mode gives way to a trial scene, Conscience finally finds vindication as Meed's deleterious effects on the law are proved in open court.

The conventions of debate poetry do not govern only the larger form of the exchange between Meed and Conscience, however, in the blurring of distinctions between the two protagonists and the resistance of the conflict to definitive closure. The generic expectations of debate also shape the language of this conversation. The exchange between Conscience and Meed frequently turns not so much on the terms of scholastic or even legal debate as on the trading of insults, a feature which points to the affinities between this part of Langland's poem and the 'flytyng' or 'ritualised [exchange of] invective'.[33] Conscience (who reveals his misogynist streak particularly at the end of passus 3, where he heaps scorn on Meed as untutored female reader) apparently finds a series of sexual slanders levelled at Meed not beneath his dignity (B.3.122–33). Meed is generally rather more ingratiating, but 'pilour' stands out in her riposte to Conscience quoted above (B.3.195), a word glossed by George Kane as a 'term of abuse'.[34] The insult possesses a particular sharpness, given that Conscience is meant to be a knight. During the Hundred Years' War 'pillars' were typically the lower-class servants of knightly soldiers, responsible for bringing back prisoners and plunder to their masters in occupied castles. One historian of the war notes that 'to call a man a *pillar*, in those days, was a serious insult which often led to bloodshed'.[35] One of Laurence

---

[32] Cf. Reed (1990; 261).
[33] For flytyng, see Reed (1990; 100–5). Reed distinguishes flytyng from debate because it lacks 'a provision for formal judgment'.
[34] Kane (2005; s.v. 'pilour'); see also *MED*, s.v. 'pilour', 1.
[35] Wright (1998; 57).

Minot's alliterative poems celebrating the military achievements of Edward III uses the term 'pelers' to refer to the Scots at Bannockburn, indicating something of its pungency as a term of opprobrium in the period.[36] Meed isn't mincing her words.

This kind of invective is typical of debate poems. Waster calls Winner 'þou wriche' and 'caytef' (ll. 424–25), while Winner abuses 'wrechide Wastoure' as a 'false thefe', 'cayteffe', and 'wikkede weryed thefe' (ll. 326, 228, 233, 242). The emphasis Meed places on Conscience's physical weakness, taunting him for how he 'Crope into a Cabane for cold of þi nayles' (B.3.191), echoes similar insults about bodily attributes in *The Owl and the Nightingale*, where the Nightingale mocks the Owl for its short body and big head (ll. 73–74).

The insults displayed during the exchange between Conscience and Meed in passus 3 resemble not only the exchanges of abuse found in other literary debates, however, but also contemporary histories such as Thomas Walsingham's account of the Good Parliament in his *St Albans Chronicle*. Walsingham's chronicle has been described aptly by a modern historian as a 'scandalous narrative...an exceptionally rich and unrestrained account inspired by a lively desire to pillory the misdeeds of the Duke of Lancaster and his courtier friends'.[37] In his representation of the court crisis of 1376, Walsingham draws on the modes of personal invective and popular slander in much the same way as *Piers Plowman* and other debate poems. Langland and Walsingham do not necessarily allude to the same events and people, but both write 'scandalous' narratives about troubles at court.

SCANDALOUS NARRATIVES: WALSINGHAM'S CHRONICLE AND LANGLAND'S DEBATE

The resemblance between the 'scandalous' mode of Walsingham's history and the debate between Conscience and Meed emerges most clearly through a comparison of some of the more sensational accusations exchanged by Meed and Conscience with Walsingham's account of the slanders associated with John of Gaunt, William Latimer (the king's chamberlain), and Richard Stury (a knight of the chamber) around the time of the Good Parliament. Walsingham recounts, for instance, that popular opinion condemned William Latimer (who had played a central role in the renewed war effort between 1369 and 1375) as an adulterer, a plunderer (or in Meed's terms, a 'pilour'), and as a cowardly soldier:

---

[36] Minot, *The Poems of Laurence Minot*, ii, l. 15.
[37] Holmes (1975; 1).

Lord Latimer's reputation was deservedly blackened in many respects. He was certainly as adulterous as the duke himself, a slave to greed and to a love of plundering... He was no better a soldier than the duke himself, for his body could not endure hunger or cold.[38]

One might compare this accusation with Meed's claims that Conscience not only plundered the poor but was a poor soldier, unable to endure the physical privations of battle:

> Ac þow þiself sooþly shamedest hym ofte;
> Crope into a Cabane for cold of þi nayles;
> Wendest þat wynter wolde han ylasted euere;
> And dreddest to be ded for a dym cloude,
> And hastedest þee homward for hunger of þi wombe.
> Wiþouten pite, Pilour, pouere men þow robbedest.
>
> (B.3.190–95)

The charges of adultery cited against Latimer find an echo, too, in Conscience's accusations about Meed's lechery: 'She is tikel of hire tail, talewis of tonge' (B.3.131). For both Conscience and Walsingham, indeed, sexual slander figures prominently as a mode of attack. Besides castigating William Latimer for his adultery, Walsingham retails several lurid stories about John of Gaunt, who was rumoured, according to the chronicler, to have taken prostitutes to his marital bed.[39] Walsingham apparently also takes pleasure in recounting the slanders against John of Gaunt during his dispute with the city of London over its legal privileges in 1377. During this spat, the prince's arms were hung upside down in the street, to signal that he was a traitor, and libellous verses were posted around the city to 'damage [his] reputation, and make his name all the more hateful' ('unde... fama ducis denigraretur, atque nomen eius magis detestabile haberetur'). Perhaps somewhat closer to the forms of invective found in the first vision of *Piers Plowman*, Walsingham also repeats the rumour that Gaunt was the illegitimate son of a Flemish woman.[40] This personal attack on its victim's parentage resembles the charge earlier in *Piers Plowman* (one refuted by Theology) that Meed is illegitimate.

Also similar in mode to the court slanders reported by Walsingham are the rather more 'political' accusations made by both Conscience and Meed. One of Conscience's most provocative claims about Meed sees

---

[38] '[F]ama domini de Latymer est multipliciter denigrata merito. Erat utique non secus quam dux adulteriis deditus, auaritie seruiens et rapinis...Ad bella plus quam ipse dux nichil ualuit, nam corpus eius impatiens inedie et algoris extitit'. Walsingham, *Chronicle*, pp. 26–7. The 'duke', of course, is John of Gaunt, persistently castigated by Walsingham as an adulterer.

[39] Walsingham, *Chronicle*, pp. 12–13.

[40] Walsingham, *Chronicle*, pp. 90–1, 98–9, 60–1.

her implicated in the death of the king's father and in the poisonings of popes:

> Youre fader she felled þoru3 false biheste,
> Apoisoned popes, apeired holy chirche.
>
> (B.3.127–28)

This charge Meed hotly denies:

> For killed I neuere no kyng, ne counseiled þerafter,
> Ne dide as þow demest; I do it on þe kynge.
>
> (B.3.187–88)

Indeed, Meed seems to implicate Conscience as well. Galloway finds in Meed's rejoinder, 'ne counseiled þerafter', a covert counter-accusation, an implicit suggestion that *Conscience* counselled or colluded in the former king's murder.[41] As typically in Middle English debate poems, counter-accusation follows accusation, each side adopting the opponent's arguments to advance their own cause.

Walsingham reports some similar and equally inflammatory claims in his account of rumours current at the time of the Good Parliament. During the course of the parliament, Walsingham informs his reader, it was reported that Richard Stury had attempted to stir up hostility against the knights who led the attack in Parliament by telling the king that they were taking steps to depose him, and 'to do with him as they had previously done with his father'.[42] In a similar vein, Walsingham accuses John of Gaunt of contemplating murder in order to secure his own succession to the throne in the last days of Edward III's reign. Following the death of the Black Prince, Walsingham claims, Gaunt would stop at nothing in trying to secure the throne at the expense of the Prince's young son Richard:

> He reflected upon the age of the king, whose death was close, and the youth of the son of the prince, whom, it was alleged, he contemplated poisoning if he could not himself attain the throne any other way.[43]

These lurid allegations about conspiracies to murder are very similar in manner to the accusations made by both Conscience and Meed in passus 3 of *Piers Plowman*. But the two writers need not necessarily share any specific historical reference. Conscience's claim that Meed

---

[41] Galloway (2006; 318).
[42] '[U]t facerent cum eo, sicut quondam fecerant cum patre suo'. Walsingham, *Chronicle*, pp. 30–1.
[43] '[C]onsiderauit enim senectutem regis, cuius mors erat in ianuis et iuuentutem filii principis, quem, ut dicebatur, impotionare cogitabat, si aliter ad regnum peruenire non posset'. Walsingham, *Chronicle*, pp. 38–9.

killed the king's father most likely alludes to the deposition and murder of Edward III's father, Edward II. But the threat that the fate of Edward II might be repeated was not made only in 1376 when, as Walsingham reports, Richard Stury claimed that the Commons was planning to depose Edward III. The same threat was also redeployed a decade later. In 1387, Richard II put a series of questions to a panel of judges concerning the proceedings of the parliament of 1386, which had established a commission to undertake the functions of government. The ninth question asked: '[H]ow ought he to be punished who in parliament moved that that statute be sent for whereby King Edward [II], son of King Edward and great-grandfather of the present king, was in time past adjudged in parliament'.[44] Edward II's murder clearly retained political currency over a long period of time, so that Conscience's and Meed's apparent allusions to it need not have any particularly local reference. And of course, as Myra Stokes points out, Conscience's accusation that Meed has killed a king also makes a more general claim in any case: Meed 'destroys the very sources of rule, social and spiritual'.[45] The similarity between Walsingham's history and the accusations about regicide exchanged by Conscience and Meed is a formal similarity. It need not imply that, as Cargill had argued, *Piers Plowman* was being recited in the streets of London as the Good Parliament sat.

ALICE PERRERS, THE ROLLS OF PARLIAMENT, AND RUMOUR AT COURT

Not only Walsingham's chronicle, but also another contemporary historical document shares with the first vision of *Piers Plowman* a 'scandalous' mode in its representation of court rumour and court factions. This history is the account in the Rolls of Parliament of the trial of Alice Perrers in 1377.

The first vision of *Piers Plowman* shows Meed carefully establishing alliances around the court. Together with earlier sequences in passus 2, Meed's conference with her friar-confessor in passus 3 provides a dramatic recreation of the spread of rumour and the formation of factions at court. The friar promises to carry Meed's messages and specifically to help to destroy Conscience (or his reputation), here imagined as a member of an opposing court faction:

---

[44] '[Q]ualiter est ille puniendus qui in parliamento movebat quod mitteretur pro statuto per quod rex Edwardus filius regis Edwardi proavus regis nunc erat alias adjudicatus in parliamento'. *Westminster Chronicle*, pp. 200–1). [45] Stokes (1984; 117).

> 'I shal assoille þee myself for a seem of whete,
> And ek be þi baudekyn and bere wel þyn erende
> Amonges clerkes and kny3tes Conscience to felle'.
>
> (B.3.40–42)

One may assume from the same conversation Meed's familiarity with rumour and slander at the court: she tells her friar-confessor that lechery is the sin most readily forgiven, for 'Who may scape þe sclaundre, þe scaþe is soone amended' (B.3.57). Earlier, before Meed's arrival in London in passus 2, Sothness overtakes her party on the road to bring news of its approach to Conscience at the court:

> Sothnesse sei3 hem wel and seide but litel,
> And priked forþ on his palfrey and passed hem alle
> And com to þe kynges court and Conscience tolde,
> And Conscience to þe kyng carped it after.
>
> (B.2.189–92)

In these scenes preceding the debate between Meed and Conscience, Langland builds a picture of the spread of gossip at the court and of how court factions could be formed and manipulated.

The account of Alice Perrers' trial in the Rolls of Parliament presents a very similar picture of the networks and alliances at court, and gives a similar prominence to court rumour and slander. In 1377, Perrers was brought to trial in Parliament. She was accused on two counts. Firstly, it was claimed that she had used her influence with the king to prevent Sir Nicholas Dagworth investigating charges against her husband, William Windsor, whose misrule as lieutenant of Ireland had resulted in numerous complaints. Secondly, she was accused of persuading the king to restore to Richard Lyons certain property that had been confiscated at the time of his impeachment during the Good Parliament.[46]

Among those testifying at the trial was John of Gaunt, who swore that although he had not been present when Lyons was pardoned, he was sure that Perrers had been behind it. Philip la Vache, a knight of Edward's chamber (and possibly the 'Vache' addressed in the envoy of Chaucer's poem 'Truth'), testified that he had not heard Alice talking about the Dagworth affair to the king, but that she had spoken of it around the court. As for the Lyons affair, again he had not actually witnessed the incident, but it was commonly said around the court that Perrers was responsible. John Beverley, an esquire of Edward's chamber, recorded that he had not heard Alice speak to the king on either matter. Nevertheless, he too believed that she was behind it all.

---

[46] The account here is based on Given-Wilson (1986; 142–6).

The episode of Perrers's trial as recorded in the Rolls of Parliament offers a representation of court factions and alliances much like the one found in the first vision of *Piers Plowman*. As I have indicated, Langland shows Meed attempting to secure herself supporters around the court before facing Conscience in passus 3. Conversely, the account of Alice's trial illustrates that in 1377, she had been abandoned by men such as Alan Buxhill, a chamber knight, and John of Gaunt. Both of these men had made Perrers gifts in the past, but nevertheless both testified against her in 1377. Moreover, the account of Perrers's trial in the Rolls of Parliament, like Langland's debate between Conscience and Meed, gives particular prominence to court rumour and slander. Conscience's invective against Meed draws on what appears to be, as I discuss further below, popular clamour against her crimes (since he implies at B.3.168 that other complainants would come forward were it not for the fact that she prevents them from getting a fair hearing at law). In just this way, the evidence against Alice recorded in the Rolls of Parliament without exception derives from hearsay and gossip. None of the witnesses supplied first-hand testimony. Rather, each voiced the popular rumours and slanders of the court. Chaucer might well, one imagines, have urged la Vache to 'Flee fro the prees and dwelle with sothfastnesse'.[47] But in Langland's poem, 'Sothness' (who brings news of Meed's arrival) himself dwells within the 'prees' of the court.

One should not, perhaps, be at all surprised to find in these parliamentary records an interest in gossip, slander, and invective, a focus that *Piers Plowman* and other debate poems share. As Reed shows, debate poetry is closely related to legal and parliamentary (as well as academic) debate. All of these kinds of texts may well have been read in similar social situations by the same audiences.[48]

'ÞOW HAST FAMED ME FOULE': PETITION AND SLANDER

The debate between Conscience and Meed resembles parliamentary documents and historical narratives not only in the way it incorporates slander and invective, but also in its use of the related, but rather more formal,

---

[47] 'Truth', in Chaucer, *The Riverside Chaucer*, l. 1.
[48] Reed (1990; 21, 88–96). I discuss the implications of Langland's use of the debate mode for the possible audience of *Piers Plowman* in the Conclusion. Langland's interest in slander in the first vision is part, of course, of a broader preoccupation throughout *Piers Plowman* with deviant speech. For discussion of Langland's use of the discourse on 'sins of the tongue' drawn from pastoral literature, see Craun (1997).

legal modes of complaint and petition (forms perhaps more consistent with the idea of 'conscience' as legal accuser/witness). Conscience begins his attack upon Meed with a list of charges that resembles in form other contemporary complaints about abuses of the law and the activities of over-powerful royal favourites:

> In trust of hire tresor she teneþ wel manye.
> ...
> She dooþ men lese hire lond and hire lif boþe;
> And leteþ passe prisoners and paieþ for hem ofte,
> And gyueþ þe Gailers gold and grotes togidres
> To vnfettre þe fals, fle where hym likeþ.
> ...
> She may neiȝ as muche do in a Monþe ones
> As youre secret seel in sixe score dayes.
> She is pryuee wiþ þe pope, prouisours it knoweþ;
> ...
> Ther she is wel wiþ þe kyng wo is þe Reaume.
> (B.3.124, 136–39, 145–47, 153)

As a comprehensive list of charges, Conscience's speech here resembles the textual form of a petition, perhaps something rather similar to the 'bille' presented by Peace in passus 4 (B.4.47ff).[49] One may find many of the charges Conscience here elaborates echoed in petitions recorded in the Rolls of Parliament. The abuses perpetrated by gaolers (B.3.138), for instance, were also cited during the Good Parliament, when the Commons complained that the innocent were being wrongfully imprisoned and forced to pay fines to secure their release.[50] The complaint that Meed can do as much in a month as the king's privy seal in 'sixe score dayes' (B.3.145–46) finds an echo in the charge, also in 1376, that the treasurer used letters under his own seal to countermand the king's letters under the privy seal.[51] Grievances about provisors (B.3.147) were aired perennially in the parliaments of the fourteenth century. The parliaments of 1344, 1346, and 1347 all saw petitions presented on the subject, before the Statute of Provisors of 1351 upheld the king's right to fill a vacant office or benefice if a bishop was unable or unwilling to act because of a

---

[49] Peace's bill appears to be a bill of trespass, containing both criminal and civil elements. However, some elements, especially the violence alleged and the implication of a trespass against the king's peace, suggest an appeal for felony. See Harding (1975; 71-7). On Peace's bill, see also Stokes (1984; 140) and Galloway (2006; 386–90).

[50] *PROME*, II, 335b. All references to the Rolls of Parliament are to the electronic edition, by volume, page, and column number of the printed edition, divisions which the digital version preserves.

[51] *PROME*, II, 355a.

papal provision.[52] Despite this legislation, complaints re-emerged in a later period. In 1376, the Commons petitioned the king to cause the statute to be renewed, complaining (with some exaggeration) that the Pope had 'generally reserved all the benefices of the world to his own collation'.[53] In its general themes, but more importantly in its textual form as a list of charges, Conscience's opening speech against Meed resembles an oral petition, of which there were many instances in medieval parliaments.[54]

As a 'petition' inserted into Langland's poetic narrative, Conscience's opening speech about Meed also approximates in mode historical narratives that incorporate similar parliamentary documents. So far, I have used Walsingham's history of the Good Parliament to illustrate the resemblance of the exchange between Meed and Conscience to various kinds of court rumour. I now turn to an earlier history, the *Vita Edwardi Secundi* attributed to John Walwayn, to show the formal affinity of Conscience's opening speech against Meed to more formal discourses.

For the year 1311, Walwayn provides a transcription of the ordinance banishing Piers Gaveston from the kingdom, 'word for word as it was read out publicly, in the following form' ('de uerbo ad uerbum, prout fuerat in audiencia publicatum, interserui sub forma que sequitur'):

> Piers Gaveston has led the lord king astray, advised the lord king badly, and persuaded him deceitfully and in many ways to do wrong; in gathering to himself all the king's treasure which, moreover, he has exported from the country...Also he maintains robbers and homicides and obtains the lord king's pardons for them, and so encourages other evildoers to greater boldness in crime...he has blank charters sealed under the king's great seal to the deception and disinheritance of the king and the crown.[55]

This text closely translates the ordinance as it appears in the Rolls of Parliament, and as a condemnation of the crimes and influence of an overweening royal favourite, it displays an obvious general resemblance to Conscience's accusations against Meed. Langland incorporates the textual form of a

---

[52] A provisor was 'The holder of a provision or grant from the pope giving him the right to be appointed to a benefice as soon as a vacancy occurred'. See Alford (1988a; s.v. 'provisour') and further Pantin (1955; 47–75, 82–98).

[53] '[I]l ad generalement reservez a sa propre collacioun touz les benefices du monde'. *PROME*, II, 339b.   [54] Myers (1937; 385–6).

[55] 'Petrus de Gauestone dominum regem male duxit, domino regi male consuluit, et ipsum ad male faciendum deceptorie et multiformiter induxit, contractando sibi totum thesaurum regis, quem eciam extra regnum elongauit...Sustinet eciam predones et homicidas ipsisque cartas domini regis de pace adquirit, et sic aliis malefactoribus magis delinquendi prebet audaciam...albas cartas sub magno sigillo regis facit consignari, in capcionem et exheredacionem regis et corone'. Walwayn, *Vita Edwardi Secvndi*, pp. 34–5; for the possible authorship of the text, see pp. xxiv–xxv.

petition into his poetic narrative in the same way as Walwayn incorporates the ordinance against Gaveston into his historical narrative, and just as the ordinance was also enrolled into the records of Parliament.[56]

Conscience seems to intend that his 'petition' should have legal efficacy as a formal 'document' initiating a trial or impeachment. His speech suggests that he means specifically to imply Meed's notoriety, in the sense of being the subject of multiple complaints, as the basis for legal proceedings against her. In the case of Chief Justice Willoughby in 1341, it was ruled that the notoriety of the abuses against the operation of justice with which he was charged might be established by bills from the Commons rather than from named individuals. In such cases, the notoriety of the accused, indicated by the 'clamour' of the people, was sufficient to have him or her put on trial without the need for an indictment (a written complaint by an individual victim or by a jury).[57] In a similar vein, Conscience cites multiple complainants against Meed or, more accurately, multiple potential complainants, since one of Meed's worst abuses is to prevent any but the rich getting a fair hearing: 'For pouere men may haue no power to pleyne þou3 hem smerte' (B.3.168). Conscience's speech is perhaps supposed, then, to resemble the kind of bill or petition from the Commons that established the notoriety of Chief Justice Willoughby in 1341, or of Adam Bury and William Latimer in 1376. On this latter occasion, the Commons used, for the first time, the process of impeachment, based upon the 'notoriety' of the defendant.[58] William Latimer and Adam Bury were 'empeschez et accusez par clamour des ditz communes' ('impeached and accused by the charge of the said commons').[59]

The king, at least, interprets Conscience's speech as possessing a specific legal force. One may infer as much from his hint that, unless Meed can disprove the charges just enumerated, she will be banished forever from the court. The generic marker the king uses to describe the speech that he has just heard also implies that he interprets it as a particular kind of legal utterance:

---

[56] Compare Emily Steiner's discussion of Langland's documents. She suggests that Langland's text resembles a chronicle or cartulary in the way it 'enrols' and glosses a variety of documents. Steiner largely concerns herself, however, with those documents in the poem that are concerned with man's 'contract' with God. She does not discuss the lines I have called Conscience's 'petition', since she includes only those examples which are figured explicitly as physical documents of various kinds. See Steiner (2003; 93–142).

[57] Plucknett (1942, 65–7, 71); Harding (1975; 79). Willoughby was accused of having 'perverted and sold the laws as if they were oxen and cows'. He was also said, like Meed, to have harboured known felons in his retinue. See Crook (2004, 16, 21).

[58] For the process of impeachment, see Musson and Ormrod (1999; 27); for its development from the practice of using the 'notoriety' of the accused as the basis for a trial, see Plucknett (1942).   [59] *PROME*, II, 324b, 330a.

> The kyng graunted hire grace wiþ a good wille.
> 'Excuse þee if þow kanst; I kan na moore seggen,
> For Conscience accuseþ þee to congeien þee for euere.'
>
> (B.3.172–74)

'Accusen' is legal diction, 'To charge...with an offence; to impugn; to indict'.[60] Here, it perhaps suggests a successful impeachment: one may compare the fate of William Latimer, 'empeschez et *accusez* par clamour des ditz communes'.[61]

However, Meed responds by contesting not the truth of the charges, but their discursive mode. Conscience's 'petition' does not constitute, she appears to argue, evidence of the 'clamour' sufficient to warrant a trial on the basis of the notoriety of the accused, but merely defamation:

> ...þow knowest, Conscience, I kam no3t to chide,
> Ne to depraue þi persone wiþ a proud herte.
> ...
> Ac þow hast famed me foule bifore þe kyng here.
>
> (B.3.178–79, 186)

Meed's strategy was one also attempted in historical cases involving notoriety. As Wendy Scase shows, in such instances the question of whether or not libels could constitute a legitimate category of legal complaint itself became an issue, for libels might be used as a means of attempting to demonstrate the popular outcry required to prove the notoriety of the defendant.[62] John of Gaunt used the same argument as Meed does when he found himself the victim of the Londoners' libels I mentioned above. The libels against Gaunt implied a charge of treason, but he responded in Parliament by stating his willingness to defend himself should anyone make an appeal of treason against him. His response implied, as Scase argues, that he did not view the libels as 'clamour' answerable in court.[63] During the debate between Meed and Conscience, the fine line between malicious invective and legitimate legal complaint similarly becomes a

---

[60] Alford (1988a; s.v. 'accusen'). Alford points out that the term in fact occurs in the poem only in collocation with Conscience and denotes his special mode of operation *in foro conscientiae*. 'Accusen' is the verb also used in describing Conscience's denunciation of corrupt priests in the C Prologue; see Galloway (2006; 102), and my discussion of this passage in Chapter 5. One may compare the similar legal diction, particularly the verb 'chalengen', used in connection with Conscience in B.15.31 (quoted in the Introduction).

[61] *PROME*, II, 324b (my emphasis). Giancarlo (2003; 145) refers to Conscience's speech as an 'impeachment', but he does not elaborate on the description and calls it merely an 'attack' in his later revision of the essay (2007; 191).

[62] Scase (2007; 64, 79–81).

[63] Scase (2007; 64–5); see also p. 121 for another case in which the accused sought to demonstrate that evidence of notoriety in fact constituted 'disclaundre.'

point at issue.[64] Conscience presents his accusations against Meed in the form of a petition or bill, but in places, as I have argued, they resemble various forms of court slander. Meed exploits this generic ambiguity to argue that what Conscience presents as legitimate grounds for legal action against her is in fact defamation: *malicious*, not honest, accusation. As Stokes suggests,

> Mede is slyly asserting the propriety of her own pleading methods, and covertly impugning those of Conscience, who, she implies (with some justice) has improperly taken refuge in malicious insult.[65]

If 'conscience' signifies a (legal) witness or accuser, Meed implicitly calls Conscience's allegorical identity into question by claiming that he has failed to follow the proper procedures of formal legal accusation.

Langland's emphasis here on what does and does not constitute a proper mode of legal and argumentative procedure again shows the resemblance between *Piers Plowman* and the literary debates that Reed demonstrates to be so closely related to parliamentary and legal disputation. Typically, debate poems place greater emphasis on the procedures of argument than on their substance or outcome.[66] So one finds in other debate poems, too, moments such as Meed's challenge over Conscience's mode of argument. In *The Owl and the Nightingale*, the Nightingale tries to establish some proper modes of procedure, based on 'faire worde' rather than mere abuse and squabbling:

> Ac lete we awei þos cheste,
> Vor suiche wordes boþ unwreste,
> & fo we on mid riȝte dome,
> Mid faire worde & mid ysome.
> þeȝ we ne bo at one acorde,
> We muȝe bet mid fayre worde,
> Witute cheste & bute fiȝte,
> Plaidi mid foȝe & mid riȝte.[67]

Later on, the Owl attacks the Nightingale for not following proper form, accusing her of lying (ll. 837–40). The way Langland highlights the contested boundaries between legitimate legal accusation and mere

---

[64] Forrest (2009; 142–8) has recently discussed how 'defamation' could refer both to 'actionable slander', the malicious imputation of a crime, and the legitimate public 'clamour' or widespread belief in a person's guilt that could initiate judicial investigation of a crime.

[65] Stokes (1984; 118). Stokes points out that pleaders in medieval courts were required to swear an oath that they would not proceed in malice.

[66] Reed (1990; 45, 73); cf. Hanna (2005; 263).

[67] *The Owl and the Nightingale*, ll. 177–84.

defamation is typical of the debate genre, with its interests in the mechanics of disputation and what constitutes an acceptable form of argument.

Typical of the debate mode, too, as I suggested earlier in this chapter, is the king's response to Meed's argument over the legal efficacy of Conscience's 'petition'. Whereas the king had been prepared, moments earlier, to have Meed banished from his kingdom, by the end of her speech he seems to have forgotten that Meed might have any case to answer: 'by crist, as me þynkeþ,/Mede is worþi, me þynkeþ, þe maistrie to haue' (B.3.228–29). Langland's king is capable of endorsing *both* speakers in turn (B.3.173–74, 228–29) and, as I have already indicated, he ultimately breaks off their debate at the head of passus 4 with a *Wynnere*-like judgement that claims both speakers as his own:

> 'Cesseþ,' seide þe kyng, 'I suffre yow no lenger.
> Ye shul sauʒtne, forsoþe, and serue me boþe.
> Kis hire,' quod þe kyng, 'Conscience, I hote!'
>
> (B.4.1–3)

The king attempts, indeed, to bring the pair to a reconciliation that looks much like the easy 'peace' that, greeted with disgust by Conscience here (B.4.4–5), will ultimately be rejected in passus 4. However, Conscience is by no means yet vindicated at this dissolution of the debate at the beginning of passus 4. The king's insistence that Conscience produce Reason (B.4.6–12) indicates that he is at least as suspicious of Conscience as of Meed. Only when the debate mode gives way to the trial scene of passus 4 is Meed finally condemned by the clamour of the commons (B.4.166).[68] The collective voice of the court, proclaiming Meed a notorious whore,[69] at last endorses Conscience's petition as more than mere defamation. Finally, he shares in Reason's victory, promoted from the position of mere debater to an authoritative, judicial role perhaps more befitting his name.[70]

The trial scene in passus 4 confirms the justness of much of Conscience's invective against Meed by exposing her deleterious effects on the

---

[68] For the literal noisy 'clamour' here, and its relation to the technical term associated with the process of impeachment, see Giancarlo (2007; 196 and n. 35).

[69] Conscience's status as a lone voice in passus 3 (as at the poem's conclusion) may be the major cause of his difficulties. As Ian Forrest recently points out (2009; 148–9), 'just' defamation generally referred to a collective, not individual opinion, the *public* clamour that secured the impeachments during the Good Parliament. A lone voice would have difficulty in establishing that his or her accusations amounted to public fame. Only by enlisting the help of Reason and eventually securing the support of all the assembled can Conscience finally see Meed defeated.

[70] At least in the C text, where Conscience is appointed the king's Chief Justice (C.4.186). Conscience's new judicial role chimes with the legal diction Langland employs to describe the action of 'conscience' in B.15.31–32, a passage that I discussed in the Introduction.

operation of justice. As the king recognizes, by trying to make monetary 'amends' on behalf of her retainer Wrong so that he may escape punishment, Meed has almost destroyed the law (B.4.174, 176). Nevertheless, Conscience does not get the final word at the end of the first vision. As typically in debate poetry, ambiguities and uncertainties remain at this conclusion. These hesitations point to the possible limitations of the 'scandalous' mode of the first vision, particularly for a poem that subsequently expands from a single-vision satire on 'topical' themes to a multi-vision spiritual quest for Truth. For, of course, slander is by definition not the same as Truth, as Meed insists when she defends herself from Conscience's attack (B.3.180–88). Langland introduces Conscience into the poem as the counsellor and spokesman of Truth (B.2.138–39), and the reader sympathizes with his moral outrage at Meed's abuses of the law. Yet Conscience's invective against Meed nevertheless necessarily involves a degree of falsification. His slurs on the character of Meed as a personified figure oversimplify the ethical dilemmas surrounding the giving and receiving of reward.

Conscience insists in passus 3 that earthly reward properly should be 'mesurable' (and in such cases not called 'meed' at all, B.3.256). In passus 4, Reason reiterates this argument that reward should be in accordance with merit (*Nullum malum inpunitum* and *Nullum bonum irremuneratum*, B.4.143–44). Yet Conscience had nevertheless also implied that God's reward might be a kind of 'meed', because not strictly merited or earned:

> 'Ther are two manere of Medes, my lord, bi youre leue.
> That oon god of his grace gyueþ in his blisse
> To hem þat werchen wel while þei ben here.
> ...
> Ther is [anoþer] Mede mesurelees þat maistres desireþ;
> To mayntene mysdoers Mede þei take.'
>
> (B.3.231–33, 246–47)[71]

These lines are admittedly ambiguous: it is unclear whether Conscience means to say that corrupt earthly 'meed' is *like* God's reward in being 'mesurelees', or unlike God's reward in being measureless.[72] But if Conscience implies that man cannot strictly or 'measurably' earn heavenly reward, then man must necessarily rely upon the 'mercy' that Meed tries to obtain for Wrong in passus 4. Piers implicitly acknowledges this

---

[71] I have here supplied in square brackets the majority B-text reading of line 246, 'Ther is anoþer Mede mesurelees'. Kane and Donaldson needlessly emend to agree with the A-text reading.
[72] For the ambiguity, see Stokes (1984; 128).

dependence when he tears up the pardon and throws himself upon God's mercy at the end of the second vision. At the conclusion of passus 4, Peace apparently receives no redress for his injuries, which suggests that there might be something wrong with Conscience's insistence on strict 'measure' and Reason's rejection of mercy. Of course, Meed's particular form of mercy, because she attempts to buy it for cash, cannot be condoned. But even in rejecting it, Reason hints that there are circumstances in which mercy might be accommodated, if 'mekenesse [not meed/money] it made' (B.4.142). I have already shown how the debate mode tends towards accommodation of both speakers, and in the seeming inadequacy of the solution of Reason and Conscience to the problem represented by Meed, Langland hints at the need to accommodate the 'mercy' and 'amends' that Meed proposes.[73]

Certainly, although Meed herself does not appear in the poem again, Conscience's subsequent appearances point to an accommodation of the amends-making and special treatment for one's retinue that Meed had earlier represented. But these now take spiritualized forms, within the divine economy. As I will show in more detail in Chapter 2, the banquet at Conscience's house in B 13, his next appearance in the poem, puts forward new spiritualized forms of household and retinue relationship. In this new scenario, lords will no longer abuse the law by obtaining easy 'mercy' for their retainers. Rather, they will retain those who offer them corrective spiritual counsel. Minstrelsy and household entertainments assume the paradoxical form of penitential meditation and sober tales of saints and the passion. Through these, lords may obtain *heavenly* mercy or 'largesse', in contrast to Meed's purely monetary mercy and 'gifts'. When Conscience appears for the third time in B 19, he delivers a speech on Christ as knight, king, and conqueror that again points to newly spiritualized forms of retinue. As I discuss further in Chapter 3, Conscience here presents the redemption as Christ's act of lordly largesse, an act by which he obtains a special legal remedy (the pardon he gives to Piers Plowman, B.19.182–90) for his retinue. His, however, is not a retinue composed of over-powerful favourites who are allowed to operate above the law. Rather, Christ's retinue comprises all baptized Christians who make true amends for wrongdoing by paying back what they owe.

Indeed, common to all Conscience's subsequent appearances in the poem is an exploration of the themes broached in the first vision—justice,

---

[73] For the 'equivocal' ending of the scene and its similarity to that in *Wynnere*, see Hanna (2005; 269–73) and also Kennedy, K.E. (2003; 185). Kennedy suggests that Langland leaves open the possibility that the king retains Meed, as well as Conscience and Reason, at the end of passus 4.

mercy, and reward—and of the central social institution through which Langland interrogates these themes in the debate with Meed: the noble household or retinue. Conscience's final appearance in B 20, as I will show in Chapter 4, again reiterates, like B 13–14 and B 19, the themes of his debate with Meed. Here, Langland exposes the prominent place of friars in the retinues of the powerful and their failure to insist on the hard penance put forward in Conscience's earlier appearance in B 13–14. Like Meed, the friars allow 'mercy' to be purchased with cash.

In all of these appearances, Langland composes Conscience as a figure who is himself involved in the social institution of the lordly household/ retinue. Albeit in slightly different guises, Conscience appears throughout the poem as originally introduced: as a king's knight. Conscience remains a knight in B 13 when he holds a banquet at his 'court' (B.13.23), when he acts as a herald describing the arms and victories of the knightly Christ in B 19, and when he reappears as castellan of Unity in B 20 and admits the friar into the household. Thus while many readers have argued for Conscience's 'development' as a character during the course of the poem, I shall be insisting, in analysing his later appearances in the following chapters, that Conscience remains fundamentally unchanged from his original appearance in the debate with Meed in the first vision. Each of his subsequent appearances simply reiterates, in a new context, the themes within which he first appears in the poem. As I argued in the Introduction, Langland composes 'type scenes': repeated conjunctions of character and theme in which the themes of the poem develop, not the character himself. Conscience remains true to knightly type throughout. All that changes is the mode within which Langland composes the figure. Langland 'spiritualizes' the themes within which he presents Conscience by transforming them in a variety of different discourses as the poem develops. So Conscience metamorphoses from king's knight in B 3–4 to penitential knight in B 13–14 as Langland turns to the new penitential mode within which he presents the newly spiritualized forms of household and retinue of this part of the poem. In B 19, he becomes a herald and preacher within the homiletic mode on which I argue Langland draws in order to present Christ's transformation of the noble retinue into a new spiritualized form based on faith. Finally, in B 20, as castellan of Unity, Conscience becomes one of those lords who, according to contemporary polemic, admit friars into their retinues, as Langland returns at the poem's end to the 'topical' satirical interests of the first vision. On the allegorical level, Conscience is transformed, as Langland moves from 'topical' satire to spiritual quest, from 'conscience' as legal witness/accuser to 'conscience' as the accuser of sins in the *divine* law. In B 13–14 and B 20, Conscience in part stands for the consciousness of guilt that precedes contrition, the institutionalized form of remorse and the first part of the sacrament of penance. Conscience himself, however, is not 'spiritualized' in these later scenes in the way that Higgs implies:[74] he does not develop like a character in a novel. Many readers have observed that Conscience seems to have changed dramatically when he makes his second appearance in the poem in B 13–14: he appears humbler, less priggish.[75] But his new humility is predetermined by the penitential discourse upon which Langland draws in composing this part of the poem. As I will show in the next chapter, Conscience changes from the self-righteous accuser of Meed to humble penitent and pilgrim only as Langland moves away from the invective of the first vision to a new, penitential mode in the fourth.

[74] Higgs (1993; 140), cited in the Introduction.
[75] Cf. Harwood (1992; 91).

2
Penitential Texts and Vernacular Conscience in B 13–14

In the second vision of *Piers Plowman*, Langland turns from the depiction of 'topical' controversies at court to the contemporary rural scene. As all readers of the poem notice, the second vision broadly mirrors the first.[1] During the ploughing of the half acre, Piers confronts the same dilemma raised by the Meed episode. That dilemma is the compatibility of justice with showing mercy to one's 'affinity'—although now the 'affinity' of all one's fellow Christians, 'blody breþeren for god bouȝte vs alle' (B.6.207; cf. the question Piers poses to Hunger at B.6.229–30). But if the thematic interests of the second vision resemble those of the first, the discourse within which Langland now broaches these themes differs from the debate mode of the first vision, with its gamesome interest in the procedures of argumentation. In the second vision, Langland takes up the controversial contemporary discourse surrounding labour (cf. the invocation of 'þe statut' at B.6.320), a mode far removed from Conscience's abstract arguments about 'mesurable hire' and the divine economy (B.3.256).[2] Little room exists for the king's knight Conscience in this scene of rural manual labour. Piers's knight, sharing Conscience's courtly 'kynde', proves predictably ineffectual at enforcing order on the half acre (see B.6.164, where the knight displays the same courtesy that Conscience shows to the friar at the end of the poem).[3] Knights and 'wasters' simply speak in entirely different, mutually incomprehensible, modes (B.6.159–70).

With the transition from the various literary modes with which he is linked in the first vision to the labour discourse of the second, Conscience thus disappears from the poem. He receives a brief reprise at the beginning of the sequence of sermon, confession, and ploughing in passus 5 of the

---

[1] The best account of the symmetry of the two first visions is provided by Middleton (1997; 233–34).
[2] Aers (1980; 8–9) describes Conscience's discussion of reward as a 'bland statement' that 'simply ignores' contemporary labour disputes.
[3] Although Langland's narrative implies that famine/Hunger in any case acts as the only truly effectual enforcer of labour (B.6.203–6). I discuss Conscience's courteous treatment of Friar Flatterer in Chapter 4.

A text (which Langland expands and translates into the terms of labour legislation at the beginning of C 5).[4] But in the B version, Conscience appears in the second vision only referentially, in Piers Plowman's invocation of Conscience, Kynde Wit, and Abstinence as his teachers (B.5.539, 7.138–39). This solely referential, not actual, appearance Langland develops when Conscience reappears in B 13–14 as, apparently, Piers Plowman's friend and disciple (B.13.131–32).

The allusion to Conscience as Piers's teacher explains why Conscience should also remain absent throughout the third vision. Piers's confrontation with the priest at the end of the second vision establishes the contours of the poem's subsequent exploration of the value of two different modes of knowledge. This confrontation poises 'academic', learned, institutionalized modes, associated with the priest, who wishes to bring his 'professional' expertise to bear on the interpretation of the pardon, against a 'kyndely', instinctual, lay-oriented kind of knowledge, professed by Piers and linked with Conscience (B.7.136–39).

In the third vision, Will explores principally the first, 'academic', institutionalized form of knowledge. His serial encounters with Thought, Wit, Study, Clergy, and Scripture in passus 8–11 interrogate the rational faculties of the soul and the institutions of learning, testing their value to the pursuit of salvation. Conscience, originally presented in the poem as a layman, a 'courtly' character, and subsequently linked in the second vision with Piers's non-academic mode of knowing, has no logical place within the dominant academic mode of the third vision, notwithstanding the efforts of some readers to associate him with the faculty discussions of academic theology.

Only with the movement away from academic to more 'affective' modes of knowledge in the fourth vision does Conscience reappear.[5] The third vision has exhausted the possibilities of academic discourses. These seem capable only of reiterating the necessity of obedience to God's law, and they lead to Will's despair at the seeming inadequacy of man's efforts before God's justice.[6] In the fourth vision, Langland accordingly turns to a new, penitential mode, one that resembles Piers's earlier lay-oriented form of knowledge.

---

[4] See the Introduction for further discussion of Conscience's appearance in the second vision in A and its later revisions. I discuss the 'autobiographical' episode in C 5 in Chapter 6. For the second vision's sequence as corresponding to the three parts of penance, contrition, confession and satisfaction, see Burrow (1969; 209–27). Middleton (1997) provides the fullest account of the 'autobiographical' episode in C 5 and its relation to the 1388 Statute of Labourers.

[5] The best-known treatment of the transition from 'academic' to 'affective' modes of knowledge at this point in the poem is Simpson (1986a).

[6] Cf. Simpson (2007; 102).

This particular kind of penitential discourse, exemplified in vernacular texts like Richard Rolle's *Form of Living* and the anonymous texts *The Chastising of God's Children*, *The Cleansing of Man's Soul*, and *Memoriale credencium*,[7] re-presents pastoral materials, originally designed for the use of the priest, in newly 'laicized' terms for direct use by religious and ultimately by lay people.[8] Within this new mode, Conscience remains a knight, as he originally appeared in the poem; the penitential 'feast' in B 13 takes place in his 'court' (B.13.23). But he is now transformed into an embodiment of the virtuous layman put forward in contemporary vernacular texts. Conscience's reappearance in B 13–14 reprises the moment at which that other virtuous layman, Piers Plowman, named Conscience as his teacher and renounced his ploughing in favour of penitential prayer. The feast hosted by Conscience in B 13 presents a conflict, like the earlier clash between Piers and the priest, between academic, theoretical knowledge and more pragmatic, 'laicized' forms of knowledge.

CONSCIENCE, CLERGY, AND PATIENCE IN B 13–14

Two speeches by Conscience and Clergy in passus 13 establish the opposing terms of the two different kinds of knowledge at work in this part of the poem, which were earlier glossed by Ymaginatif as 'clergy' and 'kynde wit':

> Pacience haþ be in many place, and paraunter knoweþ
> That no clerk ne kan, as crist bereþ witnesse.
> (B.13.134–35)

*

> I shal brynge yow a bible, a book of þe olde lawe,
> And lere yow if yow like þe leeste point to knowe
> That Pacience þe pilgrym parfitly knew neuere.
> (B.13.185–87)

---

[7] Rolle, *The Form of Living*, in *Richard Rolle: Prose and Verse*, pp. 3–25; *The Chastising of God's Children and The Treatise of Perfection of the Sons of God*; *Memoriale credencium*. For *The Cleansing of Man's Soul*, I have consulted the copy in Oxford, Bodleian Library, MS Bodley 923.

[8] For introductions/overviews on pastoral manuals, see Pantin (1955; 189–243); Bloomfield (1952); and Wenzel (1967; 68–96). For Middle English versions, see Jolliffe, *Check-list*, pp. 61–5 and 67–79; Robert R. Raymo, 'Works of Religious and Philosophical Instruction', in *Manual of the Writings in Middle English*, VII, 2255–378, 2467–582; and Patterson (1978).

Clergy's academic expertise, his precise textual analysis, contrasts with what Patience has learned on the road, through a life lived implicitly according to gospel precept ('as crist bereþ witnesse'). The latter, of course, represents the same kind of non-academic, experiential knowledge earlier embodied by Piers Plowman, and Piers himself has here 'impugned' Clergy's academic knowledge with the 'science' of love (B.13.120–30).[9]

Conscience, performing the role of orchestrator and judge of the debate, clearly favours the experiential knowledge of Patience and Piers over the academic knowledge of Clergy, even before he takes the dramatic decision to reject Clergy's 'pak of bokes' (B.13.201) and leave the banquet to go on pilgrimage with Patience. As Traugott Lawler shows, Conscience appears thoroughly non-academic in this scene.[10] He utters no riddles, and he admits that he does not fully understand Clergy's report of Piers's teaching about Dowel, based on the grammatical term 'infinite':[11]

> 'For oon Piers þe Plowman haþ impugned vs alle,
> ...
> And demeþ þat dowel and dobet arn two Infinites,
> Whiche Infinites wiþ a feiþ fynden out dobest,
> Which shal saue mannes soule; þus seiþ Piers þe Plowman.'
> 'I kan noȝt heron', quod Conscience, 'ac I knowe Piers.
> He wol noȝt ayein holy writ speken, I dar vndertake.
> Thanne passe we ouer til Piers come and preue þis in dede.
> Pacience haþ be in many place, and paraunter knoweþ
> That no clerk ne kan.'
>
> (B.13.124, 128–35)[12]

Although unable to grasp its intellectual import, Conscience nevertheless claims that he instinctively 'knows' and trusts Piers's fidelity to holy writ. Presumably Conscience does not understand Patience's comparable riddle, which also uses terminology from Latin grammar, either:

> Kynde loue coueiteþ noȝt no catel but speche.
> Wiþ half a laumpe lyne in latyn, *Ex vi transicionis*,
> I bere þer, in a bouste faste ybounde, dowel
>
> (B.13.150–52)

---

[9] In the C-text version of the banquet, of course, Piers himself briefly appears.
[10] Lawler (1995; 97).
[11] For 'two Infinites' as a grammatical concept, see Middleton (1972).
[12] I follow Schmidt's punctuation of this speech in his edition of the B text, since I assume Conscience is still speaking in lines 133–35. Kane and Donaldson punctuate these lines as a separate speech (presumably by Clergy). Lawler (1995; 91 n. 10) also queries Kane and Donaldson's punctuation here.

As Andrew Galloway argues,[13] Langland appears to allude here to a Latin riddle that appears in British Library, MS Harley 3362 and which is also referred to, among other places, in John Bromyard's *Summa praedicantium*. The 'half a laumpe lyne in latyn' (B.13.151) alludes to the first part of this riddle, '*Lune dimidium*', 'half a moon' or the letter 'c'. The riddle as a whole spells out the three letters of the Latin word for 'heart', 'cor'. '*Ex vi transicionis*', in the same line, is a phrase from Latin grammar: it refers to the grammatical concept of 'regimen', the 'power' or 'vis' by which one word governs the case of another.[14] Here, though, the phrase seems to refer, as Galloway argues, to the various transpositions of letters and divisions of words that solving riddles of this type involves.

The riddle certainly requires a very specific kind of knowledge to unravel—one that has long proved elusive, indeed, to modern scholars of *Piers Plowman*. Conscience's admission that he cannot understand Clergy's report of Piers Plowman's 'two Infinites' suggests that he would not be able to work out the solution to Patience's riddle either. Nevertheless, in another sense, the solution to Patience's riddle, 'cor', is in plain sight throughout his speech. Something close to the answer appears in the previous line in English, 'Kynde loue' (B.13.150).[15] When Conscience says, as he sides with Patience rather than with Clergy and the Doctor of Divinity, that 'þer is no tresour þerto to a trewe wille' (B.13.193), he seems to be responding to the essence of the riddle. For despite its interpretative difficulties, the riddle in fact emphasizes the importance of the *heart* or 'wille'/affect rather than the intellect.

Conscience's preference for the non-academic 'heart'-knowledge of Piers and Patience should not really surprise, given that Piers had also earlier presented Conscience as a moral instructor distinct from knowledge of books, and as the source of his own mysterious moral literacy. In siding with Patience rather than Clergy, Conscience aligns himself with Piers, the poem's earlier representation of the virtuous layman whose moral knowledge comes independently of Clergy's 'pak of bokes'.

As I have already suggested above, Langland's presentation of Piers Plowman in the second vision, and now Conscience in the fourth, as virtuous laymen whose spiritual knowledge exists apart from any academic or institutional context may be located within more general trends in vernacular writing in the later fourteenth and early fifteenth centuries.

---

[13] See Galloway (1995). My explanation of the riddle here summarizes Galloway's interpretation, which seems to me by far the most convincing offered to date.

[14] For the phrase and its meaning in Latin grammar, see Kaske (1969) and Bland (1988).

[15] Lawler (1995; 93) also remarks that Patience seems unable to keep in the answer to the riddle.

This period saw materials previously accessible only to 'Clergy' increasingly adapted for, and appropriated by, a lay audience. Conscience's banquet in B 13 and his subsequent 'pilgrimage' (in which he and Patience offer penitential instruction to Haukin) are best read alongside vernacular penitential texts of the fourteenth and early fifteenth centuries such as Rolle's *Form of Living* and the three anonymous texts I mentioned above: the *Chastising,* the *Cleansing,* and *Memoriale credencium*. These works position themselves as offering spiritual instruction supplementary to, and largely independent of, clerical supervision, the kind of instruction the penitent might receive in the confessional. They share with each other and with *Piers Plowman* a number of themes and emphases: an emphasis on individual spiritual 'counsel', which the virtuous (lay) penitent may also dispense to his or her fellow Christian; an emphasis on the spiritual knowledge that may come from individual meditation outside of any formal instruction, and on the pursuit of the spiritual life beyond mere performance of sacramental penance; and, perhaps most significantly for my purposes, an emphasis on the individual conscience rather than academic, institutional knowledge.

Of course, similar emphases are not exclusive to the particular texts I have mentioned, and which I will be considering in more detail below. Other readers of *Piers Plowman* have pointed to similar themes in other contemporary texts. Ralph Hanna has associated Piers, for instance, with earlier London devotional texts that insist on the duty of the layman to instruct his fellow Christian. Such texts include the version of *Ancrene Riwle* adapted for a lay audience in Magdalene College, Cambridge MS Pepys 2498.[16] Andrew Cole has discussed works, both heterodox and orthodox, such as *The Fyve Wittes* and Clanvowe's *The Two Ways*, which appropriate fraternal ideals in the service of a reinvented 'lollard' discourse. This discourse emphasizes meekness, lay preaching, and living by moderate example. It 'transforms fraternal ideals into a set of lay standards, a specifically lay-oriented version of virtuous poverty and Christian discipleship'.[17] In a similar vein, Fiona Somerset has discussed how the reform movement that led to the fourth Lateran Council of 1215 and Pecham's Constitutions of 1281 ultimately resulted in the production of pastoral materials written directly for the laity. She shows how *Piers Plowman* puts the established understandings of 'clergie' and 'lewed' 'under severe strain' by presenting in Piers someone whose social position seems at odds with

---

[16] Hanna (2005; 273–77, 148–221). Cf. also Watson (2007; 105), citing Hanna, who argues that 'laicized attitudes toward spiritual perfection' offer the best analogues to Patience's speech in this part of the poem.

[17] Cole (2008; 47).

his learning—someone who is 'lewed' and yet has 'clergie'.[18] The particular texts I examine here form part, then, of a wider trend in vernacular writing in this period, and my argument develops themes that have appeared in other recent readings of *Piers Plowman*. The examples I consider, however, seem especially relevant to this part of *Piers Plowman* because they present, as Langland does in B 13–14, a form of penitence that takes place without direct clerical supervision. In their emphasis on conscience over books, these texts provide a particularly useful contemporary context in which to understand Langland's composition of Conscience in B 13–14 as an embodiment, like Piers Plowman earlier, of the virtuous layman, who lacks academic knowledge and training but who nevertheless offers penitential counsel to others. Discussions of Conscience based upon scholastic moral psychology tend to imply that Langland's use of the vernacular comes about almost by accident. By contrast, reading this part of the poem in the light of contemporary vernacular texts on penance emphasizes how Langland grounds his language, and his personifications, in changing—and sometimes contested—social practices.

'VERNACULAR' PENITENCE IN THE LATE MIDDLE AGES

The late fourteenth and early fifteenth centuries saw, as Vincent Gillespie has discussed, a 'developing interest in and ownership of vernacular religious books among the laity'.[19] Pastoral texts were being written directly for lay readers as well as for the use of their priests. Texts that originally had been composed for monks, secular clergy, or for female religious were being adapted for lay people. The texts I am examining here fit within this trend for increasingly individual access to pastoral materials. Although only one of the texts I discuss, *Memoriale credencium,* was written directly for a lay audience, all offer a form of spiritual instruction that is presented as largely independent of 'Clergy', and which would ultimately lend itself to direct use by the laity.[20]

All the texts I examine here display 'laicizing' tendencies. They address audiences (whether lay or religious) that they imagine having individual

---

[18] Somerset (1998; 28–29).
[19] Gillespie (1989; 319). For this trend, see also Gillespie (1981; 121, 128) and, in connection with *Piers Plowman*, Scase (1989; 45).
[20] For possible later lay readerships for the *Cleansing* and the *Chastising*, see Raymo, 'Works of Religious and Philosophical Instruction', 2299 and *Chastising*, p. 38. Parts of Rolle's *Form of Living* enjoyed wide circulation through their inclusion in the compilation the *Pore Caitiff*; see *English Writings of Richard Rolle*, p. 84, and Brady (1980; 426–35).

responsibility for their own spiritual welfare. Moreover, they offer themselves as spiritual counsel independent of what might be offered—but more often, the texts imply, is not—by the priest. *Memoriale credencium* (a compilation of materials including William of Pagula's manual for priests, *Oculus sacerdotis*) explicitly addresses itself to a lay readership whose knowledge of 'writtus' may be limited to what they hear being read aloud.[21] Rolle's *Form of Living*, written for the recluse Margaret Kirkby in the year before Rolle's death in 1349, addresses a rather more specialised audience. A guide to the contemplative life, it includes some material on the seven deadly sins and the sacrament of penance. This latter material has much in common with similar information presented in handbooks for priests.[22] Nevertheless, Rolle offers his text as informal spiritual counsel, something quite different from the formal instruction that a priest might offer (the *Chastising* is similar in providing materials originally designed for clerical use—'as clerkis shewe'—for personal consumption by female religious).[23] Rolle imagines his reader assuming responsibility for her own spiritual progress and advancement. He addresses anticipated questions and areas of concern, and adopts the intimate mode of address of a spiritual friend ('þou' is used throughout). Though Rolle's *Form of Living* covers some of the same material as pastoral handbooks for priests, it re-presents this material for direct use by the aspiring contemplative, offering itself as informal 'good consaille'.[24] While Rolle admittedly writes for a specialized audience, and he discusses the superiority of the contemplative to the active life. Nevertheless, his text points the way to a wider audience in stressing that despising the world is an inner state, not an outward form:

> Bot þei ben oonly holy, what estate or degree þei bene in, þe which despiseth al erthly thynges, þat is to sey loueth hit nat, and brandyn in þe loue of Ihesu Criste.[25]

---

[21] *Memoriale credencium*, p. 214, ll. 3–9. I have modernized punctuation and word division when quoting from this text. The work was written around 1400.

[22] See, for instance, its description of the goods of 'kynd', fortune and grace: Rolle, *Form of Living*, in *Prose and Verse*, p. 11, ll. 344–5. This is a topic widely dispersed in pastoral manuals; see, for instance, *The Book of Vices and Virtues*, p. 19, l. 23–p. 21, l. 10; *Jacob's Well: An English Treatise on the Cleansing of Man's Conscience*, p. 69, ll. 15–30; *Cursor Mundi*, V, ll. 27558–69; *The Parson's Tale* in *The Riverside Chaucer*, X.449–54. For the date and circumstances of composition of the *Form*, see *English Writings of Richard Rolle*, pp. 82–4.

[23] *Chastising*, p. 206, ll. 5–7. For the date of composition—probably shortly after 1382 and in any event before 1408—see *Chastising*, pp. 34–7, and also Sutherland (2005; 353–73). The text appears to be connected to Barking Abbey: *The Cleansing of Man's Soul*, a text with Barking connections, cites the *Chastising* at MS Bodley 923, fol. 145ᵛ.

[24] Rolle, *Form of Living*, p. 5, l. 107.   [25] Rolle, *Form of Living*, p. 9, ll. 238–41.

Though Rolle addresses the particular audience of the female religious, his text anticipates increasingly 'laicized' forms of religion in its suggestion that true renunciation of the world means a mental attitude as much as an institutionalized state. Such an attitude, at least implicitly, may be adopted by all, 'what estate or degree þei bene in'.

As an informal variety of spiritual 'good counsel', Rolle's text implicitly offers itself as a supplement or alternative to more formal instruction on sin and penance of the kind that might be provided by a priest. Another somewhat later vernacular penitential text, *The Cleansing of Man's Soul*, explicitly presents itself as spiritual counsel supplementary to that which ought to be provided more formally by a priest. This text, connected with Barking Abbey,[26] offers itself as a supplement to the teaching the reader may—but, its author fears, probably does not—receive from her confessor:

> I purpos to write a few wordes of þe sacrament of penaunce be þe instance & preir of such þat I haue in goostly affeccioun. For as I wene be comownyng & be experience of world outward, many men & women þere ben not lettred and of simple knowynge, but ful feruent I fynde such and stable in desire of þe loue of God, þe which ful selde and al to selde haue litel comfort of her confessours to teche hem þat spedefull were &, as me þenkith, were nedeful of þis sacrament of penaunce in which is comprehended þe mater of confessioun.[27]

This text is connected with a house of female religious, and therefore, like Rolle, addresses a somewhat specialized audience. Nevertheless it seems, again like Rolle, to anticipate a broader audience as well, for the author speaks of 'many men & women...not lettred and of simple knowynge'. The text addresses itself to the gap in the market presented by those who are 'ful feruent...in desire of þe loue of God', but who nevertheless 'al to selde haue litel comfort of her confessours to teche hem þat spedefull were &, as me þenkith, were nedeful of þis sacrament of penaunce'.[28]

All four of the works I have mentioned include materials on penance and the seven deadly sins, much like those that could be found in pastoral manuals for the use of priests. But, in keeping with their self-presentation as spiritual 'good counsel' outside of a formal institutional context, they omit materials that relate directly to any priestly role. This

---

[26] The text is a treatise on the three parts of penance written in the late fourteenth or early fifteenth century. MS Bodley 923, one of four complete copies of the work, belonged to Sibyl Felton, Abbess of the Benedictine nunnery at Barking. Felton died in 1419 and was elected Abbess in 1394. See *Chastising*, p. 37, and Doyle (1958; 240).
[27] MS Bodley 923, fol. 4^(r-v).
[28] 'Not lettred' in the passage from the *Cleansing* quoted above presumably means those unable to cope with Latin as opposed to an English text.

role is implicitly usurped by the voice of the text or by the penitent herself. The author of the *Cleansing* makes clear in his introduction, for instance (cited in part above), that he will have little to say about the office of priest.[29] Similarly, *Memoriale credencium* adapts Raymund de Peniafort's *Summa de poenitentia et matrimonio* for its section on confession, but it omits Raymund's materials on cases that are reserved to the bishop, as well as the instructions on how the priest should conduct a confession (teaching the penitent to kneel, for instance, and the female penitent to avert her face from the priest).[30] The *Cleansing*, also adapting Peniafort, preserves the material on reserved cases, but only so that the penitent will obey should her case be referred to the bishop: 'Moche more I might write of þis mater but this þat I haue written suffisith to ȝow so þat ȝe obey lowely to ȝour parish prest'.[31] Similarly, the *Chastising* passes over the subject of satisfaction as properly belonging to the priest, and thus outside the scope of the present work.[32]

Informal counsel, which the reader may give herself to her fellow Christian, takes the place of priestly supervision in these texts. Rolle, for instance, hints that his reader may be in a position herself to provide spiritual comfort and counsel. After a conventional description of the three kinds of satisfaction (fasting, prayer, and almsgiving), Rolle adds that almsgiving means not only provision of food and drink to the poor, but also 'to foryeve ham þat doth þe wronge and pray for ham, and enfourme ham how þay shal do þat ben in poynt to perisshe'.[33] The *Chastising*, similarly, offers its material 'boþe for ȝouresilf *and help to oþer*', implying, as Rolle also hinted, that its audience may themselves offer instruction to their fellow Christians.[34] Likewise, *Memoriale credencium* offers its instruction so that 'þyne owne lyf þu myȝt gouerne *and oþer mannus lif amende*'.[35] This text clearly imagines a scenario in which its lay readers, though not possessed of 'clergy', might nevertheless themselves offer spiritual counsel and correction to others. Finally, it is striking that the author of the *Cleansing* submits his work to the correction not only of 'clerkes

---

[29] MS Bodley 923, fols 4ᵛ–5ʳ.
[30] *Memoriale credencium*, p. 157, l. 19–p. 165, l. 10; cf. Raymund de Peniafort, *De poenitentiis et remissionibus*, in *Summa*, III.34.17, III.34.30.
[31] MS Bodley 923, fol. 51ʳ.
[32] *Chastising*, p. 214, ll. 24–27: 'þis maner of satisfaccion longiþ to hym to knowe þat haþ cure of soule, as it is writen in holi chirche lawe. To ȝou it nediþ nat to knowe: þerfor I passe ouer of satisfaccion'.
[33] Rolle, *Form of Living*, p. 13, ll. 407–10. For a conventional account of the three parts of satisfaction, see Raymund de Peniafort, *Summa*, III.34.34: 'Consistit satisfactio in tribus, scilicet oratione, ieiunio, et eleemosyna' (Satisfaction consists in three things, that is, prayer, fasting and almsgiving).
[34] *Chastising*, p. 206, l. 5 (my emphasis).
[35] *Memoriale credencium*, p. 219, ll. 18–19 (my emphasis).

aproued' but also 'oþer holy liuers', presumably those 'simple knowynge but ful feruent' members of his imagined audience.[36] Here, implicitly, the unlearned may potentially possess a knowledge of spiritual truth as valuable as the book-learning of the author. All four texts clearly imagine that 'holy livers' as well as 'clerks' may offer spiritual counsel to their fellow Christians.

Like the pastoral handbooks for priests, vernacular texts like these take as their starting point the contemporary inadequacy of clerical provision for instruction. But, as Somerset shows, such texts appropriate the rhetoric of the inadequacy of clerical education, which originally supported the production of texts to facilitate instruction by the priest, in order to justify the writing of vernacular works for the direct use of the penitent. Moreover, they exploit this 'rhetoric of clerical critique' in order to justify vernacular works for the laity that are considerably more advanced than anything envisaged in the formal provisions for parochial instruction.[37] There appears to be not only a trend in the later fourteenth and fifteenth centuries for increasingly individual access to pastoral materials, but also a developing taste for works that offer something more than the essential elements of the faith. The texts I am considering here reflect this trend. They not only offer themselves as informal spiritual 'good counsel' independent of that which may or may not be offered formally by the priest, but also go beyond the basic elements by presenting the sacrament of penance as merely a preliminary step in a more extensive pursuit of the spiritual life.

Rolle's *Form*, for instance, falls into two parts.[38] The first, lines 1–488, provides material on matters such as the classification of sins of the heart, speech, deed and omission, and the three parts of penance. But the second half contains more spiritually advanced material. It is given over to a treatment of love, especially the three degrees of love by which the reader may obtain spiritual perfection. This second section points to an ongoing spiritual journey, for Rolle would have his reader 'euer clymynge to Ihesuward'.[39] Similarly, in the *Chastising*, the author points out that it does not suffice simply to perform the satisfaction imposed by the priest; one must also improve oneself with spiritual exercises as a kind of supplementary therapy for 'purgacion of þe soule'.[40] The *Cleansing* primarily devotes itself to three main sections on the three parts of the sacrament of penance. However, the work concludes with a final chapter that provides a recapitulation of the whole text, followed by a brief discussion of 'the

---

[36] MS Bodley 923, fol. 10ʳ. [37] Somerset (1998; 14).
[38] See *English Writings of Richard Rolle*, pp. 83–84. Some copies of the *Form* divide the text into two books.
[39] Rolle, *Form of Living*, p. 10, l. 310. [40] *Chastising*, p. 215, ll. 1–5.

reforming of man's soul': reform of the mind, the reason, and the will. It becomes clear from this discussion that the author of this work, too, believes the sacrament of penance to be only the first step of a larger spiritual journey:

> After such clensinge of ȝour soule þan schall ȝe begynne to turne to our lord Ihesu Crist and seke aȝein þat was lost. For as moche as þe soule beholdith & seeth inwardly þat he was foule deformed & be vnclennes fer out from þe presence of our lord, so moche þe rather and more þe besier he trauaileth to be reformed to þat fairhede [&] goostly semelyhede which was lost.[41]

Here, counsel on the three parts of penance is followed by a more ambitious programme of ongoing spiritual reform. Of course, one might expect something rather more spiritually ambitious than straightforward accounts of the sins and penance from texts that are associated with audiences of female religious. But *Memoriale credencium*, even though it was written for a lay audience, also includes a section on meditation and contemplation, adapted from Edmund of Abingdon's *Speculum ecclesie* (a work originally written for an audience of religious):

> Ferþermore yf a man shal lyue parfitlych and holylich, hym bihoueþ to haue knowyng of hymself and knowyng of god almyȝty. To knowyng of þiself þu myȝt come þurgh holy meditacioun, to knowyng of god almyȝty þurgh pure contemplacion.[42]

Here the individual layman may implicitly attain spiritual knowledge through direct contemplation of God, without clerical mediation. This text re-presents pastoral materials for direct consumption by the laity and at the same time offers, to borrow a phrase from Somerset, 'far more "clergie" than the minimum the laity are strictly said to require'.[43]

While they offer something much more extensive than the minimum laid down in Pecham's Constitutions, these texts simultaneously downplay the place of 'clergie' in the sense of academic or institutionalized knowledge. In the passage from *Memoriale credencium* quoted above, *self-knowledge* rather than academic knowledge is emphasized. This kind of knowledge of God anyone, in theory, may attain through 'pure contemplation'. In Rolle's *Form of Living*, too, book-learning becomes largely

---

[41] MS Bodley 923, fol. 148ʳ. Compare also the discussion of the reform of reason, the first part of this section. Here the *first* stage of the reform of reason is belief in Holy Church and the sacrament of penance; but *perfection* of reason consists of an entirely unmediated, mystical knowledge of God: 'Perfeccioun of resoun in þis liif is to be rauysched aboue himself goostly to se our lord god be an inward & intellectuale knowinge' (fols 149ᵛ–150ᵛ).

[42] *Memoriale credencium*, p. 205, ll. 14–18. See *Memoriale credencium*, pp. 16–17, for the source.

[43] Somerset (1998; 14).

irrelevant, for love, as in Patience's teaching at Conscience's banquet, is all: 'The dar nat gretly couait many bokes; hold loue in hert and in werke, and þou hast al done þat we may say or write'.⁴⁴ Similarly, as I have already shown, the author of the *Cleansing* submits his work to the correction not only of clerks but also of 'oþer holy liuers', again suggesting that spiritual wisdom may differ from academic or theoretical knowledge.

Perhaps most pregnant for my purposes are the comments the author of the *Cleansing* makes elsewhere in his work, where he distinguishes academic knowledge or *scientia* from *conscientia*:

> [C]onscience is as moche to sey as þe science of þe hert...A mannes hert hath somtyme knowynge of himself and of many oþer things by þe schewynge or techynge of other men and by redynge and oþer naturel knowynge. But proprely whanne he knowith himself þan þat knowynge is cleped conscience. And whan a man knowith oþer things þan himself than is that knowynge cleped science. Manye men trauaylen for to haue þe seconde knowynge but fewe there ben þat seken besily to come to þe ferst. Therefore seith an holy clerk Hugo de Sancto Victore, 'Manye men seken science, but fewe conscience'.⁴⁵

Clearly, this work values 'þe science of þe hert', self-knowledge or conscience, over the theoretical knowledge which comes from books. As the author writes later in the work, 'a soule when hit passith oute from þe body berith wiþ him none oþer boke but the boke of conscience'.⁴⁶ By quoting Hugh of St Victor, the *Cleansing* looks back to a twelfth-century tradition, discussed in connection with *Piers Plowman* by James Simpson, 'in which authentic knowledge of the self, and therefore of God, through the conscience, is consistently placed above the knowledge gained through human instruction and books'.⁴⁷ This twelfth-century emphasis on self-knowledge underwent a revival in the late middle ages. The fifteenth century saw a growth in the number of manuscripts of earlier authors such as Abelard, Bernard, and Hugh and Richard of St Victor, all of whom stressed that knowledge of God began with self-knowledge.⁴⁸ The resurgence of interest in twelfth-century works stressing self-knowledge coincides, of course, with the increasing interest in vernacular religious books among the laity. It is, perhaps, only natural that the growth in a lay audience for religious literature should have been accompanied by an increased

---

⁴⁴ Rolle, *Form of Living*, p. 18, ll. 622–24.   ⁴⁵ MS Bodley 923, fol. 19ʳ.
⁴⁶ MS Bodley 923, fol. 22ʳ. For the 'book of conscience' in *Piers Plowman*, cf. B.15.533–37. As Clopper (1997; 187) notes, rightly rejecting the previous interpretations by Schmidt (1982) and Wilson (1983) as largely irrelevant to Langland's concerns, this passage seems to refer to 'a faculty by which the apostles knew what to do and say... without recourse to *scientia*'.
⁴⁷ Simpson (1986b; 53).   ⁴⁸ Constable (1969).

emphasis on self-knowledge rather than academic knowledge. In any case, an emphasis on self-knowledge through the conscience over the learning acquired from books forms a final characterizing feature of the 'vernacularized' or 'laicized' penitential discourse that I have been describing. Although, of the texts I have examined here, only the *Cleansing* explicitly sets *conscientia* against *scientia*, all emphasize implicitly the role of the individual conscience over institutionalized forms of knowledge and teaching.

CONSCIENCE AND VERNACULAR 'COUNSEL' IN B 13–14

Langland's presentation of Conscience in B 13–14 shares with the texts I have been exploring the 'vernacularizing' or 'laicizing' tendencies of late-fourteenth to fifteenth-century penitential discourse. One may discern as much from the beginning of the banquet at Conscience's house. As I observed above, Conscience appears here as a non-academic figure quite different from Clergy and the learned Doctor of Divinity. He ultimately sides with Patience and his experiential, practical knowledge, leaving Clergy behind with his books. Langland seems to distinguish between *conscientia* and *scientia* in much the same way as the author of the *Cleansing*, prioritizing self-knowledge ('þe science of þe hert' or 'cor' towards which Patience's riddle points) over the kind of knowledge that may be obtained from books. As Lawler indicates, Conscience's name in this scene seems to mean 'not the faculty of inner moral judgment, but "science with" or "thorough (that is, not merely academic) knowledge," or even "perfected knowledge"'.[49] Other medieval writers also distinguished similarly between *conscientia* and *scientia*: Bonaventure, for instance, argued that *conscientia* differs from theoretical knowledge ('speculativa scientia') because it is joined to desire and deed ('iuncta affectioni et operationi').[50] Langland apparently has a similar idea in mind when he shows Conscience leaving his own banquet, for Conscience says that Patience's 'will' has moved him to mourn for his sins (B.13.189–97). Conscience, that is, responds to Patience at the level of affect, not intellect. By having Will follow him and Patience from the banquet, Langland aligns his poem, at least for the time being, with Conscience as practical knowledge (knowledge joined to deeds) rather than the *scientia* that comes from Clergy's books. Like the other ver-

---

[49] Lawler (1995; 98).
[50] *S. Bonaventurae: Opera omnia*, II, 899, trans. Potts (1980; 111).

nacular penitential texts I have been examining, Langland emphasizes the individual conscience over academic forms of knowing—although, as I will show, Clergy's parting words to Conscience offer some qualifications, which are brought to the fore in Conscience's final appearance in B 20.

But Langland does not simply present Conscience here as an allegorical representation of the *conscientia* (self-knowledge or pragmatic knowledge) that other medieval writers also distinguished from *scientia*. In the first vision, as I argued in the previous chapter, Langland presents Meed not simply as an allegorical representation of 'reward', but also as the embodiment of the kind of person who (mis)uses such reward within Langland's contemporary society. So too in the fourth vision, Langland composes Conscience as an embodiment of the virtuous (lay) penitent imagined in vernacular penitential literature. Conscience is clearly figured as a lay person in this scene, as his incomprehension of Clergy's academic language would indicate. As I have already observed, the banquet is said to take place in Conscience's 'court', implying that he is here imagined as a lay lord. Nevertheless, Conscience provides penitential counsel to the guests at his banquet in the same way as texts like Rolle's *Form* and *Memoriale credencium* suggest that their readers may offer instruction to their fellow Christians. As in the first vision, Conscience appears as a knight, but Langland now presents a newly spiritualized version of knighthood in which penitential meditation and spiritual counsel become a paradoxical form of household 'entertainment' and feasting.

Conscience's banquet at his 'court' of course recalls Dame Study's earlier complaints about the absence of spiritual counsel in the contemporary hall. Friars, in particular, Study claims, show more interest in flattering the intellectual pretensions of the laity than in calling them to penance (B.10.72–76). Theological speculation has been reduced to a dinnertime game for clerks and laymen alike (B.10.52–58), while minstrelsy has degenerated from the provision of edifying tales of Tobit to the telling of crude stories (B.10.30–35, 49–50). The gluttonous Doctor at Conscience's banquet, taking a swig of wine as he answers Conscience's question about Dowel (B.13.104), clearly recalls those arrogant intellectuals whom Study had earlier described, those who 'gnawen god in þe gorge whanne hir guttes fullen' (B.10.58).

Conscience himself, in contrast with the Doctor, offers to his guests just the kind of dinner-table edification about whose demise Dame Study had earlier complained. The 'dishes' of food he offers his guests are texts from the penitential psalms, as is the 'entertainment' he offers at the feast:

> And Conscience conforted vs and carped vs murye tales:
> *Cor contritum & humiliatum deus non despicies.*
>
> (B.13.58–58a)[51]

Of course, the abjection and sorrow indicated in the psalm Conscience quotes means that these texts can only paradoxically be described as 'merry tales'. As often in the poem, Langland transforms the usual senses of words to new, paradoxical, spiritualized meanings.[52] In describing how Conscience 'conforted' his guests with 'merry tales' of penitential psalms, Langland plays on two senses of the Middle English verb 'to comfort': 'comfort' as refreshment or entertainment (*MED*, s.v. 'comforten', 3(a), 'To refresh (sb. with food or drink)' and 6, 'To entertain or amuse (sb.)') and as spiritual edification (*MED*, s.v. 'comforten', 1, 'To strengthen (sb.) spiritually'). Spiritually nourishing but unpleasantly bitter, hard penance is paradoxically transformed into 'merriment'. Just so, Ymaginatif had earlier, in another echo of Piers's pardon-tearing, described suffering God's chastising as 'murþe' for the soul (B.12.13–15; Ymaginatif cites the same psalm, psalm 22, as Piers had quoted when he tore the pardon: cf. B.7.120–21).

The transformation here of poor food and bitter penance into paradoxically 'merry tales' or entertainment anticipates the similarly paradoxical transformation of minstrelsy in the digression on 'God's minstrels' (really the poor) at the end of passus 13. By inviting the poor pilgrim Patience to his feast, Conscience presents an example of the kind of lord who invites the poor, 'God's minstrels', to his feast at the end of passus 13 (B.13.421–56). As I discussed in Chapter 1, Meed had earlier argued that Conscience, as a knight, must rely on 'meed' for the acts of largesse by which a lord secures and rewards the loyalty of his retinue (B.3.180–82, 209–14). By contrast, a lord who, like Conscience, keeps the poor as his retainers instead receives through *them* a 'largesse' from God (B.13.446–48).

The passage on 'God's minstrels' and Conscience's penitential 'feast' thus together present a transformed version of the noble household. Conscience offers, in place of feasting and entertainment, hard penance (the contrite tears Piers had earlier vowed to eat instead of bread). His penitential 'feast' contrasts with the behaviour of the Doctor, who preaches of Paul's 'penaunces' (B.13.66), yet lives off rich food and 'miswinnings' (B.13.42). (The implication seems to be that the Doctor, like the friars Conscience will encounter in the reprise of this scene in passus 20, accepts

---

[51] All of the Latin quotations in the description of the feast in B.13.53–58a come from two of the penitential psalms, 31 and 50. See Alford (1992; 83).
[52] See Simpson (1986c).

ill-gotten gains instead of insisting upon restitution.) Conscience's hard penance also contrasts, of course, with the easy 'mercy' Meed had earlier tried to obtain for her retainer Wrong with cash. The sober reflection inspired by 'God's minstrels', who tell 'of good friday þe geste' (B.13.446), like the self-abnegation of Conscience's penitential texts, allows the lord to obtain true mercy from God.

The 'comfort' Conscience offers with his paradoxical form of 'merry tales'—penitential psalms—resembles just the kind of 'comfort' or spiritual counsel that a layman might be expected to offer in the vernacular penitential texts I examined above. Langland selects the same word, 'comfort', as the author of the *Cleansing* used to describe the 'litel comfort' his audience might receive from their confessors. Conscience's banquet certainly presents a scenario similar to that imagined in the *Cleansing*, where the author hints at the inadequacy of clerical provision for instruction or spiritual 'comfort'. In *Piers Plowman*, the layman Conscience provides spiritual 'comfort' or counsel to his fellow Christians in the absence of proper clerical instruction and example from the learned Doctor. Just as Rolle imagines his reader giving spiritual counsel as well as providing food and drink to the poor (the pittance for which Patience cries at Conscience's gate, B.13.29–30),[53] so Conscience 'comforts' his guests with the 'food' of penitential psalms. These texts were widely available to a lay readership through their inclusion in books of hours and were seen as aids to private repentance.[54]

Conscience's subsequent decision to go on penitential pilgrimage also favours 'laicized' attitudes towards penitence, and again suggests how these 'laicizing' tendencies frequently looked backwards to pre-Lateran IV, de-institutionalized ideas about penance. Lawler has argued that Conscience's decision to undertake a penitential pilgrimage with Patience resembles the motif of the knight in penitential retreat (a claim which again implies that Conscience remains a consistent 'knightly' type in this scene).[55] If one accepts Lawler's argument, one might note with some interest that the penitential romances examined by Andrea Hopkins evoke a somewhat older idea of penance as a once-only 'conversion'. They emphasize the penitent's relationship with God rather than recourse to the Church.[56] This same emphasis on an individual relationship with God may also be observed, of course, in Piers's decision to renounce his

---

[53] See Rolle, *Form of Living*, p. 13, ll. 407–10, already quoted above.
[54] The small size of many of the books containing Richard Maidstone's English translation of the psalms implies that they were produced for private reading, suggesting their association with private, individual forms of spirituality. See Staley (2006; 113, 117) and *The Prymer or Lay Folks' Prayer Book*.
[55] Lawler (1995; 97).   [56] Hopkins (1990; 32).

ploughing and take up prayer.[57] Pilgrimage is itself a form of satisfaction, the third part of penance, but Conscience, like Piers earlier, imposes his penitential act upon himself rather than performing it at the instigation of a priest.

Conscience's and Patience's instruction to Haukin at the end of passus 13 and the beginning of passus 14 also strongly resembles 'vernacularized' forms of penance. When they leave the banquet, Conscience and Patience meet the 'minstrel' Haukin. After a quasi 'confession', in which they discover the stains of all seven deadly sins on his 'coat of Christendom', they provide him instruction on penance and on what Patience elaborates as 'patient poverty'. The instruction they offer is much like the materials found in pastoral handbooks for priests, but Haukin's 'confession' nevertheless takes place in a setting very different from the one imagined in those handbooks. As Lawrence Clopper points out, Conscience and Patience do not actually act as priests, nor do they try to administer the sacrament of penance. They call Haukin to penance (B.13.313–14) and Conscience then explains the parts of the sacrament (B.14.16–28). But the two teachers provide Haukin with moral exhortation rather than offering to absolve him.[58] Clopper argues that the presentation of Conscience and Patience illustrates Langland's radical Franciscanism: his 'portrayal of the two itinerants seems in keeping with Langland's opposition to the granting of cure of souls to the friars'.[59] I do not think Langland means Conscience and Patience to be imagined as friars. Although they recall Will's meeting with the pair of friars at the beginning of passus 8, nevertheless Conscience and Patience represent a pedagogical ideal that Langland consistently shows the friars not to match. Patience and Conscience are better associated here with one of the poem's other figures, Piers Plowman, who, as the untutored devout man in the second vision, also provided his fellow Christians with teaching on the basic elements of the faith, in his case the Ten Commandments (B.5.560–629).

A closer look at Conscience's instruction on penance at the beginning of passus 14 should confirm that the instruction offered by Conscience and Patience represents lay spiritual counsel rather than more formal, institutionalized instruction:

---

[57] Cf. Simpson (2007; 78).

[58] Of course, this is consistent with the allegorical meaning of 'conscience', which as consciousness of guilt leads to contrition but does not absolve the sinner of his sin. However, Langland never writes such 'pure' allegory; Conscience is not merely a series of concepts but also a series of specific instantiations within different contemporary discourses. Here he is figured, as I have argued, as an embodiment of the 'conscientious' layman who offers spiritual advice to a fellow Christian. He is not in any straightforward way Haukin's (or Will's) own conscience.

[59] Clopper (1997; 198, n. 39).

> 'And I shal kenne þee', quod Conscience, 'of Contricion to make
> That shal clawe þi cote of alle kynnes filþe:
> *Cordis contricio &c.*
> Dowel shal wasshen it and wryngen it þoru3 a wis confessour:
> *Oris confessio &c.*
> Dobet shal beten it and bouken it as bright as any scarlet
> And engreynen it wiþ good wille and goddes grace to amende þe,
> And siþen sende þee to Satisfaccion for to sonnen it after:
> *Satisfaccio.*
> Dobest shal kepe it clene from vnkynde werkes.
>
> (B.14.16–22)

Conscience's account of the three parts of penance strikes the reader as highly conventional, and it makes full use of the rhetorical devices used in the pastoral manuals. Conscience emphasizes, for instance, the triadic form of the parts of penance by associating Dowel with *Oris confessio* and Dobet with *Satisfaccio*, while Dobest will keep Haukin's coat 'clene from vnkynde werkes'.[60] In the next chapter, I compare Conscience's similar use of the three Do's in B 19 with another instructional mode, the various triadic structures of the 'modern' or scholastic type of sermon. But such triadic forms also feature ubiquitously in pastoral handbooks.[61] As the author of *The Cleansing of Man's Soul* recognizes, triadic schemes of organization are useful mnemonic devices, enabling easy learning and recall of essential information.[62] In Conscience's speech the three Do's and the three Latin phrases '*Cordis contricio... Oris confessio... Satisfaccio*'[63] work as mnemonics keying into the more detailed information presented around them. They are perhaps comparable to commonplace mnemonic verses on the 'circumstances' of sin (cited here from Raymund de Peniafort's *Summa*):

---

[60] The three parts of penance do not, it will be noticed, correspond directly with the three Do's. '*Cordis contricio*' seems to *precede* the three Do's, while Dobest comes *after* '*Satisfaccio*', a point to which I return below.

[61] Particularly close to the three Do's as positive, comparative and superlative forms is a discussion of Conscience's main theme here, contrition, found in Raymund de Peniafort: 'Contritio est dolor pro peccatis assumptus, cum proposito confitendi, et satisfaciendi... Iste dolor debet esse triplex, vt ait Bernardus, acer, acrior, acerrimus' (Contrition is a sorrow taken up for sins, with the intention of confessing and making satisfaction. This sorrow should be treble, as Bernard says, bitter, bitterer, bitterest) (*Summa*, III.34.8).

[62] Cf. MS Bodley 923, fols 73ʳ–74ʳ. The *Cleansing* author divides each sin into sins of thought, speech, and deed, so that '3e schal haue 3our synnes bettir in mynde when 3e come to confessioun'. The manuscript decoration emphasizes his tripartite division.

[63] The Latin definition of the three parts of penance is of course commonplace; cf. Peniafort, *Summa*, III.34.7.

> Circumstantias autem istas, quas praecipue debet attendere, nota in his versiculis.
> *Quis, quid, vbi, per quos, quoties, cur, quomodo, quando.*[64]

But for all its recourse to the formal devices ubiquitous in pastoral manuals, one must surely categorize Conscience's speech alongside those works designed for individual spiritual counsel rather than those for the use of priests. Conscience merely gestures, for instance, at the requirement that the priest be wise (B.14.18), a topic that receives lengthy elaboration in the handbooks for priests.[65] As I have shown, works on penance designed as individual spiritual guidance, rather than for the use of the priest, similarly omit much material of this nature. Conscience's teaching on the three parts of penance thus suggests informal spiritual counsel to a fellow Christian, comparable to that earlier offered by Piers on the Ten Commandments, rather than institutionalized instruction. The similarity between Conscience's and Piers's teaching is of course consistent with the fact that Piers cited Conscience as the source of his own non-institutional knowledge in the second vision.

Patience implicitly confirms this characterization of Conscience's teaching as lay spiritual counsel supplementary to, or outside of, clerical supervision and instruction. In passus 14, he tells Haukin that Conscience provides (penitential) knowledge that is sufficient for salvation even in the absence of sacramental penance:

> Forþi mesure we vs wel and make we feiþ oure sheltrom;
> And þoru3 feiþ comeþ contricion, conscience woot wel,
> Which dryueþ awey dedly synne and dooþ it to be venial.
> And þou3 a man my3te no3t speke contricion my3te hym saue
> And brynge his soule to blisse, so þat feiþ bere witnesse
> That whiles he lyuede he bileuede in þe loore of holy chirche.
> *Ergo* contricion, feiþ and conscience is kyndeliche dowel,
> And surgiens for dedly synnes whan shrift of mouþe failleþ.
>
> (B.14.82–89)

Patience's words of course recall the '*Cor contritum & humiliatum*' of Conscience's banquet and they also echo Piers' earlier penitential gesture with its expression of faith in God (B.7.120–21). Conscience, joined to contrition and faith—and already separated from Clergy as academic

---

[64] 'Those circumstances which need particularly to be attended to, note in these verses: who, what, where, by which means, how often, why, in what way, when?' (Peniafort, *Summa*, III.34.29). For the classical origin of these mnemonic verses on the 'circumstances' of sin and their transmission to the Middle Ages, see Robertson, D.W., Jr (1946, 1947). For the development of mnemonic verses on the points of a good confession, see Millett (1999; 205).

[65] See, for instance, Peniafort's treatment, *Summa*, III.34.28.

knowledge/*scientia* in B 13—is all that is needful to salvation. It is sufficient in the absence of sacramental penance, and perhaps also in the situation which (as I discuss further below) both *Piers Plowman* and the *Cleansing* imagine: the contemporary deficiency of formal instruction from those supposedly professionally committed to the task.

Langland presents his two lay vernacular teachers as capable of going well beyond the basics of instruction in sacramental penance. Patience's teaching perhaps most closely corresponds in this to other vernacular penitential texts. Conscience's teaching tends to resemble more basic catechesis,[66] but Patience's discourse on poverty is, by contrast, overtly difficult (note Haukin's complaint at B.14.277) and paradoxical, apparently designed, like the teaching of a Buddhist master, to shock his pupil into realization. For Patience, the three parts of penance described by Conscience represent only the beginning of a much more radical transformation, the pursuit of a more spiritual mode of life in 'patient poverty'. This state demands nothing less than the total transformation of Haukin from 'Actif' to passive/patient:

> 'And I shal purueie þee paast', quod Pacience, 'þouȝ no plouȝ erye,
> And flour to fede folk wiþ as best be for þe soule;
> Thouȝ neuere greyn growed, ne grape vpon vyne,
> All þat lyueþ and lokeþ liflode wolde I fynde
> And þat ynogh; shal noon faille of þyng þat hem nedeþ:
> *Ne soliciti sitis &c; Volucres celi deus pascit &c; pacientes vincunt &c.*'
>
> (B.14.29–33a)

In Patience's, as in Piers Plowman's original formulation, 'patient poverty' is something other than the mere performance of sacramental penance. It involves a renunciation of will, of desire/solicitude, together with a continual *reiteration* of penitential tears; as Piers had put it earlier:

> 'I parfourned þe penaunce þe preest me enioyned
> And am sory for my synnes and so shal I *euere*
> Whan I þynke þeron, þeiȝ I were a Pope.'
>
> (B.5.598–600, my emphasis)

Patience emphasizes post- or extra-sacramental pursuit of spiritual perfection through 'patient poverty', much as the four texts I discussed above present their basic teaching on penance alongside a more ambitious programme of ongoing spiritual reform through individual meditation and spiritual exercises.

---

[66] Gillespie (1981; 167–8) suggests that the presence of the Latin tags *cordis contritio*, *oris confessio*, and *operis satisfaccio* in a fifteenth-century English lyric shows 'the influence of catechism formulations'. For the relevant lyric, see *Religious Lyrics of the XVth Century*, pp. 273–7. One could make the same point about Conscience's speech.

Although his teaching is rather more basic, even Conscience gestures towards something more than mere sacramental penance. The penitential texts Conscience offered at his feast have already hinted at that ongoing penitential meditation and rumination which Piers's substitution of tears for bread had earlier implied. Conscience's presentation of the three parts of penance in connection with the three Do's also makes clear that he imagines Haukin doing more than simply performing sacramental penance. As I have indicated, such a triadic format appears ubiquitously in the penitential manuals. But Conscience's arrangement of the three Do's in connection with the three parts of penance suggests that, as in the *Cleansing,* spiritual perfection or 'Dobest' comes only *after,* not upon completion of, sacramental penance:

> Dobet shal beten it and bouken it as bright as any scarlet
> ...
> And siþen sende þee to Satisfaccion for to sonnen it after:
> *Satisfaccio.*
> Dobest shal kepe it clene from vnkynde werkes.
>
> (B.14.19–22)

Like Piers Plowman's definition of Dowel and Dobet as 'two infinites' seeking out a third, Conscience's arrangement of the three Do's implies that Dowel is an infinite *process,* not a finite object. Haukin's collapse into tears at the end of passus 14 (reiterating Piers's similar penitential gesture earlier) sees an obsession with material labour and its rewards (cf. B.13.224–46) replaced by the work of penance. This work, as Haukin recognizes (B.14.12, 326), requires continual reiteration. The understanding of 'doing well' as 'measurable' acts that had dominated Conscience's thinking in the first vision and Piers Plowman's for most of the second (as well as Will's quest for Dowel in the third) gives way to the idea of 'doing well' as an 'infinite', unmeasurable, ongoing penitential state.

Taken together, then, the instruction offered Haukin by Conscience and Patience suggests that sacramental penance is only the beginning of the pursuit of perfection;[67] the teaching of the two speakers gestures towards a spiritual life broader than that offered by catechesis in the basic elements of the faith. Here again *Piers Plowman* participates in a more general trend in the fourteenth and fifteenth centuries. Even as pastoral materials were increasingly adapted for or finding their way into direct lay use, a taste was developing for something more than basic catechesis. To adapt the commonplace medical metaphor for penance, an interest was growing in alternative and self-help therapies; a desire emerged for the

---

[67] Cf. the similar observation made by Watson (2007; 112).

presentation of information on the basics of the faith within the context of a more individual and holistic approach to spiritual health. As conventional modern medicine might be criticized for concerning itself only with morbid conditions rather than the 'whole person', so these works also show an interest in what the conventional manuals did not teach: spiritual 'wellness'. Conscience's, and even more so Patience's, self-help instruction to Haukin seems to participate in this trend. Like the four texts I have been examining in this chapter, Langland's presentation of Conscience and Patience in this part of *Piers Plowman* draws on a newly 'vernacularized' penitential discourse, in which the penitent may appropriate for direct use materials previously accessible only to 'Clergy'. These materials may indeed show a spiritual ambition far in excess of the minimum requirements offered by more official forms of religious discourse.

The most obvious, and perhaps the most important, thing that Langland's presentation of Conscience's and Patience's 'good counsel' shares with contemporary vernacular penitential texts, however, is that it takes place in the context of an acknowledged deficiency on the part of those who are officially responsible for the provision of spiritual instruction. The ignorance of the clergy was the starting point for the manuals for priests,[68] but the author of the *Cleansing*, as I have shown, draws his own more radical conclusion: that a manual for direct use by the penitent is required.[69] In *Piers Plowman*, the very presence at Conscience's banquet of the hypocritical friar bespeaks a similar institutional lack. As Lawler says, there is nothing wrong with the Doctor's definition of 'Dowel' as 'do as clerkes techeþ' (B.13.116), except that it is self-aggrandizing[70] (as well, of course, as hypocritical: the Doctor does not practice what he preaches). The Doctor embodies that intellectual and institutional arrogance of which Dame Study complained in passus 10, and which can also be seen in the self-regarding professionalism of Piers's priest in the second vision (B.7.108).

Langland hints at some possible reorientation of the contemporary institution in Conscience's parting from Clergy in B 13. Clergy promises that he will now dedicate himself not to the higher reaches of theological study, but to humbler pastoral work, staying behind to 'confermen fauntekyns ooþer folk ylered' (B.13.213). Clergy's words suggest an attempt to redefine 'Clergy' as the provision of an adequate pastoral programme, rather than the intellectual preening and professional rivalry

---

[68] The section of Archbishop Pecham's Constitutions of 1281 setting out a programme of religious instruction for the laity began *Ignorantia sacerdotum*. See Gillespie (1981; 148–51) for texts that explicitly cite Pecham's Constitutions.
[69] See MS Bodley 923, fol. 4^{r-v}, already quoted above.
[70] Lawler (1995; 90–91).

against which Dame Study railed for its detrimental effect on the provision of proper pastoral instruction (B.10.72–76). After all, Ymaginatif had suggested in passus 12 that the value of 'clergy' was largely pragmatic, as it related to administration of the sacraments: 'For goddes body myȝte noȝt ben of breed wiþouten clergie' (B.12.85). As Conscience takes his leave in B 13, Clergy insists that he will in future have need of his 'counseille' (B.13.202–4).

But as I discuss further in Chapter 6, at the poem's end, when he will indeed have cause to recall Clergy's parting words, Conscience lacks precisely someone competent in the *practice* of pastoral care, rather than merely theoretical, academic knowledge. The friars neglect (as Will complains in B.11.75–83) precisely non-lucrative pastoral work such as 'confirming fauntekyns'. Moreover, they offer just the opposite of the hard penance represented by the bitter food at Conscience's banquet. As I show in more detail in Chapter 4, the friars return Conscience and the poem to the easy 'mercy' Meed had earlier tried to obtain for Wrong. But the friars really only highlight here the absence of their alternative, a properly engaged parish clergy (cf. B.20.280–87). The second time Conscience calls for Clergy's aid (B.20.375), it is because the friar has so corrupted the sacrament of penance that Contrition is no longer contrite. But the first time he calls, it is because Unity is threatened by 'inparfite preestes and prelates of holy chirche' (B.20.229). Clergy's failure to appear tells its own story about the institutional inadequacies that are implicit in passus 13–14.[71]

In such a context, self-help in the form of spiritual counsel given freely to one's fellow Christian (Piers, unlike the friars, refuses payment; contrast B.5.556–59 with B.20.364) may indeed appear the preferable course. As Clergy predicted, Conscience will call on his aid at the end of the poem. But finally he goes in search of 'kyndely-knowing' Piers, for he needs 'Clergy' as the pragmatic knowledge sufficient to salvation, not the bookish Clergy of passus 13. As Conscience departs in pursuit of Piers, the poem ultimately puts its hope not in sacramental penance, but in 'grace', the sudden infusion of which may bring the most persistent sinner to a good end (as Will trusts it will in C passus 5).[72]

The poem clearly exposes, in B 13–14 and in B 20, the inadequacies of the contemporary clergy. Nevertheless, Clergy's parting words to

---

[71] Cf. the comments of Aers (2004; 33–36). As Aers points out, the pilgrims in the second vision who 'blustreden forþ as beestes' (B.5.514) also suggest 'a laity abandoned by their priests'.

[72] In his analysis of the revised confessions of the deadly sins in the C text, Hanna (1995; 91, 96) argues that Langland also appeals here, not to institutionalized penitential discourse but to 'a lay sorrow apart from any ecclesiastical direction'.

Conscience in B 13, fulfilled at the end of the poem, also suggest the ultimate limitations of the vernacular project initiated by Conscience and Patience in B 13–14. Conscience and Patience may offer penitential instruction and example preferable to that provided by Clergy or the Doctor, but the end of the poem makes clear that, as a layman (and as, allegorically, the consciousness of guilt that is the precondition of contrition and sacramental penance), Conscience still depends on Clergy for the administration of the sacrament. At the end of *Piers Plowman,* Conscience once again calls others to true penance as he did in B 13–14 (cf. B.19.395). But he can do little, as once again a layman and knight ('constable' of Unity, B.20.214), when those authorized to administer the sacrament are prepared (like Meed) to substitute cash payments for performance of true *pena*. From the perspective of B 20, Langland's new poetic initiative in the mode of 'vernacular penitence' in the fourth vision might look like yet another false start, although in the poem's final lines it seems to remain Langland's best hope. The collapse of the poem's final penitential sequence in B 20 necessitates another new beginning, but one that also entails a final reiteration: a second pilgrimage for Conscience in pursuit of the holy vernacular teacher Piers.

3
'Ecce Rex': Conscience and Homiletic Discourse in B 19[1]

Conscience concludes his instruction to Haukin at B.14.28. As I will subsequently argue, one should understand that he listens along with Haukin and Will as Patience delivers his praise of 'patient poverty'. Nevertheless, Conscience drops silently from the poem at some point during passus 14, and he will not appear again until the penultimate vision of *Piers Plowman*. Langland's retelling of biblical history occupies much of the intervening narrative, as *Piers Plowman* turns to that new mode of poetry, 'good friday þe geste' (B.13.446), which was projected by the transformed 'minstrelsy' of the fourth vision.[2] Conscience, created from the first vision as a character very much of Langland's own contemporary world ('cam late fro biyonde', B.3.110) and of a topical poetry in the mode of *Wynnere and Wastoure*, drops from the poem as it turns away from earlier 'topical' themes to salvation history.

But of course Will's climactic dream of the crucifixion and harrowing of hell in B 18 does not conclude Langland's poem. In the two final visions, Langland returns to the 'contemporary conditions' of the first vision. But he now seeks to assimilate the 'topical' themes of the earlier part of the poem to the biblical narrative he has just presented. The last two visions witness an attempt to transform the 'contemporary conditions' of the two first dreams into newly spiritualized terms.

With the poem's return to the interests of the first vision at the beginning of B 19, Conscience, one of the central figures of the opening dream of *Piers Plowman*, also reappears. His speech in B.19.12–210 revisits one of the major themes of his earlier debate with Meed in passus 3, the obligations of knights, kings and conquerors towards their followers. Langland now reimagines these obligations in the

---

[1] An earlier version of this chapter was published together with part of Chapter 6 as Wood (2007). It is reproduced in revised form with kind permission from Brepols Publishers.
[2] 'Geste' is Kane-Donaldson's emendation: Schmidt, *B-Text*, B.13.447 retains 'storye', the reading of RF, the only B manuscripts to attest lines 436–53.

'spiritualized' terms of Christ's conquest over death and gift of pardon to his retinue of Christians.[3]

As in the first vision, Conscience appears here as himself a knight, although now characterized as a herald. In part, the exchange between Will and Conscience at the beginning of B 19 continues a characterization that had first emerged during the interchange with Faith at the beginning of the preceding passus: Will again takes on the role of a tournament spectator and he turns to the herald for information about the jouster. Conscience, as any good herald is supposed to do, identifies the participant by his arms and provides details of his place of origin and history (B.19.12–14, 71, 101–107).[4] The king's knight of the first vision is thus transformed in B 19 into herald of the kingly Christ. Conscience becomes the herald of Christ's new law (culminating in his granting pardon to Piers Plowman, B.19.182–90) as Abraham/Faith was earlier herald of the old.[5]

In one sense, Conscience's appearance in B 19 simply reiterates in a new context the role he performed in the first vision. Conscience seems the appropriate speaker for this part of the poem not so much because, as Britton Harwood has argued, 'conscience' is a faculty that gives knowledge of God,[6] as because Langland here returns to the themes of an earlier part of the poem in which Conscience was also central. Just as in passus 3–4 Conscience bore witness to Meed's corruption of the law, so here he bears witness to Christ's rewriting of the law.[7]

Conscience's presence in B 19 as well as in B 3–4 highlights the parallels as well as, of course, the crucial differences between Meed and Christ as leaders of retinues. While Meed attempts to secure a false form of 'pardon' (because obtained by cash) for her retainer Wrong, Christ obtains a true pardon for his 'affinity' of all baptized Christians. This pardon requires that his followers should make true 'amends' by paying back what they owe (B.19.183–87).

In his representation of Meed and her retinue, Langland briefly evoked the formulaic diction of the alliterative tradition (cf. esp. B.3.14, 'Busked

---

[3] Conscience's speech has recently received extensive treatment in Barney (2006; 100–33). See also especially Weldon (1989) for the relationship between this part of the poem and the liturgy of Holy Week. For further echoes of the liturgy, see St Jacques (1977).

[4] See Wagner (1939; 26).

[5] Much of the early part of Conscience's discussion—his identification of Piers's arms, and the language of enfranchisement of Christians versus thraldom of Jews—originates with Faith, and Conscience himself points to the resemblance when he says, 'Faithly for to speke...' (B.19.70).

[6] See Harwood (1992; 117): 'Will finds the converting knowledge of God in Conscience'. Cf. also pp. 137–8.

[7] For Conscience, from 'con-scire', as a witness, see Potts (1980; 2).

hem to þe bour þer þe burde dwelleþ'). Correspondingly, Conscience's depiction of Christ as knight, king, and conqueror reinvents one typical subject matter of alliterative poetry: the deeds of those other knights and conquerors, the Nine Worthies.[8] Langland presents a new, Christianized version of the predominantly non-Christian Nine: the feats that typically characterize the infancy of the hero in romance are here converted into the gospel miracles. The young knight Jesus is shown to be the descendant of, but also to surpass in prowess, one of the Nine, King David (B.19.96–135).

This newly spiritualized version of the conventional themes of alliterative poetry and of topics that were central to Conscience's earlier debate with Meed required a new mode of writing, something quite different from the debate and invective of the first vision. Langland found this new mode in the language of sermons. Discussions of sermon form in the medieval *artes praedicandi* offer parallels for some of the rhetorical structures of Conscience's speech,[9] while its subject matter, Christ as knight, king, and conqueror, also has analogues in homiletic discourse, particularly in sermons for Advent.[10] Such writing offered Langland a useful mode in which 'topical' concerns could be subsumed within biblical narrative:[11] in both contemporary sermons and in Conscience's speech, political themes and biblical history meet in the person of Christ the king. In B 19, Conscience draws on a variety of homiletic commonplaces in order to extend the examination of secular law and government in the first vision into the spiritual realm.[12]

---

[8] Cf. Barney (2006; 113) and see especially the account in *The Parlement of the Thre Ages* in *Alliterative Poetry*.

[9] Weldon (1989; 49, 64) argues that the repetition in the passage of forms of the verb 'to kneel' suggests the rhetorical figure 'concordia verborum' associated with the *artes praedicandi*. But his analysis of Conscience's speech is confined to the figure of kneeling and does not pursue further parallels with homiletic discourse.

[10] My choice of Advent sermons may need some explanation, given the close parallels which have been demonstrated between B 19 and the Holy Week liturgy. Advent and Holy Week are in fact closely related in the liturgy of the church (and the themes of *de tempore* sermons are generally taken from the Epistle or Gospel for the Mass). First Advent and Palm Sunday shared the same Gospel reading, because the entry into Jerusalem was understood to signify allegorically Christ's coming into human flesh. See Spencer (1993; 27–28).

[11] My identification of his speech as a sermon and Conscience as a preacher again points to the continuities between this part of the B text and one of Conscience's appearances earlier in the composition of the poem. In A passus 5, Conscience was explicitly identified as the preacher of a sermon and, as I argued in the Introduction, Langland seems to have had this passage in mind when composing the later speech for Conscience in B passus 19.

[12] The roles of preacher and herald, incidentally, are not necessarily incompatible; they may indeed be regarded as complementary. In a commonplace of *de tempore* sermons for Advent, the *Northern Homily Cycle* (I, ll. 379–80, 389, 393–94) compares the Advent of Christ with the coming of a great king. Just as messengers bring word of a king's arrival, so too are preachers 'Cristes messangeres'.

B.19.1–212 AND THE *ARTES PRAEDICANDI*

Medieval sermons have been central to the study of *Piers Plowman* ever since G. R. Owst described the poem as the 'quintessence of English mediaeval preaching'.[13] Elizabeth Salter observed that many of the allegorical characters are often overtly preaching, and that many forms of verbal repetition, as recommended in the *artes praedicandi*, form part of Langland's usual poetic practice.[14] A. C. Spearing suggested that features such as digression and even the poem's overall form—returning to the point at which it began—could be compared with those of sermons. He, too, pointed out that the poem's personified figures often appear as preachers: 'They do not have to be interpreted allegorically themselves, but are more likely to *use* the medieval preacher's technique of allegorical exegesis on Scriptural texts'.[15] One should not be surprised, therefore, to find in Conscience's discussion a number of similarities with the formal devices recommended by the guides to sermon composition, or to discover that it shares with sermons some traditional subject-matter. A comparison of Conscience's speech with medieval sermons reveals how Langland drew, in composing this figure, on materials that are commonplace in Latin and vernacular texts. These are materials quite different from the scholastic sources typically adduced in readings that interpret Conscience's role in the poem in straightforward allegorical terms.

Conscience's speech most strikingly resembles the form of medieval sermons in its triadic structure. In keeping with the triadic form of its central scheme, Conscience's discussion of Christ as knight, king, and conqueror falls into three sections, although none corresponds directly with any one part of the triad. The first part, lines 26–68, introduces and defines each term of the trio knight, king, and conqueror, before recapitulating the events presented in the previous passus. Conscience alludes to the Crucifixion (lines 41, 49–50) and harrowing of hell (lines 52–57), and briefly to Christ's ministry on earth (lines 44–47). He concludes this first section with an explanation of the significance of the cross as a weapon against temptation (lines 63–68).

The second section of Conscience's speech, lines 69–107, presents a life of Christ, beginning with his birth and the Epiphany and providing an account of the allegorical significance of the gifts of the Magi. Already, at the moment of his birth, the three kings acknowledge Jesus as 'souereyn/

---

[13] Owst (1926; 295). Wenzel (1988) surveys the major discussions of this subject.
[14] Salter (1963; 24–57).
[15] Spearing (1972; 111). Similarly, Alford (1977) examined Langland's use of verbal concordance in his Latin quotations, and suggested that Langland drew on preachers' handbooks for his material.

Boþe of sond, sonne and see' (lines 77–78; cf. B.18.237–50). But, Conscience explains, he did not fully assume the roles of king and conqueror until he had grown into manhood (lines 96–98). Lines 99–104 take the form of a description of a young knight, with some chivalric touches (cf. the earlier description of Christ as 'a knyght þat comeþ to be dubbed' at B.18.13), although they also fall under the rubric of conqueror. Conscience explains that the granting of 'good and... heele' is the 'kynde... of a Conquerour' (line 106).

The third section, beginning at line 108, continues the discussion of Christ's life while introducing a second triad, Dowel, Dobet, and Dobest. Dowel corresponds to Christ's first miracle, the wedding at Cana (line 110), which Conscience presents as an allegorization of the new law, 'to louyen oure enemys' (line 114). Dobet (line 129) involves further miracles: feeding the five thousand and healing the sick. Christ's superlative achievement, Dobest, sees him granting pardon to Piers Plowman (lines 182–90).

The triadic structure of Conscience's discussion resembles one of the formal characteristics of the 'modern' or scholastic type of medieval sermon.[16] In his *Forma praedicandi*, Robert of Basevorn recommends that a preacher should base his sermon on a text (the sermon's 'theme') that can provide material for a sermon of three parts:

> For a good Invention of the Theme the following are required: that it concur with the feast, that it beget full understanding, that it be on a Bible text which is not changed or corrupted, that it contain not more than three statements or convertible to three.[17]

Basevorn suggests various reasons why a tripartite form should be preferred, ranging from respect for the Trinity ('pro reverentia Trinitatis') to the more practical reason that three parts are 'more convenient for the set time of the sermon' ('tempori sermonis requisito convenientius').[18]

In Advent sermons, this triadic form receives special emphasis because it coincides with the idea of the triple advent of Christ, understood to be his coming in human flesh, his coming into the hearts of the faithful, and his coming at the last judgement. As the *Speculum sacerdotale* explains:

---

[16] For discussion of the terminology, and for general accounts of sermon form, see Wenzel (1986; 61–100); Spencer (1993; 228–68); and *Middle English Sermons*, pp. xliii–lv.

[17] 'Bene inveniendo themati illa requiruntur: ut festivitati congruat, ut plenum intellectum generet, ut sit de textu Bibliae, non mutato nec perverso, ut non contineat plures dictiones quam tres vel tribus convertibiles'. Basevorn, *Forma praedicandi*, in *Artes praedicandi*, p. 249, trans. Krul in *Three Medieval Rhetorical Arts*, p. 133. Thomas Waleys provides a slightly different version of this triadic form in his *De modo componendi sermones*, in *Artes praedicandi*, p. 356.

[18] Basevorn, *Forma praedicandi*, p. 254; trans. Krul, in *Rhetorical Arts*, p. 138.

Knowe that the aduent of oure Lord is in þre maners. The first is in his flesche; the secound in hertes of his trewe peple, the whiche aduent is iche day by the Holy Gost; and the thridde aduent is when he schall come at the day of dome in his maieste.[19]

Perhaps reinforced by this triadic scheme, some sermons provide other three-fold divisions of the life of Christ. The Nativity sermon in John Mirk's *Festial* explains that Christ was born for three causes, 'forto 3yue pes to men of good wyll, forto lyghten hom þat loken ill, and forto draw men so wyth loue hym tylle'.[20] Similarly, Mirk's Advent sermon falls into three parts, corresponding to three stages in Christ's life and the three causes for which he came into the world:

> [He] was borne, and trauayld, and dyet. He was borne to bryng man out of sekenes ynto euerlastyng hele; he trauaylde forto bryng man ynto euerlastyng reste; he was ded forto bryng man ynto þe lyfe þat neuer schall haue ende. Þys was þe cause of Crystys fyrst comyng ynto þys world.[21]

In presenting Christ's life under the triadic rubric of knight, king, and conqueror and in a discourse structured in triadic form, then, Conscience follows the method of structuring a sermon recommended by the *artes praedicandi*. This triadic form was readily combined with three-fold schemes for Christ's life, much like the biography of knight, king, and conqueror provided by Conscience.

The triad 'knight, king, and conqueror' itself also invites comparison with the guides to sermon composition. Conscience presents knight, king, and conqueror as three degrees or grades, so that 'To be called a knyght is fair', 'To be called a kyng is fairer', 'Ac to be conquerour called, þat comeþ of special grace' (B.19.28–30). In so doing, Conscience follows the advice given by writers like Basevorn. Basevorn recommends that the parts of a sermon be generated through the use of comparatives in much the same way: 'Per comparationem sic. Primum bonum, secundum melius, tertium optimum' ('Through comparison, as follows: good, better, best').[22] Of course, as I suggested in commenting on Conscience's use of the three Do's at the beginning of passus 14 in the previous chapter, similar triads commonly serve as mnemonic devices in other didactic literature too. Langland develops here

---

[19] *Speculum sacerdotale*, p. 4, ll. 19–23.
[20] *Mirk's Festial*, p. 21, ll. 16–17.
[21] *Mirk's Festial*, p. 1, l. 27–p. 2, l. 3.
[22] Basevorn, *Forma praedicandi*, p. 276; trans. Krul, in *Rhetorical Arts*, p. 163. Basevorn's example, as Spearing (1972; 118) indicates, also resembles the second triad introduced by Conscience in passus 19 and ubiquitous in earlier parts of the poem, Dowel, Dobet, and Dobest.

Conscience's role as instructor or counsellor from his previous appearance in B 13–14.

One might also observe how Conscience's speech begins as a response to Will's questions on Christ's names:

> 'Is þis Iesus þe Iustere', quod I, 'þat Iewes dide to deþe?
> Or is it Piers þe Plowman? who peynted hym so rede?'
> (B.19.10–11)

> 'Why calle ye hym crist, siþen Iewes called hym Iesus?'
> (B.19.15)

> 'Is crist moore of my3t and moore worþi name
> Than Iesu or Iesus þat al oure Ioye com of?'
> (B.19.24–25)

This series of questions may be compared with one of the Middle English sermons in the collection edited by Woodburn Ross, on the text 'Natus est rex'. Taking the key word of its theme, 'rex', this sermon presents four questions based upon the name of king:

> [Q]uis est rex iste? qualis est? quantus est? et vbi?
> The first question is of is personall dignite;
> the secound of is maner of lyvynge;
> the third is of is auctorite;
> and þe fourth of is dwellynge.
> This is þan þe first question, qwhat maner of person is þis kynge?
> the secound, of qwhat powere and of qwhat maner of lyvynge?
> the third, how is he to oþur princes in auctorite?
> and the fowrte, qwere trowe we þat is dwellynge be?[23]

Conscience's 'sermon' develops out of similar questions relating to Christ, his names, and his 'maner of lyvnge'. Nicholas de Aquavilla's sermon for First Advent, on the text 'Dicite filiae Sion, "Ecce rex tuus venit tibi"' (Matthew 21:5: 'Tell ye the daughter of Sion: Behold thy king cometh to thee'), takes a similar form. Aquavilla generates his material as a response to the question, 'Who is this "king"?': 'quis est iste "rex"...et quomodo appelletur? Iste rex Christus est et appellatur Iesus, i.e. saluator mundi' (who is this king...and what is he called? This king is Christ, and is called Jesus, that is, the saviour of the world).[24] Again, one might compare Will's questions, 'Is þis Iesus þe

---

[23] *Middle English Sermons*, no. 39, p. 225, ll. 4–11. Ross, the sermon's editor, prints this text as prose, but I have presented it as verse to illustrate how it uses the rhymed divisions recommended by the *artes praedicandi*, a device Basevorn calls 'colouration'. For discussion of this technique, see Basevorn, *Forma praedicandi*, p. 321, and Wenzel (1986; 84–85).

[24] Aquavilla, *Sermones dominicales moralissimi*, fol. a_2^v. For this edition, see Coates and others, *Catalogue*, IV, N-045. For the sermon, see Schneyer, *Repertorium*, IV, no. 1. For Aquavilla, see Sharpe, *Handlist of the Latin Writers*, no. 1076.

Iustere…Why calle ye hym crist, siþen Iewes called hym Iesus?' (B.19.10, 15). Basevorn also recommends that sermons be based upon questions like 'quis', 'qualis', and 'vbi': 'Isto modo solent antiquitus themata declarari et dividi: quis, quid, qualiter' ('Traditionally themes are wont to be declared and divided this way: who, what, and how').[25] As the marginal annotation 'Questio 2a' in the sermon printed by Ross suggests, this method of setting out questions derives from the scholastic methods out of which the modern or university sermon developed.[26] Will thus initiates Conscience's speech, as Stephen Barney indicates, 'in the schoolish form of a *quaestio*', and he receives a gentle rebuke from Conscience (B.19.26) for the academic pretensions he has frequently displayed elsewhere.[27]

Finally, one should notice that Conscience's 'sermon', although it begins as a discourse addressed only to Will, concludes with a collective prayer. Here, too, it follows the formal methods recommended in the guides for preachers: Basevorn stresses that a sermon should properly conclude with a prayer.[28] Langland also added a long concluding prayer to Repentance's sermon in B passus 5, perhaps after composing this sequence in B 19 (B.5.477–505; cf. A.5.251–54).[29] Alan Fletcher is surely right in pointing to the increasing formal prominence of the sermon in passus 5, and perhaps more generally, as Langland revised the poem.[30]

'KNYGHT, KYNG, CONQUEROUR' AND 'RESON AND RIGHTWISNESSE AND RUÞE': SOME HOMILETIC COMMONPLACES

As well as a number of formal features, Conscience's speech also shares with medieval sermons some conventional subject matter.[31] His discussion of the names 'Jesus' and 'Christ' (B.19.15–62, 69–70), for instance, prompted by Will's question, 'Why calle ye hym crist, siþen Iewes called hym Iesus?' (B.19.15), was probably a commonplace in the medieval pulpit.[32] Discussions of the meanings of the two names appear frequently

---

[25] Basevorn, *Forma praedicandi*, p. 279; trans. Krul, in *Rhetorical Arts*, p. 166.
[26] *Middle English Sermons,* p. 226, l. 24.
[27] Barney (2006; 109, 112).
[28] Cf. Basevorn, *Forma praedicandi*, p. 307; trans. Krul, in *Rhetorical Arts*, p. 198.
[29] See the Introduction for further discussion and Alford (1993).
[30] Fletcher (2001; 66).
[31] For reasons of space, I do not examine here the major debt that Conscience's sermon owes to homiletic discourse, the image of the Christ-knight. See Woolf (1962).
[32] Under its heading for 'Jesus', for instance, the Lollard handbook for preachers, the *Floretum*, poses the similar question of why the followers of Christ are called Christians and not Jesuans. See Oxford, Bodleian Library, MS Bodley 448, fol. 100vb. Bloomfield (1962; 217, n. 3) cites a sermon of Wyclif that presents the same question.

in sermons and in handbooks for preachers,[33] although of course the topic appears in other texts as well.[34] One can take as exemplary Jacobus de Voragine's third sermon for the Feast of the Circumcision, on the text 'Vocabitur nomen eius Emmanuel' (Is. 7:14; cf. Matt. 1:23):

> [His] proper names are Christ, Jesus, the Son of God and Emmanuel. Therefore his first name is Jesus, which is interpreted as 'salvation'... The second name is Christ, which is interpreted as 'the anointed one'... The third name is the Son of God... The fourth name is Emmanuel, which is interpreted as 'God with us'.[35]

As Derek Pearsall suggests, in explaining how this knight was first called Jesus and later acquired or 'com to' the name Christ (B.19.69–70) Conscience alludes to this 'traditional distinction of the names Jesus and Christ'. But he does not, however, give the conventional interpretations of the two names.[36] As an interpretation of 'Christ', Conscience offers not 'the anointed one', but 'conquerour' (B.19.62). He presents, indeed, a full alternative set of names, 'knyght, kyng, conquerour' (B.19.27).[37] Nevertheless, Conscience still follows here similar discussions of Christ's names in sermons. Jacobus de Voragine's fourth sermon for the Feast of the

---

[33] On 'Jesus' as 'salvator' or 'saveoure', see, for instance, *Fasciculus morum*, p. 408, l. 88; the *Floretum*, MS Bodley 448, fol. 100va; *The Northern Homily Cycle*, I, ll. 3874–78; *Speculum sacerdotale*, p. 16, ll. 16–17. On 'Christ' as 'the anointed', see *The Middle English Translation of the Rosarium Theologie*, p. 94, ll. 1–6 and Jacobus de Voragine's second sermon for First Advent from his 'Sermones de tempore', in *Sermones de tempore et de sanctis et Quadragesimales*, I, fol. 2va. For this edition of Jacobus de Voragine, see Coates and others, *Catalogue*, IV, J-083. For the sermon, see Schneyer, *Repertorium*, III, no. 3.

[34] The meaning of 'Jesus' could also be found in the 'Interpretationes nominum Hebraicorum', the list of Hebrew names found at the back of many medieval bibles. The distinct meanings of the two names 'Jesus' and 'Christ' also appear, for instance, in *Cursor Mundi*, V, ll. 25013–20.

[35] 'Propria nomina sunt Christus, Iesus, Filius Dei et Hemanuel. Primum ergo nomen eius est Jesus: quod interpretatur salus... Secundum nomen est Christus: qui interpretatur vnctus... Tertium nomen est Filius Dei... Quartum nomen est Hemanuel: quod interpretatur nobiscum Deus'. Jacobus de Voragine, 'Sermones de sanctis', in *Sermones de tempore et de sanctis et Quadragesimales*, II, fol. D_7^{ra-b}(31^{ra-b}). For this volume, see *Catalogue of Books Printed in the XVth Century now in the British Museum*, XII, 73. For this sermon, see Schneyer, *Repertorium*, III, no. 347.

[36] Pearsall, *C-text*, p. 345, n. 14. As Barney (2006; 114–15) argues, Conscience seems to distinguish between 'Jesus' as a proper given name and 'Christ' as an acquired or official title, like king or conqueror.

[37] Skeat found in line 62 evidence of Langland's ignorance that 'Christus' meant 'anointed' in Greek; see *Parallel Text*, II, 266, n. 14. But as Barney argues (2006; 111), this was surely commonplace knowledge. Schmidt suggests that Langland simply associated 'conqueror', as the 'superlative degree' of knight, with ideas of kingship and hence anointing. See Schmidt, *B-text*, p. 485, n. 62.

Circumcision, for instance, distinguishes personal from official names. He explains that Christ has four 'nomina officialia' designating the various roles he performs for mankind: 'angelus' (referring to Christ's role as messenger), 'magister' (teacher), 'medicus' (physician), and 'aduocatus' (advocate).[38] Conscience's trio of names—knight, king, and conqueror—constitutes a similar series of titles of office. And it is not really surprising that Conscience seems more interested in the 'nomina officialia' of knight, king, and conqueror than in the conventional interpretations of the names 'Jesus' and 'Christ'. After all, he earlier appeared in the poem as a king's knight (B.3.110). In outlining the responsibilities of the offices of knight, king, and conqueror, Conscience returns, as I have already argued above, to one of the themes of his debate with Meed in the first vision. His discussion of the conqueror's obligation 'To make lordes of laddes of lond þat he wynneþ' (B.19.32) belatedly answers Meed's argument that the king ought to ennoble his retinue with the profits of war, to make 'The leeste brol of his blood a Barones piere' (B.3.205).[39] As in the banquet at Conscience's house, which I discussed in the previous chapter, the retinue politics of the first vision here take on new, paradoxical, spiritualized forms. In passus 3, Meed had insisted on the centrality of 'meed' to acts of lordly largesse, and had berated Conscience for his involvement in military failures. But here defeat becomes, paradoxically, a victory. The blood he sheds in his death on the cross constitutes Christ's act of largesse to his retainers, just as in B 13 the humble poor, 'God's minstrels', earn for their lordly masters a 'largesse' from God.

Sermons, especially Advent sermons, also provide analogues for another of Conscience's important topics, his description of the Nativity and Epiphany and his allegorical interpretations of the gifts of the Magi:

> Aungeles out of heuene come knelynge and songe,
> *Gloria in excelsis deo &c.*
> Kynges come after, knelede and offrede sense,
> Mirre and muche gold wiþouten mercede askynge
> Or any kynnes catel; but knowelichede hym souereyn
> Boþe of sond, sonne and see, and siþenes þei wente
> Into hir kyngene kiþ by counseil of Aungeles.
> And þere was þat word fulfilled þe which þow of speke,
> *Omnia celestia terrestria flectantur in hoc nomine Iesu*;
> For alle þe Aungeles of heuene at his burþe knelede,
> And al þe wit of þe world was in þo þre kynges.
> Reson and Rightwisnesse and Ruþe þei offrede;

---

[38] De Voragine, 'Sermones de sanctis', fols D$_7$^{vb} (31vb)—D$_8$^{ra} (32ra). For this sermon, see Schneyer, *Repertorium*, III, no. 348.

[39] Cf. Simpson (1985; 472–75, 2007; 195).

> Wherfore and why wise men þat tyme,
> Maistres and lettred men, *Magi* hem callede.
> That o kyng cam wiþ Reson couered vnder sense.
> The seconde kyng siþþe soopliche offrede
> Rightwisnesse vnder reed gold, Resones felawe;
> Gold is likned to leautee þat laste shal euere
> For it shal turne tresoun to riȝt and to truþe.
> The þridde kyng þo kam knelynge to Iesu
> And presented hym wiþ pitee apperynge by Mirre;
> For Mirre is mercy to mene and mylde speche of tonge.
>
> (B.19.74–93)

This moralization of the three gifts of the Magi as three attributes of Christ ('Reson and Rightwisnesse and Ruþe') resembles similar discussions that appear in a variety of texts and frequently in sermons. As Morton Bloomfield notes, the gifts were often taken to symbolise Christ's three aspects as king, God, and mortal man, as in *The Three Kings of Cologne*:

> By þese iij glorious ȝiftes, þat is to seye Gold, Ensense, and Mirre, is schewed in one lord Crist diuine Mageste, kyngis powste, and mannys mortalite. Ensense perteyneþ to sacrifice, Golde perteyneþ to Tribute, and Mirre perteyneþ to sepulture of dede men.[40]

Along similar lines, the *Speculum sacerdotale* allegorizes the gifts in terms of Christ's triple kingship: 'And they seide: "Yif he be erthely kyng, he woll take golde; yf he be heuenly kyng, he woll take sense; and ȝif he be a dedely kyng, he schall take the myrre" '.[41]

These traditional interpretations do not correspond particularly closely with the meanings of 'reson, rightwisnesse and ruþe' put forward by Conscience.[42] But as, implicitly, royal virtues,[43] Conscience's 'reson, rightwisnesse and ruþe' do find broad parallels in the discussions of similar qualities as kingly attributes of Christ that occur in many Advent sermons. In his sermon for the first Sunday in Advent, for instance, the Oxford preacher John Felton takes the text 'Ecce rex' in order to explain that Christ is described as a king because he possesses five qualities that every good king ought to share: ' "Rex" iste Christus est, qui habet quinque conditiones

---

[40] *The Three Kings of Cologne*, p. 79, ll. 1–5; cf. Bloomfield (1962; 218, n. 9). For other versions of this interpretation, see *Mirk's Festial*, p. 49, ll. 21–25; *The N-Town Play*, I, no. 18, 'The Magi', ll. 239–58; *The Towneley Plays*, I, no. 14, 'Offering of the Magi', ll. 231–45.

[41] *Speculum sacerdotale*, p. 20, ll. 27–30.

[42] Although *The N-Town Play* does offer an interpretation of the gold very similar to Conscience's 'Rightwisnesse vnder reed gold, Resones felawe' (B.19.88), which perhaps points to a common source: 'I wyl hym offere þe rede golde,/As reson wyl me teche' (ll. 35–36).

[43] Cf. Barney (2006; 117) and Schmidt, *B-Text*, p. 485, n. 86.

quas debet habere quilibet bonus rex...scilicet, iusticiam, sapientiam, potenciam, mansuetudinem, et humilitatem' ('This 'king' is Christ, who has five qualities which every good king ought to have...namely, justice, wisdom, strength, mildness, and humility').[44] Some of these qualities have an obvious resemblance to those discussed by Conscience. Along similar lines, the Middle English sermon on the text 'Natus est rex' that I discussed above[45] begins with an appeal to 'prynce' Jesus that lists a triad of qualities much like those discussed by Conscience (although this sermon was apparently for Epiphany rather than Advent):

> O þou victorius prynce of powre almyghty! O þou most wisse and discrete, rewlyng prudently al þinge! O þou most benigne Lord, gracious and full of mercy.[46]

Perhaps closest to Conscience's 'reson, rightwisnesse, and ruþe', although not in triadic form, is Jacobus de Voragine's second sermon for First Advent, on the text 'Ecce rex'. This example explains that Christ has his office as king not in order to judge severely but with mercy.[47]

Conscience, then, departs from the allegorical interpretations of the gifts conventional in homiletic discourse. But the royal virtues he discusses nevertheless find echoes in the similar kingly or princely attributes frequently presented in Advent and related sermons. Langland apparently relies on the expectation of allegorical readings of the gifts, but adapts the traditional interpretations to the interests of his poem. As Barney indicates, Langland's 'Reson and Rightwisnesse and Ruþe' correspond to three of the Four Daughters of God, Truth, Rightwisnesse, and Mercy, in the previous passus of the poem.[48] Christ, of course, there presented himself as the kingly agent who reconciles justice and mercy, or Conscience's rightwisnesse and ruþe: 'I may do mercy þoru3 my rightwisnesse and alle my wordes trewe' (B.18.389, and cf. the analogy with royal pardons at B.18.379–83). Conscience's discussion of the gifts takes place under the rubric of 'prynce' or knight (B.19.96–98), but it implicitly confirms the poem's earlier presentation of Christ as a king who reconciles the

---

[44] Felton, *Sermones dominicales*, Oxford, Bodleian Library, MS Lat. th. e. 7, fol. 8^r. Felton is here following Nicholas de Aquavilla's First Advent sermon (fol. a$_3^r$ in the edition quoted above). For Felton, see the study of his career in Fletcher (1998; 58–118) and Sharpe, *Handlist*, no. 689.

[45] *Middle English Sermons*, no. 39. (cf. Note 23).

[46] *Middle English Sermons*, p. 220, ll. 22–24.

[47] 'Quarto debemus ipsum libenter suscipere propter officium: quia non habet officium severe iusticie sed pie misericordie' (Fourthly we should welcome him freely on account of his office: because he does not have the office of harsh justice but of piteous mercy). Jacobus de Voragine, 'Sermones de tempore', fol. 3ra. See Schneyer, *Repertorium*, III, no. 3.

[48] Barney (2006; 117).

conflicting demands of justice and mercy that troubled the secular realm in the poem's first vision.[49]

KINGSHIP AND HOMILETIC DISCOURSE IN THE B-TEXT PROLOGUE

In B 19, as I have been arguing, Langland returns to the concerns of the first vision, and Conscience's 'sermon' on Christ as knight, king, and conqueror in B 19 is closely related to his earlier role as a king's knight at the beginning of the poem. One may see the intimate connection between these two parts of *Piers Plowman* in the close parallels, recently discussed by Barney, between Conscience's speech and the 'founding of the commonwealth' sequence in the Prologue (B.Prol.112–45). Langland probably inserted this sequence, new to the B text, into the original Prologue following the composition of (or contemporaneously with) B passus 19.[50] The sequence shows the king conferred with the authority to rule and presented with counsel by a lunatic, an angel, and a goliard. As Barney points out, this passage resembles Conscience's speech in B 19 in its discussion of 'royal titles... and their relation to the appellated virtues of justice and mercy'.[51] As Ralph Hanna has argued, the two passages probably also share the same topical allusions. Since J. A. W. Bennett, critics have generally agreed that the founding of the commonwealth in the B Prologue in part refers to the coronation of Richard II in July 1377. But Hanna suggests that Conscience's 'sermon' also alludes to that event. At the end of his speech, Conscience instructs Will to sing the hymn '*Veni creator Spiritus*' (B.19.210), echoing the moment in Richard's coronation service at which the same hymn was sung.[52] Barney argues for a further allusion to Richard's coronation in Conscience's allegorization of the three gifts of the Magi as 'reson, rightwisnesse and ruþe'. These closely resemble, he claims, the three virtues—justice, mercy, and truth—that Richard II swore to uphold in 1377.[53]

---

[49] In an essay which in part responds to an earlier version of this chapter, Burrow (2009) points out that the gifts are presented to the infant Jesus, who is imagined as a knight. He argues that 'Reson and Rightwisnesse and Ruþe' are therefore to be understood as the proper qualities of knighthood, rather than as royal virtues. According to Burrow, only a small part of Conscience's speech, lines 44–49 and 124–41, concerns itself with kingship. I maintain, however, my insistence on the importance of kingship as a theme in the passage as a whole (a theme which links Conscience's speech to the first vision, as I argue in more detail below). The analysis of kingship, indeed, extends throughout passus 19, recurring in Conscience's encounter with the tyrannical king in B.19.465–79a.

[50] For this chronology, see Hanna (1996; 233–34) and Barney (2006; 102, 109).

[51] Barney (2006; 109).

[52] Bennett (1943b; 55–64); Hanna (2005; 250).   [53] Barney (2006; 117).

But as well as sharing allusions to topical events, the two passages also share analogues in homiletic discourse and the kinds of commonplaces (transcending any immediate topical resonance) that I have discussed in connection with Conscience's speech in passus 19. Talbot Donaldson, for instance, pointed out the resemblance between the Angel who counsels the king in the B Prologue (B.Prol.128–38) and the mechanical golden angel that was lowered to offer Richard a crown in Thomas Walsingham's account of his pre-coronation procession through London.[54] But the Angel of the Prologue might equally bring to mind the angels who appear in Conscience's account of those who acknowledge Christ at his birth and resurrection:

> Aungeles out of heuene come knelynge and songe,
> *Gloria in excelsis deo &c.*
>
> (B.19.74–74a)

*

> That Aungeles and Archaungeles, er þe day spronge,
> Come knelynge to þe corps and songen
> *Christus rex resurgens*
>
> (B.19.150–52)

The contents of the Angel's speech, too, might recall the kinds of material that I have put forward as analogues for Conscience's 'sermon' in B 19. The Angel's warning to the king that he must temper justice with piety or pity ('*Nudum ius a te vestiri vult pietate*', B.Prol.135)[55] closely resembles those discussions I cited above that emphasize Christ's combination of justice and mercy, or in Conscience's terms, reson and ruþe.[56] The Angel, indeed, explicitly invokes the kingly Christ of the Advent sermons and of Conscience's speech in B 19. He reminds the king that he administers the laws of a higher, heavenly king:

> *O qui iura regis christi specialia regis,*
> *Hoc quod agas melius, iustus es, esto pius!*
>
> (B.Prol.133–34)[57]

---

[54] Donaldson (1949; 117–18) also suggested that the Angel's speech might allude to Richard's coronation oath. Owst (1961; 578–79) identified the Angel with Thomas Brinton.

[55] I have followed the translation of Galloway (2006; 127), 'Naked law needs to be clothed by you with piety [*or* pity]'.

[56] Other parallels between the speech of the Angel and homiletic discourse are noted by Alford (1992; 33) and by Somerset (2005; 120).

[57] 'O you who administer the sublime laws of Christ the King, in order to do that better, as you are just, be pious!' (trans. Galloway (2006; 127)).

That the coronation sequence in the B Prologue draws on the same discourses that I have suggested as parallels to Conscience's 'sermon' in passus 19 need not necessarily conflict with the view that the sequence also alludes to contemporary events. Indeed, one might argue that the contemporary events to which B 19 and the B Prologue perhaps allude themselves also drew on the same modes of representation of the royal Christ which I have been discussing. As Barney indicates, the citizens of London 'carefully assimilated' Richard II to Christ in their civic pageants, and Gordon Kipling comprehensively demonstrates that the imagery of Advent played a central role in this assimilation.[58] Equally, Advent sermons frequently presented the coming of Christ as the civic entry of a king.[59] It is perhaps not surprising that the Angel in the B Prologue should recall both Richard's coronation procession and the language and imagery of Advent sermons when events such as the 1377 coronation themselves figured the king in terms that closely resemble the royal Christ of the Advent sermons and of Conscience's 'sermon' in B 19. What *Piers Plowman* has in common with a text like Walsingham's history of Richard II's coronation is not so much (or not only) shared allusions to topical events as a shared mode of representation, a mode in which contemporary politics could be aligned with biblical narratives.

One further example may confirm that the 'founding of the commonwealth' in the B Prologue mirrors Conscience's sermon in B passus 19 not only in the contemporaneity of its composition but also in shared analogues in homiletic discourse. This example is the etymology of the name of king, rex, provided by the Goliard: '*Dum rex a regere dicatur nomen habere/Nomen habet sine re nisi studet iura tenere*' (B.Prol.141–42).[60] In her study of the theme of government in *Piers Plowman,* Anna Baldwin argued that a parallel for this etymology in the work of the jurist Bracton demonstrated the 'political tenor' of Langland's coronation scene.[61] But a similar etymology, one should notice, also occurs in Basevorn's *Forma praedicandi*, as an example of an Advent sermon. Basevorn suggests that a

---

[58] Kipling (1998; 15–21) and *passim*; Barney (2006; 109, 116). Mann (1994) also discusses the connections between Christ's 'adventus' at the gates of hell in B passus 18, the Palm Sunday Entry into Jerusalem, the celestial Jerusalem of the Second Coming, and royal civic entries.

[59] See, for instance, Felton's First Advent sermon (here following Nicholas de Aquavilla), MS Lat. th. e. 7, fols 11ᵛ–12ʳ; Jacobus de Voragine's first sermon for First Advent, 'Sermones de tempore', fol. 1ʳᵇ (Schneyer, *Repertorium*, III, no. 2); and a similar example quoted by Owst (1961; 32).

[60] 'Since *rex* [king] is said to have its name from 'rectification' [*regere*], it has the name without the substance unless he is zealous to uphold the laws' (trans. Galloway (2006; 128)).

[61] Baldwin (1981; 14–15).

preacher might take the standard text, 'Ecce rex', in order to show how Christ provides an example of humility. We name Christ king (rex) from ruling (regendo), and no one is ruled better than by humility, through which one distinguishes a king from a tyrant:

> The theme could be: *Your king comes*, and the development thus...Christ.. is proposed to us in the foresaid words as an example against pride. He is described as preserver of humility against pride, because he is *king* (rex) which comes from *ruling* (regendo). Now no one is better ruled by any virtue than by humility through which a king is seen to differ from a tyrant.[62]

Rather than belonging exclusively, as Baldwin implies, to a political field of discourse, the discussion of the title 'rex' also apparently featured regularly in the pulpit. Andrew Galloway points out that the same etymology also appears in Bromyard's *Summa praedicantium* and suggests that its presence there implies that verses similar to the Goliard's were 'common in homiletic discourse'.[63]

Of course, Galloway's observation need not invalidate Baldwin's argument for the political resonance of this apparently commonplace discussion of the derivation of the name of 'king'. The same play on the noun *rex* and the verb *regere* also turns up in a sermon by Thomas Brinton on what his editor describes as 'the unhappy state of the Kingdom' in the last years of Edward III's reign. This context suggests that sermons offer a mode in which biblicism and critique of contemporary politics could be combined.[64] The close relationship between B 19, the climax of the poem's bible-narrative, and the B Prologue, its re-engagement with 'contemporary conditions', implies that homiletic discourse provides a powerful tool for assimilating the events of contemporary political life to biblical narrative. The citizens of London attempted just such an assimilation in idealizing mode in their pageants for Richard II. The connection between B 19 and the B Prologue suggests an effort at reform like that presented by Conscience's messianic speech at the end of passus 3. Here, Conscience reimagines society in the contours of bible narrative: '*Conflabunt gladios suos in vomeres*' (B.3.308a).[65]

---

[62] 'Potest esse thema: *Rex tuus venit*, et prosecutio sic...Christus...in verbis praedictis nobis proponitur in exemplum contra superbiam. Contra superbiam describitur implicite humilitatis conservativus, quia *rex*, qui dicitur a *regendo*. Modo nulla virtute regitur quis melius quam humilitate per quam videtur rex a tyranno differre'. Basevorn, *Forma praedicandi*, pp. 314–15; trans. Krul, in *Rhetorical Arts*, pp. 205–6.

[63] Galloway (2006; 129). For further examples of the rex/regere etymology, see Alford (1992; 33–34) and Hanna (2005; 249).

[64] *Sermons of Thomas Brinton*, I, 46; the sermon was preached in 1374 or 1375.

[65] As Hanna (2005; 274) indicates, 'The language promises a society predicated on bible-lore'.

Conscience's speech in B 19 draws on the language of preaching in order to re-present the 'topical' themes of the first vision in newly 'spiritualized' terms. Correspondingly, in the new B Prologue, the same mode reminds the king of his obedience to a higher law, and points to the need to re-establish contemporary institutions along properly spiritual lines.

But the narrative of B 19–20, of course, sees the project of refounding contemporary institutions in new spiritualized terms fail. Conscience perhaps believes that the reformed society he imagined in B 3 really has come about when in B 19 he once again urges Christians to communal labour ('Conscience comaundede þo alle cristene to delue', B.19.364). But the conclusion of passus 19 sees Unity already unravelling in competing individual interests. Homiletic discourse gives way to the broad mode of 'contemporary critique' within which Langland had framed the two first visions. The Brewer's reply to Conscience, 'Ye? baw!...I wol noȝt be ruled' (B.19.396) in this second ploughing scene echoes Waster's reply to the knight during the first: 'I was noȝt wont to werche...now wol I noȝt bigynne!' (B.6.167). Just as Piers's knight failed to keep order on the half-acre, so in passus 20 Conscience's own knightly courtesy ultimately leads, as I discuss in more detail in the next chapter, to the collapse of Unity at the hands of the friars.

4

'To a Lord for a Lettre Leue to Haue': Lordly Conscience and the Friars in B 20[1]

Ultimately, as Langland gives Conscience the final word in *Piers Plowman,* the poem settles on one controversial contemporary mode, antimendicant satire. As Penn Szittya shows, in his presentation of Conscience's failure to defend Unity against Friar Flatterer, Langland draws on a tradition of satire against the friars that originates with William of St Amour. Sire *Penetrans domos* derives his name from William's controversial exegesis of 2 Timothy 3.[2]

The poem finally turns to antimendicant discourse because the friars, with their profession of poverty and their avowed interest in the sacrament of penance, represent the nearest contemporary examples to the language of 'patient poverty' expounded in B 14. But the friars of course embody, as the catastrophe of B 20 makes clear, the de-sanctified, grossly materialized version of Patience's idealized language of patient poverty. The kingly Christ of Conscience's sermon in B 19 insists that his retainers pay back what they owe if they wish to have a share in the pardon he gives as the spoils of his victory. Quite in contrast, the friars allow mercy to be bought for cash, just as Meed had attempted to make merely monetary amends for her retainer Wrong in passus 4.

With the return to the themes of his original debate with Meed, Conscience again becomes central. Langland returns to the concerns of the first vision by suffusing his account of the friars' corruption of Unity with the language of retainership that also permeated the poem's first vision. The last vision returns to a topic central to the first to treat the problem represented by the friars as a question of retinue politics.[3] Langland draws in this part of the poem on a particular strand of antimendicant satire that

---

[1] An earlier version of this chapter appeared together with an essay by Ralph Hanna; see Hanna and Wood (2010; 224–38). It is reproduced in revised form here with kind permission from Nicholas Rogers and the original publisher.

[2] Szittya (1986; 3–10).

[3] Other readers have, of course, noted the broad resemblances between the first and last pairs of visions in the poem; Barney (2006; 101–2) offers a summary, while perhaps the best account of this symmetry is provided by Middleton (1997; 269–71).

dwells on the friars' positions in the retinues of the great and their interference with the consciences of the rich. Thus on one level of the allegory in passus 20, as Britton Harwood argues, Conscience is the accuser of, or sense of remorse for, sins (as distinct from Contrition, the institutionalized form of remorse that forms the first stage of the sacrament of penance).[4] But as earlier a king's knight and now castellan of Unity, Conscience is also implicitly, within this particular antimendicant mode, transformed into a specific instantiation of 'conscience'. He here becomes an example of a lordly conscience easily misled by friars.

At least one medieval reader of *Piers Plowman* seems to have noted the connection for which I am arguing between Conscience's bouts with Meed in the first vision and with the friars in the last—between the representation of lords and friars at the poem's conclusion and of Meed and her retinue at its inception. In the third passus of the text of *Piers Plowman* in MS Bodley 851, Meed responds to Conscience's accusations against her with a lengthy tirade in which she attacks Conscience for his behaviour towards the friars:

> Freres fyndeth the a frend that thow furst blamedest:
> Thyselue art asentaunt that they schal men schryue.
> Furst thow corue hem a cope, Conscience, thyselue,
> Ant comawndest vche couent coueytyse to lete,
> Ant nyme nat of no man but as nede hascheth.[5]

In his review article on the 'Z text', George Kane argues convincingly against the view, proposed by George Rigg and Charlotte Brewer, that these lines represent an authorial first draft of the poem written before the A text. As he demonstrates, the passage rather reflects 'the preoccupation of another mind' with one of the most troubling episodes of the poem, the moment at which Conscience admits Friar Flatterer to Unity in B 20, with disastrous consequences.[6] 'Freres fyndeth the a frend that thow furst blamedest' clearly recalls B.20.318–23, where Conscience first rejects the friar and then in the same breath admits him. It also echoes Conscience's long speech at B.20.244–72, in which he 'blames' the friars at length for 'coveting cure' and for their excessive numbers. The last line quoted above, 'Ant nyme nat of no man but as nede hascheth', responds to Conscience's final words at the very end of the poem, when he expresses the wish 'þat freres hadde a fyndyng þat for nede flateren' (B.20.383).[7]

In their immediate context in passus 3, the lines in Bodley 851 thus make little narrative sense, and it is difficult to explain away the fact that

---

[4] Harwood (1992; 133).   [5] Rigg and Brewer, *Z Version*, 3.151–55.
[6] Kane (1985; 922–5).
[7] For the echoes of B passus 20 in these lines, see Kane (1985; 924 and n. 24).

at this point in the poem, Conscience simply has not yet 'blamed' the friars.[8] Nevertheless, the author of the text in Bodley 851 was not so far from the mark in implicitly presenting an interpretation in which the debate between Meed and Conscience in passus 3 anticipates Conscience's run-in with the friars in passus 20.[9] In B 20, the connection between the two episodes is signalled, for instance, by the echoes of the Westminster world of the first vision in the analogy Langland draws between debtors and those who confess themselves to the friars:

> shame makeþ hem wende
> And fleen to þe freres, as fals folk to westmynstre
> That borweþ and bereþ it þider and þanne biddeþ frendes
> Yerne of forȝifnesse or lenger yeres loone.
> Ac while he is in westmynstre he wol be bifore
> And maken hym murie wiþ ooþer mennes goodes.
> And so it fareþ with muche folk þat to freres shryueþ,
> As sisours and executours; þei shul ȝyue þe freres
> A parcel to preye for hem and pleye wiþ þe remenaunt,
> And suffre þe dede in dette to þe day of doome.
>
> (B.20.284–93)

As Myra Stokes discusses, the problem adumbrated here also dominates the examination of Meed's effects on the operation of the king's justice in passus 3–4. Just as Meed attempts to relax the penalties of the secular law, so the friars relax the penalties of the divine law embedded in the penitential system. Instead of enforcing penance, the friars allow those who confess to them to buy off the penalties of the law with cash.[10] The friars are 'selling God's law in a manner as destructive of the spiritual commonwealth as the sale of the law of the land was to the social' in passus 3–4.[11]

Langland further suggests the connection between the first and the last visions of the poem in the scene early in passus 3 featuring Meed and her friar-confessor. This scene presents in miniature the same corruption of the sacrament of penance brought about by the friars at the end of the poem. As Stokes argues, the connection between Meed and the friar at this early point in the poem points to the parallel between the corruptions each practices, 'the relaxation of *pena*, punishment legal and penitential'. The sequence in passus 3, with its close conjunction of Meed and friar, helps point to what Stokes calls the 'juristic' character of the

---

[8] Cf. the arguments of Rigg and Brewer in their notes to these lines.
[9] I thus distance myself from Kane's rejection of the interest and value of the manuscript.
[10] See note 15 below.   [11] Stokes (1984; 24).

friars' malpractices in B passus 20.[12] The friar's promise to assist Meed in bringing down Conscience, here conceived as a rival at court (B.3.42), also suggests the parallel between these early scenes and the poem's last vision. By the end of *Piers Plowman*, this promise reads like a prophecy fulfilled.

The friar's promise in passus 3 is indeed quite precisely fulfilled, and the comparison between the activities of Meed and the friars made in quite specific terms, in B 20.[13] As I will show, the means by which the friars gain admittance to Unity and the language in which Conscience analyses the problems they represent both echo the earlier presentation of the activities of Meed and her retinue in passus 2–4. In analysing the problem presented by the friars in B passus 20, Langland returns to the problem of retinue politics central to the first vision of the poem: the distinction between 'maintenance' as a legitimate support or 'fyndyng' and 'maintenance' as unlawful protection, the wrongful exercise of the 'good lordship' demanded by a retinue.[14]

FRIARS AND RETAINERS IN B PASSUS 3–4 AND PASSUS 20

The means by which Friar Flatterer gains admittance to Unity suggests the close relationship between the activities of Meed and of the friars. The narrative of B passus 20 brings into prominence just the kind of 'bad lordship' also practised by Meed, and the friars' relationship with their lordly protectors here emerges as one of their chief dangers. In this part of the poem, as Stephen Barney has recently argued, 'Friars and their wealthy patrons are two sides of the corrupt absolution system'.[15] As Meed conspired with her friar-confessor in passus 3, so in passus 20 Conscience is brought down by the friars acting in concert with their aristocratic patrons.

A 'lord þat lyueþ after likyng of body' (B.20.71) becomes one of Conscience's chief opponents in the siege of Unity. The same figure or another of his kin, 'Sire leef-to-lyue-in-lecherie', first calls for Friar Flatterer

---

[12] Stokes (1984; 114–15).

[13] Although B 20 also reprises the inner dream of B passus 11, when a friar also colluded in the erosion of the Dreamer's own conscience (B.11.53–58). The *dramatis personae* of this scene reappear at the end of the poem with the arrival of Fortune, Coveitise, and Elde.

[14] On the 'easy slide' between the two senses of 'maintenance', see Hanna (2005; 265).

[15] Barney (2006; 195). Langland strikes this note, of course, as early as the Prologue, with the first appearance of the friars as 'chief to shryue lordes' (B.Prol.64). Lawler (2006; 165) comments that 'Friars as chapmen shriving lords is thus at issue at the very end of the poem as it was at the beginning'.

(B.20.311–15). The lecherous lord, of course, recalls the earlier interview between Meed and her friar in which Meed urged her confessor to show especial sympathy towards 'lordes þat lecherie haunten' (B.3.53).[16] The means by which Friar Flatterer gains admission as a confessor, however, most clearly highlights this particular cooperation of friar and lordly patron:

> The frere herof herde and hiede faste
> To a lord for a lettre leue to haue
> To curen as a Curatour; and cam with his lettre
> Boldely to þe bisshop and his brief hadde
> In contrees þer he coome confessions to here.
>
> (B.20.324–28)

Langland here describes two technical procedures. The second stage of the process, and a point of contention in the controversy between mendicants and seculars, sees the friar obtaining authority from a licensing bishop in order to hear confessions. Obtaining a licence was a requirement stipulated by the papal bull of 1300, *Super cathedram*, but the system embroiled many bishops in ongoing battles with unlicensed mendicants. In 1358–59, for instance, Bishop Grandisson of Exeter complained about false confessors, using the text from 2 Timothy 3 that forms the basis for the representation of the friar in *Piers Plowman* as Sire *Penetrans domos*.[17] Earlier in passus 20, Conscience had himself expressed the wish that friars' names and numbers might be recorded in the bishop's register (B.20.271). Arnold Williams's study of episcopal registers suggests that some bishops did indeed maintain quotas of licensed mendicant confessors and preachers, although he concludes that supervision of licences was—as B 20 implies—'normally lax'.[18]

But Langland's narrative also calls attention to another document; not the bishop's licence but the letter from the lord which, apparently, recommends the friar to the bishop in the first place. This letter from the lord appears to be an instance of what Pantin calls 'indirect patronage'. Magnates had certain benefices and ecclesiastical offices in their own gift. But they could also press a bishop to grant a living to one of their own

---

[16] Lawler (2006; 161) observes that 'the lord who lives after the lust of his body is not really a new character: he is Wrong [who raped Peace's wife]...he is the "lordes that lecherye haunteth" that the friar mentions to Meed'.

[17] *The Register of John de Grandisson*, II, 1197–98. This use of the text originated, as Szittya shows, with William of St Amour, although it might have attracted Grandisson's (and Langland's) notice via its use in the London sermons of Grandisson's protégé, Richard FitzRalph. On Grandisson's knowledge of William's work and the possible influence of FitzRalph, see Szittya (1986; 62–3, 121–2). For FitzRalph's sermons, see Walsh (1981; 415–19). [18] Williams (1960; 32–4, 91).

favourites. In much the same way, the lord in *Piers Plowman* appears to influence the bishop to grant a licence to his especially favoured friar.[19] The friar's presence at Unity, crucially, results from an act of patronage. Sire leef-to-lyue-in-lecherie and his aristocratic kin play a central role in the friars' destruction of Unity.[20]

Plentiful literary evidence offers support for such a narrative in which the rich and powerful are the friars' central supporters. The wealthy seem to have shown a particular enthusiasm for friars, which drew much fire in contemporary texts. Edward III, for instance, employed Dominicans from King's Langley as his personal confessors until the end of his life.[21] Richard II drew most of his confessors from the Dominican order, including Thomas Rushook, who was twice banished from court for his influence over the king, and Alexander Bache, whom the Westminster chronicler criticised for his haughty manner.[22] John of Gaunt appointed his confessors from the Carmelite order.[23] The London Greyfriars church enjoyed a good deal of noble patronage, and the Bohun family employed Augustinian friars as confessors and manuscript illuminators at Pleshey Castle.[24]

This apparent preference of the powerful—like the lecherous lord of B 20 and Lady Meed—for friar-confessors, and the seeming preference of friars for the wealthy, provoked much contemporary complaint.[25] Richard FitzRalph attacked the friars' association with kings and queens and dukes and duchesses in his fourth London sermon of 12 March 1357.[26] In Wycliffite writings, friars are often suspected of using their influence in the confessional to sinister ends: 'þei leeden prelatis, lordis and ladies, justisis and oþer men by confessioun'; 'þei maken prelatis and lordis, bi here fals flateryng and lesyngis in confessions and preuei conseils, to lette prestis to preche goddis lawe'.[27] Wyclif himself attacked the friars' role as

[19] Pantin (1955; 32–4).
[20] For Lawler too (2006; 154), 'a lord in cahoots with a friar' epitomises the corrupt 'system' of absolution.
[21] Ormrod (1989).
[22] Saul (1997; 320–1); Barney (2006; 138).
[23] For these men, see *BRUO*, III, 1571–72; *BRUO*, II, 1077; *BRUC*, p. 188.
[24] John Stow's *Survey of London* lists the fourteenth-century monuments to prominent figures in Greyfriars church. See Stow, *Survey of London*, p. 286. For the Bohuns' employment of Augustinians, see Sandler (2004; 19).
[25] Cf. Lawler (2006; 153), linking Reason's scathing reference to the king's confessor (B.4.145) with Richard II's unpopular confessors.
[26] Gwynn (1940; 87).
[27] 'Fifty Heresies and Errors of Friars', in *SEWW*, III, 385; 'Of the Leaven of Pharisees', in *EWW*, p. 5. I am indebted in the following paragraphs to the references on the topic of friars and their association with the rich collected by Pamela Gradon and Anne Hudson in *English Wycliffite Sermons*, IV, 138; see also Barney (2006; 242). On Lollard hostility towards the friars, see Hudson (1988; 348–51).

confessors of kings, princes, and the powerful in one of his sermons.[28] In his commentary on Matthew 23, Christ's curse on the scribes and pharisees, he wrote that friars used confession to acquire the secrets and possessions of secular lords; the rich may go laughing to confession, he claimed, because—like Meed in passus 3—they expect to be absolved in exchange for a small donation:

> [A]nd thus the rich can go laughing to caesarean confessors and believe that they are absolved, for a pittance and without grief, of all the sins they have committed, whilst holding the intention of sinning again.[29]

Langland would surely have agreed: in passus 3 Meed goes 'shamelees' to her friar, and he absolves her 'for a seem of whete' (B.3.40, 44) and a donation to the friary. *Piers Plowman* sharply contrasts those wealthy individuals who thus laughingly obtain absolution for money with the grief of the '*cor contritum & humiliatum*' exemplified in Conscience's 'banquet' of poor food in B 13.

Complaints that the friars were motivated by Meed-like impulses in seeking out the great also appear ubiquitously in contemporary polemic. That friars flattered the rich and failed to reprove their sins was held to be axiomatic: according to the Wycliffite commentary appended to an English translation of the Franciscan Rule and the Testament of Francis, 'men knowen wel þat freris wile flatere & spare to reproue scharply synnes of grete men for drede of los of worldly goodis or frendischipe or fauour'.[30] According to 'Fifty Heresies and Errors of Friars', they 'seken faste, by grete giftis and veyne costis, to be calde maysters of dyvynite, and speke bifore lordis, and sitte at þo mete wiþ hom'.[31] This last comment, of course, recalls both the friar who is the guest of honour at Conscience's banquet in B passus 13 and Dame Study's earlier complaint that legitimate aristocratic patronage centred on the great hall has declined along with the rise of such 'Freres and faitours' (B.10.72), who encourage both learned and lay to regard theological speculation as dinner-table entertainment.

Langland also seems to have been drawing on contemporary polemic when he yoked Friar Flatterer with Sire leef-to-lyue-in-lecherie. Friars were frequently accused of tolerating or actively encouraging aristocratic

---

[28] Wyclif, *Sermones*, II, 121, ll. 11–14.
[29] '[E]t sic divites possent ridendo adire confessores cesareos et credere quod pro parva porcione pecunie de omnibus peccatis commissis sine dolore, ymmo cum iterum peccandi proposito absolvuntur'. *Exposicio textus Matthei xxiii*, in Wyclif, *Opera minora*, cap. ii, p. 318, ll. 20–2 and p. 318, l. 37–p. 319, l. 3. The Middle English adaptation of this text, 'Vae Octuplex', is edited by Gradon in *English Wycliffite Sermons*, II, 366–78.
[30] *EWW*, p. 50.   [31] *SEWW*, III, 396.

lechery. The Wycliffite tract 'On the Seven Deadly Sins' notes that the second estate is

> smyttid wiþ lecchorie, as ben gentilmen and hor wifes bothe, as if þei holde it bot a gamen, one to lye by oþers wyf. And if freris enterlasen, þo synne is more perilouse.[32]

As noted above, Lady Meed had earlier asked her friar-confessor for particular indulgence towards 'lordes þat lecherie haunten' and 'ladies þat louen wel þe same' (B.3.53–54). In offering to be her 'baudekyn', Meed's friar perhaps hints at the role of go-between also implied by the Wycliffite text.

Richard Firth Green argues that John of Gaunt might have suggested Langland's figure of Sire leef-to-lyue-in-lecherie.[33] But it seems unlikely, as I discuss further below, that he is the only contemporary figure noted for the vice. Aristocratic lechery also formed a central theme, for instance, of Thomas Brinton's sermon preached during the Good Parliament. Brinton claimed that no country was so noted for adultery as England, and that few men, especially lords, were contented with their wives.[34] And the friars' general association with lechery is an antimendicant commonplace.[35] According to 'Of the Leaven of Pharisees', friars 'norischen ryche men and wymmen in lecherie and auoutrie for monye and to haue here owne lustis'. They 'seyn to nyse wymmen þat it is lesse synne to trespase with hem þan with oþere weddid men'.[36] 'How Religious Men Should Keep Certain Articles' makes the same complaint about the friars' tolerance of lechery, with the additional point that they fail to insist on restitution and do not excite the 'shame' proper to a good confession. The text implies, as does Meed's confession to the friar in passus 3, that friars accept donations to their own foundations instead of insisting on the restitution of ill-gotten gains; the author goes on to say that the friars 'haue part of þis robberie, & make worldly festis & wast houses aȝenst here pouert & profession'.[37]

Their popularity with the nobility meant that contemporaries often suspected friars of involvement in various kinds of court and political intrigue. Such intrigue resembles Meed and her friar plotting against Conscience in passus 3, but it is perhaps also reminiscent of the collusion of lord and friar in the fall of Unity. In 1384, the Carmelite friar John

---

[32] *SEWW*, III, 164. 'Enterlasen' is glossed by Arnold as 'to interfere'; cf. *MED*, s.v. 'enterlacen', 1 (c), 'to join, or become involved in, a crime or conspiracy; to conspire (with someone)'.
[33] Green (1997).   [34] *Sermons of Thomas Brinton*, II, 318.
[35] Stokes (1984; 135, n. 23) provides further examples.
[36] *EWW*, p. 6. Might Meed's claim that lechery is the sin most readily forgiven (B.3.58) perhaps come from the teaching of a friar?
[37] *EWW*, p. 224.

Latimer told Richard II that John of Gaunt was plotting his murder. (Latimer seems, as Richard II's most recent biographer suggests, to have been manipulated as a 'pawn in a grander game played by the rivals for power at court'.)[38] Wyclif reported a similar rumour which implicated friars in a plot to murder Gaunt himself.[39] I have already suggested (in Chapter 1) the close resemblance of the action of passus 3 to various forms of court slander, and Meed's encounter with the friar, whose help she enlists against Conscience as a rival at court (B.3.41–42), clearly belongs to this discourse. On the evidence presented above, friars seem regularly to have been implicated in this discourse during the period.[40] The collusion of friar and lord in passus 20, though, also resembles contemporary political intrigues involving friars. It thus precisely fulfils the earlier suggestion that Meed and her friar would 'felle' Conscience at court (B.3.42). The poem returns, at its conclusion, to the political themes of its first vision.

An especially notable contemporary intrigue, and one particularly reminiscent of Meed's friar-confessor in B passus 3, is Thomas Walsingham's claim that Alice Perrers, Edward III's notorious mistress (and long suspected as a model for at least some aspects of Meed's characterization) was in league with a Dominican friar. With his aid, Walsingham reports, she had induced the king into an illicit relationship by magic.[41] During the course of the Good Parliament of 1376,

> parliament was informed that Alice had over a long period of time kept in her company a man who was a brother in the Order of Preachers who displayed the appearance of a physician, and professed that skill; but he was an evil magician, dedicated to evildoing, and it was by his magical devices that Alice had enticed the king into an illicit love-affair with her...It was said, furthermore, that this brother had made wax effigies of the king and Alice, and that...he used these with the juices of magical herbs and his words of incantation to enable Alice to get whatever she wanted from the king.[42]

---

[38] Saul (1997; 131–2). Goodman (1992; 100) suggests in his biography of Gaunt that the friar may have had a grudge against Gaunt on account of his preferment of rivals within the Carmelite order, or because he supported Wyclif. (The Carmelites, as I discuss further below, had a tradition of anti-Wycliffite polemic in the period.)

[39] *De Ordinacione Fratrum*, in Wyclif, *Polemical Works*, I, cap. ii, p. 95, ll. 1–2.

[40] See also Scase (1998; 240) for a case in 1387 in which named friars were accused in libels of murder, sodomy, and treason. Thomas Thornton, one-time prior provincial of the Austin friars, appears also to have been involved in some variety of political intrigue. He was summoned to appear before the king's council in 1360. His successor, Geoffrey Hardeby, probably enjoyed the support of Alice Perrers as well as the favour of Edward III; see Gwynn (1940; 125, 128–9).

[41] Huppé (1939; 51) also mentions the episode involving Alice and her friar in connection with the depiction of Meed.

[42] '[N]unciatum est in parliamento dictam Aliciam secum a multis temporibus quendam fratrem de ordine Predicantium detinuisse, qui speciem pretulit fisici et artem

Alice's Dominican partner in crime closely resembles Meed's friar in passus 3, both for his complicity in lechery and for his involvement in intrigues at court. But his powers as a physician-magician also provide a close parallel for Friar Flatterer, 'phisicien and surgien' (B.20.315; cf. 'The frere wiþ his phisyk þis folk haþ enchaunted', B.20.378). Green identifies Friar Flatterer with Friar William Appleton, surgeon to John of Gaunt, and would on this basis revise the customary dating of the B text to some time after Appleton's murder during the Peasants' Revolt of 1381. But the story involving Alice's friar shows that Appleton is by no means the only prominent friar-physician of the period. Indeed, the capture of Alice's friar turned specifically on his profession as a physician. He was eventually entrapped and brought before parliament by Sir John de la Mare and Sir John Kentwood, who arrived at the friar's place of refuge on Perrers's estate asking where they could find a man who knew how to cure diseases: 'The brother who was standing in an upper room, seeing that they were carrying urinalia in their hands, reckoned that he would make a lot of money out of them, so he soon admitted that he was the doctor whom they sought'.[43] He was, of course, immediately captured.

It is worth pointing out that the object upon which the story of Alice's friar turns, the urine flask, forms part of the depiction of Sire *Penetrans domos* in Bodleian Library, MS Douce 104. John Friedman suggests that this illustration might represent topical satire, both on Friar William Jordan, whom Marcett identified with the Doctor of Divinity in B passus 13 (another name for the uroscopy flask was a 'jordan'), and possibly also the Dominican Henry Daniel, who composed a treatise on urine in 1379. Friedman also provides evidence of a tradition of anti-Dominican satire centring on the uroscopy flask, and Walsingham's story about Alice Perrers's friar perhaps depends on similar associations.[44] But whilst I do not offer him as a direct model either for Meed's friar or for Friar Flatterer, Alice's friar seems at least as likely a candidate as those offered by Friedman and Green. His rise to notoriety closely coincides with the latest datable allusions in the B-text continuation and revised Prologue

---

profitebatur eandem; set magus erat nequissimus maleficiis deditus, cuius experimentis eadem Alicia dominum regem allexerat in suum illicitum amorem...Dicebatur enim eundem fratrem cereas fecisse effigies, regis uidelicet et eiusdem Alicie, quibus, per herbarum potentium succos et incantamina sua loquens...effecit ut dicta Alicia potuit a rege quicquid uoluit optinere'. Walsingham, *Chronicle,* pp. 46–9. The English translation here obscures the sense of 'detinere' as 'to retain': Walsingham identifies the friar as a member of Alice's retinue.

[43] 'Frater uero ille stans in solario, cum uidisset homines ferentes in manibus urinalia, ratus se lucraturum grandem pecuniam, mox fatetur se esse medicum quem querebant'. Walsingham, *Chronicle,* pp. 48–9.

[44] Marcett (1938; 57–64); Friedman (1994).

(that is, to the events of 1377), although 1376 is probably too late a date for him to have inspired directly the portrait of Meed's friar, already present in A passus 3. The Dominican's profession as physician and his status as an accessory to Alice's affair with Edward III means that William Appleton and John of Gaunt offer by no means the only historical parallels to Friar Flatterer and Sire leef-to-lyue-in-lecherie. Indeed, after the exposure of Alice and her friar accomplice, Gaunt was, according to Walsingham, primarily concerned not with his own reputation for lechery but with the scandal in which Edward was involved: the duke 'was more concerned about his father's notoriety as an adulterer...than about his own ill-repute, for although he was licentious himself he wanted it to be thought that he detested this vice'.[45] But of course, the poem need not allude to any particular historical figure at all (and *Piers Plowman* does not, of course, present the historical 'facts' about the friars). That Friar Flatterer is a satiric type was doubtless recognized not only by the annotator of one manuscript of *Piers Plowman* who glossed 'Sire *Penetrans domos*' as 'a general name for a friar'.[46] The metaphor of the confessor as physician is conventional (as Szittya shows, it pervades FitzRalph's works, for example).[47] The Wycliffite texts 'Of the Leaven of Pharisees' and 'How Religious Men Should Keep Certain Articles' suggest the conventional status, too, of the claim that friars feigned expertise in medicine in order to gain intimacy with women. The latter text accuses friars of being 'to homly wiþ gentil wymmen bi colour of fisik'.[48] It seems likely that Walsingham as much as Langland drew on antimendicant commonplaces in his portrait of Perrers's friar.[49]

Other contemporary intrigues also suggest broad parallels for the collusion of friar and noble patron in B passus 3 and passus 20. Walsingham mentions not only the scandal involving Alice and her friar, but also the greatest conspiracy theory of them all, that the friars were responsible for the Peasants' Revolt.[50] Conversely, the Carmelite history of Lollardy, the *Fasciculi zizaniorum*, accused Wyclif and his followers of having incited the rebellion.[51] This atmosphere of accusation and counter-accusation

---

[45] '[P]lus pendens patris infamiam, qua dicebatur adulter, quam suam propriam quamuis et ipse luxuriosus existeret, tamen ut uideretur hoc uitium detestari'. Walsingham, *Chronicle,* pp. 50–1.
[46] Huntington Library, MS HM 143, cited Scase (1989; 180, n. 1).
[47] Szittya (1986; 283, n. 58).
[48] *EWW,* pp. 10, 224.
[49] See Barney (2006; 241), for further potential candidates for Friar Flatterer, assessment of Green's and Friedman's proposals, and for the sensible reminder that in the poem the 'whole conception of confessor as physician is metaphorical'.
[50] Walsingham, *Chronicle,* pp. 504–5; quoted Dobson (1983; 368–9).
[51] *Fasciculi zizaniorum,* p. 272, cited Dobson (1983; 376).

offers a further example of how the friars might use their influence with the rich and powerful, for in 1382 they appealed to John of Gaunt for aid. Although in this case Gaunt remained silent, the Carmelite Stephen Patrington, who delivered the friars' letter, would later receive £100 a year for life from Gaunt and serve as confessor to Henry V.[52]

Rumours involving friars, particularly Franciscans, continued in a later period, too. In the early years of the reign of Henry IV, friars frequently appear as alleged plotters against the king. In 1402, a Franciscan preached that Richard II was still alive. A Franciscan from Aylesbury was brought before the king where he pluckily declared his readiness to take up arms in the cause of the usurped Richard. In Leicester in the same year, eleven Franciscans had planned to join a gathering intending to go looking for Richard. The Leicester conspirators were charged with preaching that Richard was still alive; with stirring up the populace to go looking for Richard in Scotland; and with imposing as a penance the task of looking for Richard in Wales.[53] Walsingham remained suspicious of the friars' activities in these years, reporting that the Franciscans had used black magic to produce bad weather in the mountains of Wales in order to impede the movement of English troops (the Franciscans of Anglesey had indeed joined the Welsh rebellion).[54]

The influence the friars were felt to exert upon some of the most powerful figures in the land, then, clearly fed suspicions about their involvement in court and national affairs at the very highest level. Alexander Bache, Richard II's confessor from 1389–94 and also bishop of St Asaph from 1390, perhaps offers the nearest example to the kind of influence with the nobility enjoyed by Friar Flatterer. In November of 1390, Bache obtained from the king a number of privileges for the clergy of his diocese, which Chris Given-Wilson describes as 'an interesting example of how a courtier might use his influence'.[55]

Langland's depiction of Friar Flatterer gaining admission to Unity under the patronage and protection of a lord resonates with many of these contemporary anxieties about the extent of the influence enjoyed

---

[52] Workman (1926; II, 246–7). Wyclif of course had particular reason to resent the friars' influence; of the seventeen doctors of theology who sat on the Blackfriars Council in 1382, sixteen were friars, and several enjoyed royal patronage and influence. John Kenningham, who delivered the closing sermon of the Council, was one of Gaunt's confessors as well as one of Wyclif's early opponents in Oxford and the author of several tracts against him. In earlier years, before his own preferment, he had sneered at the favour Wyclif then enjoyed from Gaunt. See Workman (1926; II, 120–1, 260–1) and *Fasciculi zizaniorum*, p. 3; the relevant tracts are printed in *Fasciculi zizaniorum*, pp. 4–103.
[53] *Eulogium historiarum sive temporis*, III, 389–93; Wylie (1884; I, 274–8); McNiven (1987; 95).
[54] McNiven (1987; 96), Davies (1995; 212).   [55] Given-Wilson (1986; 179).

by friars under the patronage and protection of the great. But it also presents the problem posed by the friars in terms of a theme central to the debate between Meed and Conscience in passus 3 and to the ensuing action involving Peace and Wrong in passus 4: the politics of the retinue. In passus 4, Meed attempts to intervene in the case of Peace v. Wrong to protect her retainer, Wrong, from the full force of the law; in passus 20 the lord secures the friar's position with a letter to the bishop. The 1346 Ordinance of the Justices underlines the close relationship between the activities of Meed and of the friars (albeit that these activities take place in the different spheres of the secular and ecclesiastical law). The 1346 ordinance both forbade that any should 'take in hand Quarrels other than their own, nor the same maintain by them nor by other', and commanded that the justices should henceforth 'do equal Law and Execution of right to all our Subjects, rich and poor, without having regard to any Person, and without omitting to do right for any *Letters* or Commandment [lettres ou mandementz] which may come to them from Us, or from any other'.[56] The action of B passus 20, then, not only reflects contemporary anxieties about the friars' influence with the powerful, but broadly replays the action of the first vision. It exposes the friars as the beneficiaries of a position much like the one occupied by Wrong and Meed's other followers—one of whom was, of course, a friar-confessor. The similarity between the two sequences of the poem suggests, on a literal level, that the friars enjoy corrupt, Meed-like forms of patronage or maintenance. But it also points, at a deeper level, to the connection between Meed's and the friars' abuses. As Meed 'maintains' her retainers in their Wrong, so the friars maintain their wealthy patrons—including Meed herself—in their sin. The 'pryuee paiement' given to the friar at B.20.364 is an exact analogue to the 'present' offered to Peace by Meed (B.4.95). As Traugott Lawler suggests, in passus 4 Peace 'is a kind of stand-in for the friar-confessor, offering forgiveness in return for a donation'.[57] Moreover, in B 20, Peace will again be won over by lordly Hende Speche (B.20.348–55), just as he was earlier seduced by Lady Meed's gold. Langland reprises the character of Peace in B 20 within a situation that echoes the original scene in which he appeared in B 3–4. Just so, Conscience's presence at the beginning and end of the poem highlights the parallels between the activities of Meed and the friars. The successive appearances of both characters serve to underline recurring themes within the poem.

---

[56] *Statutes of the Realm*, I, 20 Edward III, c. 1, c. 4, pp. 303–4 (my emphasis).
[57] Lawler (2006; 152).

RETAINERSHIP AND A 'FYNDYNG' FOR THE FRIARS

The language in which Conscience discusses the friars' position, and the suggestions he offers for a remedy, also point to the connection between B 20 and the retinue politics examined in the earlier Meed episode. On their first arrival at Unity, Conscience argues that the friars must have some sort of regular living, which he will later refer to as a 'fyndyng':

> And if ye coueite cure, kynde wol yow telle
> That in mesure god made alle manere þynges,
> And sette it at a certain and at a siker nombre.
> And nempnede hem names, and noumbrede þe sterres:
> *Qui numerat multitudinem stellarum et omnibus eis nomina vocat.*
> Kynges and knyghtes þat kepen and defenden
> Han Officers vnder hem, and ech of hem a certein.
> And if þei wage men to werre þei write hem in noumbre;
> Wol no tresorer take hem wages, trauaille þei neuer so soore,
> But þei ben nempned in þe noumbre of hem þat ben ywaged.
> Alle oþere in bataille ben yholde Brybours,
> Pylours and Pykeharneys, in ech a parisshe ycursed.
> ...
> It is wikked to wage yow; ye wexen out of noumbre.
>
> (B.20.253–63, 269)

Conscience here alludes to a central antimendicant topic. Richard FitzRalph had also used the biblical text to which Conscience alludes at B.20.253–55, Wisdom 11:21, to argue that the friars multiplied 'wiþoute eny ende' as a result of their mendicant existence, which did not require them to make provision for a secure living or 'fyndyng' for any of their number, and thus placed no natural restraint on their growth.[58]

But if Conscience here adverts to a controversial antimendicant gloss on a biblical text, the example he gives of the arrangements made by kings, knights, and their officers for paying men-at-arms belongs firmly within his earlier debate with Meed in passus 3, and the discussion there of war and retinues. Conscience here refers to the indentured or contract army, the paid military service that was increasingly replacing customary obligatory service. The nobility contracted to supply given numbers of men to be paid at standard rates specified in the agreements drawn up between leaders and the king: as Conscience says, 'A certein for a certein'

---

[58] See the Middle English translation of his *Defensio Curatorum* in Trevisa, *Dialogus inter Militem et Clericum*, p. 59, l. 30–p. 60, l. 1. The resemblance to FitzRalph is discussed by Frank, Jr (1957; 110, n. 6); Bloomfield (1962; 145–6); Szittya (1986; 280–2); and Scase (1989; 36–7).

(B.20.267).⁵⁹ If the friars were given a similar kind of regular 'wage', Conscience argues, if they were accommodated, metaphorically, to something like this regular indentured retainership, they would no longer have to pillage their living from their penitents like irregulars on the battlefield. They would no longer engage in that Meedish 'maintenance' of sin that allows the guilty to escape the law. The proposal possesses a clear logic, since plunder was frequently regarded as a legitimate substitute for wages when pay fell in arrears.⁶⁰ 'Wage' the friars, and they will no longer need to pillage.

The solution Conscience proposes to the problem presented by the friars implicitly connects their activities with those of Meed, for a similar solution was also proposed to the problem of 'maintenance' when it re-emerged during the reign of Richard II in the form of an anxiety about the proliferation of noble liveries. The statute of 1390 that attempted to address this problem stipulated that no livery was to be awarded unless its recipient was retained by indenture for life in peace and war, or was alternatively a 'Domestic and Familiar [mesnal & familier] abiding in [the lord's] Household'.⁶¹ The statute attempts to deal with the problem of maintenance by distinguishing between legitimate kinds of retainer and those whose only attachment to their lord consisted in receipt of his livery and fee. Just so, Conscience attempts to address the problem posed by the friars as a question of retinue politics, seeking, metaphorically, to assimilate the friars to one regularized form of retainership.⁶²

But the echoes in B 20 of passus 3 and the debate between Meed and Conscience should give one pause when assessing the likelihood of success for Conscience's proposal. With its emphasis on a divinely sanctioned order—measured numbers and agreed wages as opposed to numberless friars—Conscience's proposal here resembles his earlier effort to distinguish 'mesurable hire' or equitable wages (B.3.256) from the proliferation of Meed (developed in the C text, as I discuss in the next chapter, in terms of conformity to grammatical gender, case, and number). But just as Conscience's terms in passus 3 have been described as a 'bland statement' having 'no obvious application to the complexities of Langland's milieu',⁶³

---

⁵⁹ Hewitt (1966; 33–4); and see Baldwin (1981; 25, 78).   ⁶⁰ Hewitt (1966;105).
⁶¹ *Statutes of the Realm,* II, 13 Ric II, Stat. 3, pp. 74–5; and see Dunham (1955; 69–70).
⁶² Stokes (1984; 24–7) points out that the connection between the first and last visions, between the problems posed by Meed to secular justice and by the friars to the divine law of the penitential system, is emphasized by the similarity of the solutions Langland offers to the twin problems of venal judges and venal friars. Both must be provided, the poem insists, with a regular income to prevent them abusing their offices.
⁶³ Aers (1980; 8–9).

so, too, the solution Conscience puts forward in B 20 glosses over the complexities of contemporary social practice.

To begin with, Conscience's reference to battlefield pillagers, 'Pylours and Pykeharneys' (B.20.263), should remind one of Meed's accusation in passus 3 that Conscience himself plundered the poor as a king's knight:

> Wiþouten pite, Pilour, pouere men þow robbedest
> And bere hire bras at þi bak to Caleis to selle.
>
> (B.3.195–96)

As I suggested in Chapter 1, the accusation Meed makes against Conscience resembles charges made against members of the court during the Good Parliament. I do not claim that Langland intended a specific allusion to that event in passus 3. Nevertheless, both the events of 1376 and Meed's similar accusation against Conscience in passus 3 imply that the system of wages for men-at-arms may not have operated as tidily as Conscience imagines in B 20. Certainly, it did not prevent pillaging. Conscience apparently imagines that the system of contracting and accounting for soldiers offers an ideally regulated system contrasting with the friars' numberless proliferation. Yet failures of this system and its accountability were precisely at stake in the Good Parliament. John Neville was impeached for multiple breaches on just this score. Firstly, he had failed to supply the right quantities and quality of men, even though he had received the full agreed payment for them (thus violating Conscience's neat formula, 'A certein for a certein', B.20.267). Secondly, he had allowed his troops to cause destruction in the county of Hampshire.[64] Although the Good Parliament stands out as perhaps the most prominent contemporary instance, these were not unique breaches: armies were frequently tempted to similarly lawless behaviour before embarking for battle.[65]

The echo in B 20 of Meed's accusation about Conscience's pillaging, then, suggests that the organization of war did not proceed in the ideally ordered way Conscience imagines. Just like 'mesurable hire' in passus 3, his formula here tends to gloss over the complexities of contemporary practice. It must have been difficult, in reality, to distinguish between the illicit activities of irregulars and the pillaging tolerated or even ordered from above. The destructive raid constituted, after all, a major tactic of the war, and supplies for men and horses to live on had also to be seized from the invaded territory. As H. J. Hewitt puts it, 'In all wars of the period, in the absence of specific prohibition, leave to plunder was probably taken for granted'.[66] The necessity of 'living from the land' on foreign

---

[64] *PROME*, II, 329a. [65] Hewitt (1966; 44). [66] Hewitt (1966; 105).

territory 'regularized theft' quite as easily as Need does at the beginning of B 20,[67] and one wonders quite how Conscience imagines those used to pillaging will learn to be contented with more meagre, if more regular, wages. In B 19, Conscience had presented Christ at the head of a newly spiritualized form of retinue, and he seems to believe in B 20 that the friars might be accommodated to a similarly idealized form of retainership. But in presenting the friars and their lords replicating Meed's abuses, Langland seems not to share Conscience's optimism about the possibility of reforming the noble household.

Moreover, Conscience's attempt to contain the friars within some regular form of metaphorical 'retainership' simply ignores one obvious fact about them. For on the literal level, as Friar Flatterer and his lord illustrate, the friars' popularity with the nobility meant that they were *already* in the retinues of lords and knights—not the indentured retainers to whom Conscience refers, but resident members of noble households in receipt of annuities. The king's confessor, for instance, enjoyed an established position within the royal household.[68] On his appointment as Edward III's confessor in 1376, William Siward received an annuity of £69 10s 6d.[69] John of Gaunt's confessors were also counted 'among the most important officers of the household'.[70] Gaunt's *Register* records annuities to 'nostre cher en Dieu frere William de Baddby nostre confessour', who received £10 per year, probably for life.[71] Gaunt retained William Appleton for life as his 'phisicien et surgien'.[72] Many of these men rose to prominence through such connections. Gaunt's confessor Walter Disse, for instance, served as a papal nuncio in England, Castile, Navarre, Portugal, and Aragon, positions which suggest his association with Gaunt's claims to the throne of Castile.[73]

In *Piers Plowman*, Langland also briefly figures the friars as members of Antichrist's retinue: 'Freres folwede þat fend for he gaf hem copes' (B.20.58). On the literal level the friars' copes, as Lawrence Clopper shows, played an important role both in antimendicant polemic and in internal debates over the observance of poverty within the Franciscan order.[74] But in the immediate context, with Antichrist represented as a king or leader rallying knights to his banner on the battlefield (B.20.69), the copes he offers the friars also suggest the livery that might be worn by

---

[67] Hewitt (1966; 94). Need's speech is analysed by Adams (1978).
[68] Given-Wilson (1986; 12).   [69] *BRUO*, III, 1704.
[70] Armitage-Smith (1904; 176).
[71] *John of Gaunt's Register*, II, 116–17; *BRUO*, I, 90.
[72] Green (1997; 88).   [73] *BRUC*, p. 188.
[74] For the internal disputes and external criticisms surrounding the Franciscan habit, see Lambert (1961; 213–14) and Clopper (1997; 46–7 and n. 47).

retainers. Robes were a regular grant both to household residents and also to those Meedish retainers whose only connection to their lord consisted in the wearing of a livery and acceptance of a fee.[75] Friars, then, *already* receive incomes from knights and lords; they already enjoy the kind of favour extended by Meed to her own friar-confessor. The exact mechanism by which Conscience hopes to alleviate the friars' neediness, the cause of their corruption, thus becomes increasingly less clear, for as Ralph Hanna has recently argued, in *Piers Plowman* employments themselves, not the lack of them, cause the contemporary crisis which the beginning of the poem announces.[76] In B 20, as Lawler argues, Contrition himself is a lord, thoroughly implicated in the corrupt 'system' of absolution.[77] One might add that Conscience, apparently also a lord and certainly all too susceptible to lordly Hende Speche, does little better. Like too many of his peers—at least according to contemporary polemic—lordly Conscience welcomes the friar right into the household. Conscience's allegorical role as accuser of sins is fatally compromised by the literal level of his presentation as a knightly figure easily seduced by a friar. No wonder the author of the version of the poem in Bodley 851 expresses dismay at his apparently inconsistent behaviour.[78]

The precise nature of the 'fyndyng' Conscience imagines for the friars remains, then, deliberately opaque, characteristic of his tendency to gloss over the material conditions of the present.[79] Nevertheless, the language of retainership in which Conscience couches his solution to the friars' predicament may cast some light on what the 'fyndyng' entails. Typically, readers have assumed that Conscience means that the friars should have 'property and ecclesiastical livings like the rest of the church'.[80] But Clopper has argued against such a view, pointing out that Conscience could not intend for the friars to receive endowments when he has earlier

---

[75] In passus 13, Haukin complains that as a minstrel unable to perform any of the usual entertainments offered by members of that profession he has received few robes 'or furrede gownes' (B.13.227).

[76] Hanna (2005; 255) and cf. B.Prol.64–65, 87–94.

[77] Lawler (2006; 165).

[78] Many readers would try to smooth over the abruptness of Conscience's change of heart in first accusing the friars and then allowing Friar Flatterer to enter Unity, by appealing to scholastic discussions of the faculty of conscience. These discussions point out that conscience may err (see the Introduction for further discussion). I think Conscience's behaviour is meant to seem inconsistent in the way that the author of the 'Z text' sees. Just as Contrition ceases to be contrite because of the friar, so Conscience's lordly sympathy for the friar causes him to stop behaving as conscience should (witnessing against sins and against corruption). As Jenkins (1969; 140) puts it, he starts behaving like 'a literal rather than an allegorical example of Conscience'.

[79] A tendency discussed in connection with B 20 by Hanna (2005; 299).

[80] Szittya (1986; 286), a view recently cited with approval by Barney (2006; 247). I return to this question in Chapter 6 below.

insisted that Francis and Dominic renounced lordship.[81] As David Aers observes, the poem suggests both that the Constantinian endowment of the church is 'venom', and that the poverty of the friars 'has become a source of the drug that poisons the church'. Reform of the friars is linked to reform of the church: the church's endowments should be removed and a 'fyndyng' provided for the clergy through 'dymes' (cf. B.10.322–35, B.15.553–64).[82] The metaphor of retainership Conscience applies to the friars might lend support to the view that he intends that the 'fyndyng' should secure a living for the friars without involving endowments and the exercise of dominion.[83] The practice of retaining men by indenture and awarding cash annuities enabled the lord to avoid alienating any of his property,[84] and as applied to religious, the *metaphor* of retainership was perhaps always understood as denying the existence of dominion. English friars seem to have drawn on a similar metaphor by claiming that they held their lands only at the will of lay lords, like villeins.[85]

Whether or not Conscience's use of the metaphor of retainership in connection with the friars can be associated with a similar argument, it is clear that the comparison between the friars and *corrupt* forms of retainership and the practice of 'maintenance' was recognized by other writers. The Wycliffite dialogue between a secular priest and a friar in Dublin, Trinity College MS 244 compares voluntary mendicancy, such as that practised by the friars, to the maintenance of thieves: 'We seyn þat siþ biggynge wiþouten nede as is stronge bigging is ensaumple & mayntenynge of þeues'.[86] This comparison, of course, belongs to the broader trend, extensively discussed by Wendy Scase, which drew into the controversy over religious mendicancy the language of the secular law, particularly the emerging law on vagrancy.[87] As I have argued, the language of retainership that suffuses Langland's account of the friars in B passus 20 makes similar connections between the mendicant controversy and the problems caused by 'maintenance' in the secular law. Friar Flatterer and his lord inevitably call to mind Meed and her friar, and the central role

---

[81] Clopper (1997; 295). Pearsall (*C-text*, p. 23) describes the 'fyndyng' as 'the provision of regular unsolicited alms', a view consistent with, for instance, B.15.307–12.

[82] See Aers (2004; 138, 156).

[83] Clopper, however, takes 'waging' the friars to mean patrimony and the granting of privileges, and argues that Conscience says the friars should *not* be 'waged'. I take his 'It is wikked to wage yow' (B.20.269) as implying the *difficulty* of waging/accounting for seemingly numberless friars, not that it is 'wicked' in the modern sense to do so.

[84] Dunham (1955; 52–3).

[85] Little (1934); Scase (1989; 103).

[86] Dublin, Trinity College, MS 244, fol. 216ʳ. I am most grateful to Anne Hudson for the characteristic graciousness with which she loaned me her microfilm and transcript of this manuscript. For this text, see Hudson (1988; 222). [87] Scase (1989; 69–72).

Conscience plays in both the first and the last visions establishes a clear analogy between the friars' corruption of the sacrament of penance and Meed's perversion of the secular law. In both scenes, though, Conscience seems to be implicated in the very corruptions against which he rails. In passus 20, Conscience accuses the friars for their abuses as he had earlier accused Meed. But within the antimendicant discourse of this part of the poem, he implicitly becomes one of those very lords whose consciences are, according to contemporary polemic, led astray by friars: himself part of the problem, rather than the solution.

5
New Modes in the C Text: Clerical 'Suffraunce' and Vernacular Counsel

If Conscience's final appearance in *Piers Plowman* B can be viewed as the reiteration, in a new mode, of his original representation in the first vision of the poem, the revisions to Conscience's role in the first vision of the C text may be analysed in much the same way. Langland composes *Piers Plowman* both as a reiterative series of episodes and as a reiterative series of versions. Just as Conscience is transformed during the composition of B within a variety of different discourses, so too Langland transforms him in C by the insertion of new materials in alternative modes.

In the first vision of C, Conscience remains a knight, as he was in the first vision of B. But Langland develops his presentation of the figure with two new passages. In Conscience's new speech on Hophni and Phineas in the C Prologue, Langland introduces a new discourse. This discourse draws on legal terminology in order to connect—as B 20 also had done—clerical negligence in enforcing the divine law with the practice of maintenance in the secular law. In C 3, Langland inserts the famous 'grammatical metaphor'. In this interpolation, Conscience again attempts to align contemporary earthly institutions—including labour relations and the king's relationship to his people—with God's eternal law.

These two insertions in new modes early in the C text transform the way Conscience appears in this part of *Piers Plowman*. As Andrew Galloway argues, the intrusion of the passage on Hophni and Phineas develops the specifically legal position of Conscience ('conscience' as witness or accuser), while the insertion of the grammatical metaphor transforms the debate with Meed into something more like a sermon.[1] Taken together, these two new passages develop a theme that had emerged during Conscience's banquet in B 13 and his encounter with the friars in B 20. Like those earlier sequences in B, the two additions in C emphasize the need

---

[1] See Galloway (2006; 362): in C 3 Conscience 'is less the prosecuting attorney of Meed that he is in A and B, and more a teacher or preacher of the court as a whole, and particularly the king'. Galloway (2006; 103) observes that the insertion in the C Prologue 'stresses a legal force and posture, distinctly more prominently and technically than does B'.

for that which Conscience himself increasingly offers in the early part of C: counsel and correction.[2] As I will show, however, Conscience does not necessarily have all the right answers, and the new discourses in C do not sit entirely comfortably with the debate mode in which Langland originally composed Conscience's first appearance in the poem.

MAINTENANCE AND 'SUFFRAUNCE': CONSCIENCE, MEED, AND CLERICAL NEGLIGENCE IN THE C-TEXT

In C.Prol.95–124, lines newly interpolated in the C text, Conscience uses the example of Hophni and Phineas to attack those clergy who fail to correct sins because of their own covetousness. Conscience rebukes in particular those who 'suffer' the sin of idolatry 'for loue of ʒoure coueytise' (C.Prol.103)—that is, because this idolatry yields the valuable offerings of cash and candles.

One should compare this passage, first of all, with another addition to the C text that also deals with the toleration of sin by the clergy. This addition, in passus 9, blames bishops for the proliferation of 'lollares and lewede Ermites' (C.9.241) going about dressed like friars:

> The cause of al this caytiftee cometh of many bischopes
> That soffreth suche sottes and oþere synnes regne.
> Certes, hoso durste sygge hit, Simon *quasi dormit*;
> *Vigilare* were fayrere for thow haste a greet charge.
> For many wakere wolues ar wriþen into thy foldes;
> Thy berkeres aren al blynde that bringeth forth thy lombren:
> *Dispergentur oues*, þe dogge dar nat berke.
> The tarre is vntydy þat to þe tripe bylongeth;
> Here salue is of supersedeas in sumnoures boxes.
>
> (C.9.256–64)

These two newly-interpolated passages on clerical negligence in the C Prologue and C 9 introduce two related terms from legal discourse, 'suffraunce' and 'supersedeas'. Langland also employs both these terms, in C passus 3 and 4, in connection with Meed's obstructions of justice in the secular realm.

Conscience's speech in the C Prologue turns on the question of 'soffraunce' (C.Prol.124); some form of the verb 'sufferen' appears four times

---

[2] I reserve until the subsequent chapter discussion of the third interpolation affecting Conscience in C, the 'autobiographical' passage at the beginning of C 5 (in this case poised in a waking interlude between the first and second visions).

in the speech (C.Prol.96, 101, 109, 119). The passage I have quoted from C 9 employs the same verb ('soffreth', C.9.257), along with another term, 'supersedeas' (C.9.264). These two terms occur in conjunction again in lines that Langland also added to the C text. In passus 4, Reason specifies as a condition of his service of the king 'þat vnsittynge suffraunce ne sele ȝoure priue lettres/Ne no supersedias sende but y assente' (C.4.189–90). Earlier, in passus 3, in lines also new to C, Conscience briefly personifies 'vnsittyng soffraunce' as Meed's sister:

> Vnsittyng soffraunce, here suster, and heresulue
> Han almest mad, but marye the helpe,
> That no lond ne loueth the and ȝut leeste thyn owene.
>
> (C.3.208–10)

Galloway follows Skeat's gloss of 'vnsittyng soffraunce' here, 'Unseemly Tolerance (of evil men)'.[3] But 'suffraunce' also has a more specific meaning within legal discourse: 'Improper indulgence; licence implied from the omission or neglect to enforce an adverse right'.[4] The legal force of 'suffraunce' emerges clearly in Reason's warning to the king not to let 'vnsittynge suffraunce' seal his privy letters. As Galloway argues,

> The warning against *vnsittynge suffraunce* cautions the king from improper indulgence of fraud or other crime, using a phrase elsewhere inserted into C...and here perhaps especially related to his power to pardon crimes since transmitted via his *priue lettres*.[5]

As John Alford shows, the oath of the justices that was appended to the 1346 Ordinance of the Justices acknowledges the problem of ' "vnsittynge suffraunce" authorized by letters sent under the king's seal'. The oath requires of justices 'that Ye deny to no Man common Right by the King's Letters, nor none other Man's, nor for none other Cause'.[6] Moreover, the Ordinance of the Justices itself (already cited in Chapters 1 and 4) reveals that the 'suffraunce' transmitted by royal letters is closely connected to Meed's own particular crime, maintenance at law. Both 'maintenance' and 'vnsittyng soffraunce' hinder the proper operation of justice:

> Because that, by divers Complaints made to Us, We have perceived that the Law of the Land, which We by our Oath are bound to maintain, is the less well kept and the Execution of the same disturbed many times by Maintenance and Procurement, as well in the Court as in the Country; We, greatly moved of Conscience in this matter, and for this cause desiring as much for the pleasure of God, and ease and quietness of our Subjects, as to save our

---

[3] Galloway (2006; 314).   [4] Alford (1988a; s.v. 'suffraunce').
[5] Galloway (2006; 424).
[6] Alford (1988a; s.v. 'suffraunce'); *Statutes of the Realm*, I, 20 Edward III, c. 6, p. 306.

Conscience, and for to save and keep our said Oath, by the assent of the great Men and other wise Men of our Council, We have ordained these things following: first, We have commanded all our Justices, That they shall from henceforth do equal Law and Execution of right to all our Subjects, rich and poor, without having regard to any Person, and without omitting to do right for any Letters or Commandment which may come to them from Us, or from any other.[7]

One might indeed, as Conscience does, identify 'vnsittyng suffraunce' as Meed's sister.

The second term I cited above, 'supersedeas', possesses similar connotations. As Alford shows, 'supersedeas' refers to a 'writ that stayed or put an end to a proceeding'. The writ was supposed to 'protect individual rights (e.g. to keep a litigant in one court from being arrested by order of another court), but issuance of the writ, as Langland notes, was subject to abuses such as bribery, favouritism, etc'.[8] The Rolls of Parliament sometimes refer to 'supersedeas' as an important right and a cornerstone of common law protection. In a dispute over tithes between the parson of Kneesall and the abbot and convent of Rufford in 1315, the abbot and convent repeatedly requested a writ of supersedeas so that they could pursue a prior appeal. But, they complained, 'the king's chancery have completely refused the said writ and utterly rejected what has hitherto been part of common law'.[9] More often, however, as in *Piers Plowman*, 'supersedeas' becomes virtually synonymous with delayed or obstructed justice: 'And when the justices who were appointed had enquired and found certain people indicted of the aforesaid trespasses, a writ of supersedeas was issued to the said justices, so that his suit is delayed until now', reads one complaint about its use in the Parliament Rolls.[10] In *Piers Plowman* C.2.190–92, 'supersedeas' refers to the bribery by which the writ is generally obtained. Here, Langland writes of 'Summnours...þat supersedias taketh' ('who, for the right price, hand out writs that put an end to legal proceedings').[11]

By introducing the legal terms 'supersedeas' and 'suffraunce' into the new passages on clerical negligence in the C Prologue and passus 9, Langland draws a precise connection between the absence of clerical correction

---

[7] *Statutes of the Realm*, I, 20 Edward III, c. 1, p. 303.
[8] Alford (1988a; s.v. 'supersedeas'), and see also Baldwin (1981; 52), for the proliferation of such writs in the first year of Richard II's reign.
[9] '[L]a chauncelerie nostre seignur le roi le dit brief ont tut outrement vye, e ceo q'ad este de [comune] ley cea en arier pleynement contredit'. *PROME*, I, 298b.
[10] 'Et quant les justices qi furent assignez avoient enquis et troverent certeynes gentz enditez des trespas avantditz, si vynt un bref as dites justices de supersedeas, issint qe sa seute est delaie tantqe en cea'. *PROME*, I, 300b.
[11] As glossed by Galloway (2006; 278).

and Meed's corruption of justice in the secular realm. He makes the 'suffraunce' of sin by the clergy—their failure to insist on the penalties of the divine law for the sake of their own material benefit—precisely analagous to the maintenance or 'unsittyng suffraunce' by which Meed attempts to buy off the penalties of the secular law for the members of her own retinue.

These revisions to the early part of the C text, then, further develop the identification that Langland had made at the end of B passus 20 between the activities of Meed and of the friars. As I showed in the previous chapter, the friars also enjoy protection from *letters*, like those mentioned in the Ordinance of the Justices. In the C Prologue, *Piers Plowman* again links 'maintenance' and that failure to rebuke sin which results from the covetousness of those with responsibility for correction. Indeed, Traugott Lawler suggests that Langland added the passage on bishops and 'supersedeas' in C 9 precisely in the light of the B text's conclusion:

> all the business about 'tar' or 'salve' connects this passage with the last scene of the poem. I feel certain that when Langland added this stunning passage on corrupt bishops to the C version, he had that last scene in mind, and was preparing his readers for it.[12]

I am equally certain that Langland made the insertion in the C Prologue—closely related to this other interpolation in C 9, as the similarity of their language indicates—with the final scene of the poem very much in mind.[13] One may readily perceive the similarity between the tolerance of sin that Conscience condemns in the C Prologue (turning a blind eye to sin for the sake of donations) and the practices of the friars at the end of the poem (their corruption of the penitential system by accepting 'privy payments' to themselves instead of insisting upon restitution). The poem's criticism, of course, turns in the C Prologue to the secular clergy, not the friars. Nevertheless, at the beginning of C, Conscience rails against abuses that are in essence the same as those practised by the friars in B 20, as well as by Meed in the first vision of the poem.

In drawing on language drawn from legal discourse, the newly interpolated passage on Hophni and Phineas sees Conscience assuming, as Galloway argues, an increasingly legal position. By the end of passus 4, the king has promoted Conscience, originally a king's knight, to the position of king's justice (C.4.186). Moreover, Langland employs a verb taken from legal discourse, 'accusen', to describe Conscience's new speech in the

---

[12] Lawler (2006; 187).
[13] Lawler (2006; 152, n. 36 and 157, n. 46) also notices that the phrase 'unsittyng suffraunce' is in C only, and that it 'looks towards the climactic scene of the poem'.

Prologue: 'Consience cam and accused hem' (C.Prol.95). As I discussed in Chapter 1, Langland's king had used the same verb to describe Conscience's 'petition' against Meed in B.3.174. There the use of 'accusen' suggested that Conscience meant his complaint about Meed to have specifically legal force as a prosecution or indictment. The new passage in legal mode in the C Prologue thus sees Conscience increasingly becoming a formal legal witness or accuser—rather than, as he was in B, a debater reasonably evenly matched with Meed. But Langland also introduces a second new discourse in his presentation of Conscience in the first vision of C, one which again affects how the character appears in the latest version of the poem. In this new mode, in C 3, Conscience becomes increasingly a preacher or counsellor as he appropriates Latinate grammatical discourse for vernacular instruction.[14]

MEED AND MERCEDE: GRAMMATICAL METAPHOR IN C 3

Critics of *Piers Plowman* have extensively discussed Conscience's grammatical metaphor in C 3, both for its technical terminology and for its development of Langland's ideas about reward.[15] I shall have more to say about this topic in the next chapter, where I examine the relationship between the passage in C 3 and Langland's earlier uses of grammatical analogies at Conscience's banquet in passus 13 of the B text. For now, though, I offer a review of the terminology of the passage, and consider its effects as a discourse new to Langland's composition of Conscience in the first vision of C.

In the B text, Conscience attempts to distinguish legitimate and illegitimate kinds of reward by defining the semantic possibilities of the word 'meed'. According to his definition, one may distinguish 'two manere of Medes'. The first is the reward given by God in the hereafter to those who do well while they are here, '*Qui ingreditur sine macula & operatur Iusticiam*' (B.3.237*a*). The second is a 'Mede mesurelees þat maistres desireþ' (B.3.246): the various corrupt forms of reward, tantamount to bribes, embodied in Meed the allegorical personage. Nothing else, Conscience claims, should be called 'meed' at all. Those things that appear to

---

[14] Although like the passage on Hophni and Phineas, the grammatical metaphor also uses legal terminology and examples, discussed Alford (1982).
[15] For the most important contributions, see Mitchell (1969); Amassian and Sadowsky (1971); Alford (1982); Overstreet (1984); Adams (1988); Martin (1993); Smith (1994; revised in Smith (2001; 140–70)); and Galloway (2006; 332–60).

be examples of good rewards, such as wages for labour and payment for goods, are more properly named 'mesurable hire' and 'permutacion' respectively (B.3.255–58). Conscience thus delimits the term 'meed' so that it applies only to two situations: the bad reward offered on earth, and the good reward offered by God.

In the C text, however, Langland seems to have found this original formulation unsatisfactory. It may be that both he and Conscience implicitly acknowledge the problem that I discussed in the previous chapter. There, I argued that B 20 exposes the difficulty of distinguishing what, per se, constitutes 'mesurable hire' and what is a 'mesurelees' meed (or what is a legitimate 'fyndyng' as opposed to illegitimate pillaging). Whatever his motivations,[16] in his revisions to C, Langland attempts to refine his thinking by introducing two major changes to the discussion in B. He replaces B's definition of 'two manere of Medes' with a distinction between two discrete terms, 'meed' and 'mercede'. This change effectively restricts the semantic range of 'meed' even further, to exclude *any* positive form of reward.[17] And instead of attempting to distinguish the various types of reward according to whether they are 'measurable' or 'measureless', Conscience now distinguishes legitimate from illegitimate reward ('meed' from 'mercede') according to two new principles. These two new criteria involve, firstly, the chronological sequence of the deed and the reward and, secondly, the pre-existing *relationship* between the giver and the receiver of the reward. In order to elaborate this second principle, Langland introduces the most complicated and controversial part of the revised passage. Here, he compares the two categories 'meed' and 'mercede' with two different kinds of grammatical 'relation': 'rect' and 'indirect'.[18]

The grammatical metaphor has proved notoriously difficult to interpret (even that tireless commentator Skeat threw up his hands) for two reasons. Firstly, Langland neglects to provide any clear indication of the relationship between his two terms for reward (meed and mercede) and the various grammatical terms to which he compares them. The second difficulty lies in the obscurity of some of the social and legal examples with which Conscience illustrates his argument. I make no claim to

---

[16] Adams (1988) suggests that Langland in part responds to readers of the B text who were anxious about the semi-Pelagian implications of that version.

[17] 'Mercede' appears to be Langland's own coinage from Latin 'merces' (like Conscience's grammatical terms used later, 'englisch was it neuere' (C.3.343)). The invention of new, semi-technical terms characterizes the C-text revision: compare 'lunatyk lollares' v. 'lewede Ermytes' (C.9.107, 140). Like 'meed'/'mercede', this pairing seems to be intended to draw ever finer distinctions between legitimate and illegitimate forms of begging and reward.

[18] For these 'two fresh distinctions' in C, see Adams (1988; 220).

elucidate all the difficulties of the passage here. Nevertheless, the essential outline of Conscience's discussion and its significance to the exploration of Meed in this part of the poem can be fairly readily discerned.[19] Conscience first distinguishes 'mercede', which designates positive forms of reward, from 'meed', which now refers only to negative ones. The distinction between the two categories lies in their temporal sequence. Good reward, 'mercede', is received only after the deed, and bad reward, 'meed', in advance:

> ...Gylours gyuen byfore and goode men at þe ende
> When þe dede is ydo and þe day endit.
> And þat is no mede but a mercede, a manere dewe dette,
> And but hit prestly be ypayed þe payere is to blame.
>
> (C.3.303–6)

Though the terms here have changed, the thought, as Robert Adams has argued, in fact varies little from B. Good rewards ('mercede') are available only once earned—in terms of the spiritual analogy, after death, 'When þe dede is ydo and þe day endit'. Only bad rewards, 'meeds', may be had in advance here on earth. The C text's distinction between 'meed' and 'mercede' ultimately follows much the same line of argument as B's distinction between 'two manere of Medes', the bad ones dished out on earth and the good ones awarded by God in the hereafter 'To hem þat werchen wel while þei ben here' (B.3.233).[20] As in the B text, Conscience excludes merchandise from the category of 'meed', describing it rather as 'a permutacoun', an equitable exchange of 'on peneworth for another' (C.3.313–14). Similarly, feudal 'fees' might seem to be an exception to the rule that good reward can never be received in advance. But Conscience seems to imply that these also represent something other than 'meed'. Kings' gifts of land are dependent upon an existing relationship of 'loue' and loyalty, and the giver may revoke the gift in the case of malfeasance (C.3.315–23). With the example of feudal fees, Conscience implicitly introduces the second means by which one may distinguish good reward ('mercede') from bad reward or 'meed', namely in terms of the *relation* between the giver and receiver of the reward.

In the grammatical analogy proper (C.3.333–406*a*), Conscience develops more explicitly the idea that the existing relationship between giver

---

[19] I am particularly indebted in the following explanation to Adams (1988), which to my mind is the most persuasive (and also the simplest) of the various attempts at elucidating the terms of the passage. I note points of disagreement with earlier treatments as these arise.

[20] Cf. Adams (1988; 230): 'in the world of B, the idea of good rewards *in hac vita* has *already* been repudiated. Only bad rewards, earthly meeds, are available here'.

and recipient distinguishes legitimate reward from illegitimate. He does this by comparing his terms 'meed' and 'mercede' firstly with two terms from grammar, 'indirect' and 'rect' relation, and then with the agreement between an adjective and its substantive noun:

> Thus is mede and mercede as two maner relacions,
> Rect and indirect, reninde bothe
> On a sad and siker semblable to hemsuluen.
> Ac adiectif and sustantif vnite asken,
> Acordaunce in kynde, in case and in nombre.
>
> (C.3.333–37)

As most recent critics of the passage have noted,[21] elementary Latin grammars identify four and sometimes five different kinds of grammatical accord. Langland adverts to two of these here. The fifteenth-century Middle English grammatical text called the *Accedence,* an adaptation of the *Ars Minor* of Donatus,[22] describes the different kinds of accord as follows:

> How many concordys in gramer byn þer? V. Quech v? þe fyrst betwene þe nominatiue case and þe verbe, þe secund betwene þe adiectyue and þe substantyue, þe iij betwene þe relatyue and þe antycedens, þe iiij betwen þe nowne partytyue and þe genitiue case þat folus, þe v betwene þe superlatyue degre and þe genitiue case þat folus…In how many schall þe nowne adiectyue and þe substantyue acord? In iij. Wech iij? Case, gendyr and nowmbyr. In how many schall þe relatyue and þe antycedens acord? In iij. Wech iij? Gendyr, nowmbyr and person.[23]

As this explanation shows, both the agreement between an adjective and a substantive and that between a relative pronoun and its antecedent require accord in three things: gender, number, and case; and gender, number, and person, respectively. Unlike the *Accedence,* however, Langland does not distinguish the two different types of accord. Conscience states that adjective and substantive agree in gender, number, and case ('in kynde, in case and in nombre', C.3.337), but he nevertheless goes on to say that a man is a '*relatif* rect' (C.3.355, my emphasis) if

> He acordeth with crist in kynde, *verbum caro factum est*;
> In case, *credere in ecclesia*, in holy kyrke to bileue;
> In nombre, Rotye and aryse and remissioun to haue.
>
> (C.3.356–58)[24]

---

[21] See especially Overstreet (1984; 254).
[22] See Thomson, *Descriptive Catalogue,* p. 1.
[23] *Accedence* (Text A), in *Middle English Grammatical Texts,* p. 8. See also Meech (1935; 98–101), cited Overstreet (1984; 254).
[24] I discuss below the significance of *credere in ecclesia* as an example of agreement in case.

Of course, as the *Accedence* clearly explains, a relative and its antecedent agree in gender, number, and person, not case. Notwithstanding Holy Church's rebuke in B.1.141 that Will learned too little Latin in his youth, Langland could not have forgotten the kind of mnemonic presented in a Middle English grammatical text like the one in London, British Library, MS Add. 19046: 'Say thys in Latyn: Relatiuum et suum antecedens conuenient in genere, numero et persona'.[25] Nevertheless, most recent commentators on the passage agree that Langland here compares the two types of accord between a relative and an antecedent and between an adjective and a substantive. Samuel Overstreet points out that speculative grammarians such as Radulphus Brito sometimes defined relative and antecedent as a variety of adjective and substantive.[26]

Langland seems, then, to compare the two types of grammatical accord, the agreement between a relative and its antecedent, and that between an adjective and a substantive. It also seems clear that Langland means to compare 'meed' with one type of relation—'indirect'—and mercede with the other—'rect'.[27] 'Direct' ('rect') relation means that the relative agrees in case with its antecedent as well as in gender, number, and person; 'indirect' relation denotes those instances in which the relative agrees in gender, number, and person with its antecedent, but takes a different case.[28] In purely grammatical terms, both are legitimate forms. But Conscience seems to give 'indirect' relation an entirely pejorative sense, corresponding to the entirely pejorative meaning attached to 'meed' in this version of the poem:

> Indirect thyng is as hoso coueytede
> Alle kyn kynde to knowe and to folowe
> And withoute case to cache to and come to bothe nombres,
> In whiche ben gode and nat gode, and graunte here neyther will.
> Þat is nat resonable ne rect to refuse my syre name,
> Sethe y, his sone and his seruant, sewe for his ryhte.
> For hoso wolde to wyue haue my worliche douhter
> I wolde feffe hym with here fayre and with here foule taylende.
> So indirect is inlyche to coueyte

---

[25] Text HH, in *Middle English Grammatical Texts,* p. 196.

[26] Overstreet (1984; 265). Other grammatical treatises support a similar association between the two different kinds of accord. For examples, see Thurot (1869; 359, 362). For discussion of Langland's comparison of the two different kinds of grammatical accord, see also Amassian and Sadowsky (1971); Adams (1988; 221–22); and Smith (2001; 166).

[27] Amassian and Sadowsky's effort to show that both 'meed' and 'mercede' and 'rect' and 'indirect' relation have both negative and positive senses results in a reading of the passage which seems to me barely comprehensible in its complexity.

[28] See Overstreet (1984; 254).

> To acorde in alle kynde and in alle kyn nombre,
> Withouten coest and care and alle kyn trauayle.
>
> (C.3.363–73)

With its conjunction of sex and economics in the reference to the 'foule taylende' of the daughter (presumably debts) enfeoffed to the son-in-law, this passage resembles Conscience's earlier condemnation of Meed's promiscuity. Conscience had spoken in very similar terms of Meed's willingness to attach herself to all comers (including Conscience himself).[29] The basic point Conscience makes seems clear: indirect relation represents a kind of grammatical promiscuity, in which words attach themselves to others without regard for case or number. Just so, 'meed' indiscriminately attaches itself to all, without regard for the proper or 'rect' relation that should exist between the giver and the recipient of a reward. Proper reward—'mercede' or 'relacion rect'—is possible only in the context of an existing relationship of trust and fidelity between giver and receiver:

> As a leel laborer byleueth with his maister
> In his pay and in his pite and in his puyr treuthe,
> To pay him yf he parforme and haue pite yf he faileth
>
> (C.3.348–50)

Conscience, then, no longer defines good reward narrowly as that which is strictly equitable or 'measurable'. Unlike in B, he takes account in C of the fact that a reward may not be *strictly* equivalent to the recipient's merit, but might nevertheless be felt to have been 'earned' by his best efforts. In terms of the spiritual analogy, Langland seems, as Adams argues, to imply a semi-Pelagian view: the view that God is self-obligated to reward those who have made their best efforts to please him.[30]

Despite the difficulties presented by the manner of its exposition, the immediate significance of Conscience's argument in terms of the allegorical understanding of Meed appears relatively straightforward. Conscience uses grammatical analogy to paint a clear picture of the social and moral chaos caused by 'meed' or 'indirect' relation. In proposing a marriage between Conscience and Meed, the king implicitly suggests that the use to which it is put determines the moral quality of reward ('meed' is potentially good if wedded to 'conscience' or put to a moral purpose). Conscience's grammatical analogy allows him to make a decisive riposte. According to his definition, its point of origin determines the quality of reward. It must occur in its proper sequence, following upon good deeds,

---

[29] This passage, as several readers have noted, also resembles Alan of Lille's use of grammatical metaphor to attack aberrant forms of sexual relation. See Mander (1979) and Overstreet (1984; 266–67).

[30] Adams (1988; 232).

and within the context of a proper, 'direct' relationship between giver and recipient. Conscience implicitly returns to the genealogical analogies earlier employed in the poem by Theology. But whereas Theology had argued for Meed's legitimacy as the daughter of Amends (C.2.123), Conscience uses grammar to show that Meed has no good relations; she is 'euermore a mayntenour of Gyle' (C.3.287).

Conscience does not only adopt grammatical discourse, however, in order to make a more sophisticated distinction between proper and improper reward than the one he offered in B. In keeping with the medieval belief that God had created a real resemblance between the laws of grammar and the 'laws of the Christian moral and intellectual universe',[31] Conscience also uses grammatical language in an attempt to align social practice with God's law. He does this partly through wordplay. Conscience converts his discussion of social practices, particularly the relation between the king and his subjects, into the terminology that he also used to outline grammatical concepts. In so doing, he plays on 'grammatical' and 'political' senses of words in order to produce what Alford calls 'conceptual double-entendre'.[32] For example, Conscience describes 'relacioun rect' as 'a record of treuthe', 'Folowynge and fyndynge out þe fundement of a strenghe' (C.3.344–45). But it also resembles, he suggests, the relationship between the king and the commune:

> Ac relacoun rect is a ryhtful custume,
> As a kyng to clayme the comune at his wille
> To *folowe* and to *fynde* hym and feche at hem his consayl.
>   (C.3.374–76, my emphasis)

Here to 'folowe' and to 'fynde' play on the senses Conscience used in his initial grammatical outline and alternative meanings that derive from the poem's political vocabulary (a vocabulary which Langland introduces from the 'founding of the commonwealth' in the Prologue onwards). To 'folowe' plays on the senses 'to come or occur after something' (*MED*, s.v. 'folwen', 1(a) and (b)), as the relative comes after the antecedent in the sentence, and various senses which refer to the obedience required of a king's retinue or subjects: 'to accompany', 'to attend (as a disciple, servant or helper)' (3 (a)); 'To obey or be subservient', 'to keep or observe (a rule or law)' (4 (a) and (b)). To 'fynde' plays on 'to discover, find out' (*MED*, s.v. 'finden', 7 and related senses) but also 'to procure or provide' (*MED* s.v. 'finden', 15 (a), and cf. C.Prol.143–44).

His use of grammatical discourse thus makes Conscience's speech in C more than simply a riposte to Meed and a new attempt at distinguishing

---

[31] Middleton (1972; 184–85); Alford (1982; 736–9).
[32] Alford (1982; 739). Alford treats a series of puns in the passage on grammatical terms and legal diction. On wordplay, see also Overstreet (1984; 256).

legitimate from corrupt forms of reward. The grammatical language he uses in C sees Conscience become increasingly, as Galloway argues, a counsellor or preacher to the court—and particularly to the king, to whom this speech seems really addressed.

Of course, as Galloway indicates, one may detect an element of flattery in Conscience's use of grammatical language to provide political advice to the king.[33] As 'lord antecedent' (C.3.379), the king rules or governs the 'case' of the commune; they must simply accord themselves with his law (C.3.377). Nevertheless, Conscience's grammatical teaching implicitly carries a reminder that the king is himself subject to (and must govern himself in accord with) a higher law, God/grammar: 'god, the ground of al, a graciouse antecedent' (C.3.354).[34] Conscience suggests the necessity of the king's obedience to this higher law in the exemplum of Samuel and Saul that follows the grammatical metaphor, a passage which Langland slightly expands in C. Conscience declines to elaborate upon the '*culorum* of this kaes' (C.3.433), but the story, which tells of God's vengeance on Saul for ignoring Samuel's counsel, illustrates that even a king must be obedient ('buxum', C.3.418) to God's bidding, and to those who counsel him on God's commands. The exemplum of Samuel and Saul resembles that of Hophni and Phineas in the C Prologue, in which Conscience discusses a corresponding instance of false mercy: a father's failure to rebuke his sons.[35] Both the C Prologue and C 3 serve, then, as reminders of the necessity of correction and counsel. They highlight the need for just that edifying talk which Conscience's banquet and the passage on God's minstrels in B 13 had suggested might be provided for lords. In the first vision of C, Conscience stresses the importance of just the kind of correction that Friar Flatterer failed to provide to Sire leef-to-lyue-in-lecherie at the end of the previous version of the poem.

'ENGLISCH WAS IT NEUERE': GRAMMATICAL DISCOURSE AND VERNACULAR INSTRUCTION

Conscience's developing role in the first vision of C as corrector and counsellor or preacher in part results from Langland's composition within a new poetic mode. In the grammatical metaphor of C 3, Langland adopts

---

[33] Galloway (2006; 358).
[34] As Galloway (2006; 346) indicates, 'To call God the *ground of al* uses a phrase usually associated with grammar itself'; cf. Langland's description of grammar as the ground of all in B.15.372 (C.17.108).
[35] Cf. Hanna (1996; 243) for the parallel between the passages on Saul and Samuel and Hophni and Phineas.

a homiletic style that draws on 'clerical' materials but redeploys them in the service of vernacular instruction to an interested layman: the king. Conscience takes up the Latinate grammatical tropes commonplace in contemporary homiletic discourse, but he re-presents them in the 'applied' vernacular context of political advice.

One aspect of Conscience's grammatical speech in particular may be viewed as a commonplace of homiletic themes and style. In C.3.355–62, Conscience outlines the grammatical concept 'relacioun rect' (the agreement between a relative pronoun and its antecedent) in terms of man's agreement with God in gender ('kynde'), case, and number:

> And man is relatif rect yf he be rihte trewe:
> He acordeth with crist in kynde, *verbum caro factum est*;
> In case, *credere in ecclesia*, in holy kyrke to bileue;
> In nombre, Rotye and aryse and remissioun to haue,
> Of oure sory synnes to be assoiled and yclansed
> And lyue as oure crede vs kenneth with crist withouten ende.
> This is relacion rect, ryht as adiectyf and sustantyf
> Acordeth in alle kyndes with his antecedent.
>
> (C.3.355–62)

As Derek Pearsall points out, Conscience takes his examples here from the articles of the Creed. These include belief in the incarnation, belief in Holy Church, and belief in the resurrection of the body and the forgiveness of sins.[36] Conscience's second example, '*credere in ecclesia*' (C.3.357), illustrates agreement in case. This example seems to allude to a topic that originated in commentaries on the Creed. According to this tradition, right belief in God could only be expressed by *credere* used with the accusative case and 'in'. The tradition was established by Augustine and later systematized by, amongst others, Bede and Peter Lombard. The latter may be taken as exemplary:[37]

> Aliud est enim credere in Deum, aliud credere Deo, aliud credere Deum. Credere Deo, est credere vera esse quae loquitur, quod et mali faciunt...Credere Deum, est credere quod ipse sit Deus, quod etiam mali faciunt. Credere in Deum, est credendo amare, credendo in eum ire, credendo ei adhaerere et ejus membris incorporari. Per hanc fidem justificatur impius, ut deinde ipsa fides incipiat per dilectionem operari.[38]

---

[36] *The C-text*, p. 94, n. 356–60.
[37] For Augustine, see *In Iohannis evangelium tractatus CXXIV*, p. 287; Sermo 144 (alias 61), cap. 2, in *PL*, XXXVIII, col. 788; and Mayer and others (1986; s.v. *credere*). For Bede, see *In epistolas septem catholicas*, in *Opera exegetica*, p. 198.
[38] '"Credere in Deum" is one thing, another "credere Deo," and another "credere Deum." "Credere Deo" is to believe what he says to be true, which the wicked also do... "Credere Deum" is to believe that he is God, which the wicked also do. "Credere in

In using a clause from the Creed, *credere in ecclesia,* as an example of agreement in case, Conscience seems to be thinking of this tradition of discussion of the Creed. According to such discussions, the different grammatical cases governed by the verb *credere* stand for different kinds of belief, and one particular case—the accusative—represents the proper kind of faith in God.

Nevertheless, one might notice some puzzling aspects to Conscience's presentation of this theme. Conscience appears to use *credere in* with the ablative case, rather than the accusative case favoured by Lombard (*credere in ecclesia* rather than *in ecclesiam*). The relevant part of the Apostles' Creed uses the accusative case: 'Credo in spiritum sanctum; sanctam ecclesiam catholicam; sanctorum communionem; remissionem peccatorum; carnis resurrectionem; vitam aeternam'. Conscience therefore seems to misquote the text of the Creed, as well as to use a case that differs from the one recommended for the expression of proper faith by Peter Lombard. Conscience may, however, *deliberately* misquote the Creed. As Overstreet shows, commentators felt that the use of *Credo in... ecclesiam* in the Creed was potentially problematic. By using the same grammatical form as *Credo in Deum,* it seemed to imply the same kind of belief in the Church as in God. It may be, as Overstreet claims, that Conscience deliberately uses the ablative case (rather than the accusative case that appears in the original text of the Creed) as a way of avoiding the suggestion that belief in the Church is the same kind of belief as faith in God.[39] But it is not altogether certain that Conscience deliberately misquotes here. Galloway proposes one alternative explanation: that a macron over the 'a', making *ecclesia* into *ecclesiam,* was lost at an early point in the transmission of the poem (although all the C-text manuscripts agree in reading '*ecclesia*').[40]

The precise implications of Conscience's use of *credere in ecclesia* (rather than *ecclesiam*) thus remain somewhat obscure, but it is clear that, in general terms, Langland had in mind a theme conventional in discussions of the Creed, a theme which links particular grammatical forms with particular forms of belief. Conscience's example illustrates how man may become 'relatif rect'—that is, how he may live in a proper relationship to God. It is only possible for him to do so if he agrees in grammatical case with holy church: he must hold the right sort of faith in the church and its

---

Deum" is by believing to love [him], by believing to go into him, by believing to adhere to him and to be incorporated into his body (of believers). By this faith the sinner is justified, so that henceforth this faith begins to be put to work through love'. See Peter Lombard, *Sententiarum,* liber 3, dist. 23, in *PL,* CXCII, col. 805.

[39] Overstreet (1984; 258–59).   [40] Galloway (2006; 348).

teachings, and conduct his life accordingly. The thematic implications of Conscience's use of *credere in ecclesia* bear a close resemblance to the arguments made by commentators on the use of *Credo in Deum* in the Creed. As the passage from Lombard's *Sentences* quoted above suggests, commentaries on the use of *credere* conclude that only the combination of 'in' plus accusative designates the proper kind of faith, expressed in love, and ultimately in good deeds. These commentaries invariably go on to emphasize the insufficiency of faith alone and the importance of works. False Christians and the wicked possess faith. But without love, faith is worthless, as Peter Lombard goes on to confirm with reference to St Paul: 'Si habuero omnem fidem, charitatem autem non habeam etc'.[41] Holy Church, of course, elaborated the same lesson in Passus 1: 'Chastite withouten charite worth cheyned in helle' (C.1.184); '*Fides sine operibus mortua est*' (C.1.183a, quoting James 2:26).[42] And Conscience's grammatical metaphor develops the same argument by insisting on the priority of love and the importance of good works. Lombard argues that the right sort of faith, expressed by *credere in*, initiates good works through love ('incipiat per dilectionem'). So, too, Conscience insists that if kings or popes give great gifts, 'loue is the cause' (C.3.317), and the gift remains conditional on the subsequent performance of good works:

> And yf the lele and lege be luyther men aftur
> Bothe kyng and Cayser and þe crouned pope
> May desauowe that thei dede and douwe þerwith another.
>
> (C.3.318–20)[43]

To be 'relatif rect' and to accord in gender, number, and case with God involves fulfilling in one's actions one's obligations to God, the Church, and to others.

I wish to concentrate, however, not so much on the thematic implications of this topic of *credere* and the cases it governs as on its dissemination. Overstreet, after discussing the origin of the topic in commentaries on the Creed, mentions its presence only in works that might be considered overtly 'grammatical', such as the discussion in the *Catholicon* of Johannes Balbus.[44] But one may also compare Conscience's mini-commentary

---

[41] *PL,* CXCII, col. 805, citing 1 Cor 13:2.

[42] Alford (1992; 36).

[43] In this context, Conscience's use of the word 'cause' suggests a technical vocabulary. In feudal relationships the 'cause' of the vassal's obligations towards his lord was the grant of the fief or fee. See Ganshof (1952; 138). Conscience perhaps attempts to make not the grant of a fee itself, but the love out of which it is granted, the 'cause' of the relationship between the lord and his vassal. For 'cause' as 'A legal suit or accioun; any question in litigation before a court of justice; also, a ground or reason', see Alford (1988a; s.v. 'cause').

[44] Overstreet (1984; 259).

on the Creed and his example of *credere in ecclesia* with similar discussions in sermons. The same discussion of *credere* and the cases it governs that I quoted above appears, for instance, under the entry for *credere* in the Lollard handbook for preachers, the *Floretum*.[45] The presence of the topic here suggests that discussion of the various grammatical forms associated with the verb *credere* was not confined to its original sources or to strictly 'grammatical' texts, but was also commonplace in homiletic discourse.

The grammatical topic of the cases governed by the verb *credere* certainly found its way into a sermon on one notable occasion. Thomas Brinton took up the subject in his well-known sermon preached before a convocation of the clergy during the Good Parliament in 1376. I have already shown how the topic lent itself to discussions of the sufficiency of faith versus works, and Brinton takes up the idea for the opportunity it provides to develop his theme, *Factor operis hic beatus* (James 1:25). He urges his audience at this critical historical juncture to be 'doers of the deed', not merely listeners. Having heard the parliament's pronouncements concerning the mismanagement of the kingdom, they must take remedial action.

After his introduction or 'protheme', Brinton, in the customary manner, re-states his theme, *Factor operis hic beatus*, and then proceeds to a discussion of the articles of the Creed, which all Christians must know. But it does not suffice, he warns, that the Christian should merely know the articles of the faith. He must also manifest them in deeds:

> And although the Christian might know these articles, they do not suffice to his salvation unless he has manifest works of faith, for the apostle says in James 2:26, 'Faith without works is dead.' But the Christian might say, 'I shall be saved by whatever way is given me,' (supporting his argument) by the statement of the saviour, 'He that believeth and is baptized shall be saved,' Mark 16:16. But these two things every Christian has; therefore... etc. I respond that it is one thing to believe God, another to believe God to exist, and another to believe in God. To believe God to exist is to believe just as demons and infidels do. To believe God is to believe that whatever he has promised us he will fulfil in us. But we believe in God when we trust him and truly love him and fulfil our faith in deeds.[46]

---

[45] MS Bodley 448, fol. 50rb.

[46] 'Et licet Christianus istos articulos sciat, ei non sufficit ad salutem, nisi fidei opera in se habeat manifesta, dicente apostolo, *Iacobi 2, Fides sine operibus mortua est*. Sed dicet Christianus, Quacumque via data ero saluus per illam sentenciam saluatoris, *Qui crediderit et baptizatus fuerit saluus erit. Marci vltimo.* Sed hec duo habet quilibet Christianus. Igitur, et cetera. Respondeo aliud est credere Deo, aliud credere Deum esse, aliud credere in Deum. Credere Deum est credere Deum esse sicut credunt demones et eciam infideles. Credere Deo est credere quod quicquid nobis promisit in nobis adimplebit. Sed in Deum credimus quando in eo speramus et vere diligimus et fidem nostram opere adimplemus'. *Sermons of Thomas Brinton*, II, 316.

Conscience also emphasizes, of course, 'þe doynge' (C.3.293); reward is only legitimate and an example of 'relacioun rect' when 'þe dede is ydo and þe day endit' (C.3.304). And it is tempting to speculate that Conscience's own allusion to the topic in his discussion of case in *credere in ecclesia* nods to Brinton's sermon. It perhaps forms part of an ongoing dialogue developing out of the events of 1376, if the recent suggestion that Brinton himself alludes to *Piers Plowman* be accepted.[47] In any case, Brinton's example demonstrates that the topic did find its way into sermons, and suggests that one might view Conscience's grammatical metaphor as a similar homiletic set-piece. Both 'sermons' take as their overt theme the doing of deeds, and both implicitly concern themselves with proper government.

Conscience's grammatical analogy can be compared in other ways to the themes and style of sermons. As I suggested in Chapter 3 in connection with Conscience's use of comparatives in B 19,[48] and as Alford also shows, the *artes praedicandi* frequently exploited grammar as a means of generating material for sermons.[49] Robert of Basevorn's *Forma praedicandi* devotes most of a chapter to a discussion of grammar as a device for generating sermon divisions. Nouns, verbs, adverbs, participles, and prepositions all lend themselves, he says, to treatment in sermons. (Interestingly, he excludes pronouns, whereas the relationship between pronoun and antecedent provides the major topic of Conscience's speech.)[50]

Most notably, Basevorn suggests that preachers might derive the parts of a sermon from discussion of different cases, in much the same way as Conscience uses *credere in ecclesia* as an example of agreement in case. So, for example, if the chosen theme is 'the intelligent minister is acceptable to the king' (Proverbs 14:35), its divisions can be stated

> Through case, as follows: in the first place we tell what kind of a man an ecclesiastic ought of himself to be: *intelligent*; what he should do to others: *minister*; whom he should please by this: *is acceptable to the king*.[51]

---

[47] Typically the influence has been seen as running in the opposite direction; as I mentioned in Chapter 3, Owst (1961) found a full characterization of Brinton in the B-text Prologue. But Galloway (2006; 134) has recently suggested that Brinton alludes elsewhere in his sermon to the pardon scene in *Piers Plowman*, a suggestion taken up by Hanna (2005; 251–52).

[48] 'To be called a knyght is fair'; 'To be called a kyng is fairer'; 'Ac to be conquerour called, þat comeþ of special grace' (B.19.28–30).

[49] Alford (1982; 733–36).

[50] Basevorn, *Forma praedicandi*, p. 276; trans. Krul, in *Rhetorical Arts*, p. 163.

[51] 'Per casus sic: In *primo* describitur vir ecclesiasticus qualis debeat in se esse: *intelligens*, quid apud alios facere: *minister*, cui per illa placere: *acceptus est regi*'. Basevorn, *Forma praedicandi*, p. 276; trans. Krul, in *Rhetorical Arts*, p. 163.

John Bromyard's *Summa praedicantium* also includes an example of this kind of grammatical conceit based on case in his entry for 'superbia'. The proud, he says, belong to the oblique cases, because they lean away from what is right ('obliquant a rectitudine'; cf. Conscience's 'relacioun rect'). The dative case represents those who give only in expectation of a return, either of money or of praise: 'Datiui casus sunt dantes munera vel laudes vel adulationes vt per hec consimilia vel maiora consequantur'. Those who accuse or maliciously conspire against their neighbours embody the accusative case ('Accusatiui casus sunt fratrum vel vicinorum accusatores et maliciosi conspiratores').[52] In addition to the specific topic, then, of *credere* and the cases it governs, homiletic discourse offers close parallels for the kinds of grammatical play in which Conscience indulges in C passus 3. Conscience adopts in C 3, as Galloway argues, an increasingly homiletic style and posture.[53]

But while one may compare Conscience's speech with the themes and style of the contemporary sermons and preaching manuals that I have just been examining, one might also notice one crucial difference. Where writers use grammatical analogies in sermons elsewhere, these are typically sermons intended for a clerical audience, as Alford notes.[54] Conscience's use of grammatical analogies in English poetry before a lay audience therefore represents, as Galloway suggests, a bold expansion of the possibilities of vernacular poetry. The king himself remarks on the novelty in his comment on Conscience's language, 'englisch was it neuere' (C.3.343).[55] It is striking that where grammatical materials appear elsewhere in contemporary vernacular literature, they do so in texts associated with translation projects, including the Wycliffite bible.[56] Like Conscience's and Patience's instruction to Haukin in B 13–14, the grammatical metaphor in C 3 thus points towards new vernacular audiences for materials that were originally more socially exclusive. Both Conscience's instruction to Haukin in B 13–14 and his grammatical metaphor in C 3 are forms of counsel that appropriate Latinate or 'clerical' materials for new vernacular situations. Galloway argues, indeed, that

---

[52] Bromyard, *Summa praedicantium*, s.v. 'superbia', S.xiiij, Art.iii.xi–xii. For this edition, see Coates and others, *Catalogue*, IV, J-110.

[53] Galloway (2006; 360). Galloway suggests that the conclusion of Conscience's grammatical section with a benediction at line 406a represents a turn towards a 'homiletic style' which 'may reflect how medieval Parliaments often opened with a sermon'.

[54] Alford (1982; 736): 'The use of the grammatical metaphor was intended mainly for sermons *ad clerum*'. Brinton's example, discussed above, was delivered to a convocation of the clergy.

[55] Galloway (2006; 343–44).

[56] See *Middle English Grammatical Texts*, p. xv, and chapter 15 of the Prologue to the Wycliffite bible in *Selections from English Wycliffite Writings*, p. 68.

Langland's revision in C of the original grammatical/riddling passage in B 13 'may have helped define a wider social scope for modern vernacular literature'. In the C text, Langland removes the Latin grammatical tag *Ex vi transicionis* (B.13.151), as well as Patience's taunting challenge to the Doctor of Divinity to 'undo' the riddle (B.13.157). For Galloway, this revision represents Langland's 'final, if partial, turn away' from the 'specialized Latin community of readers' that would have been capable of interpreting such materials.[57] One may observe the same widened 'social scope' for vernacular literature in Conscience's grammatical metaphor in C 3 and in Conscience's and Patience's teaching in B 13–14. Both passages implicitly address themselves to the growing lay and vernacular audience for materials that were accessible originally only to more restricted and specialized audiences.

'I KAN NO3T CONSTRUE': GRAMMATICAL METAPHOR AND DEBATE IN C 3

The grammatical metaphor may, then, be seen as a bold experiment, rather than as crabbedly obtuse, as many earlier readers (including Skeat) assumed.[58] Nevertheless, Langland's literary experiment is, arguably, not wholly successful. Conscience aspires to make of grammatical analogies a universal language, a language which would subsume heavenly and earthly patterns of reward. But in C 3, Conscience's new grammatical discourse comes into conflict with the 'topical' concerns of the debate mode within which this part of the poem was originally framed. In B 20, as I argued in the previous chapter, Conscience's wish to see the friars conform to the 'certain and...siker nombre' (B.20.255) with which God has established all else in the universe tends to gloss over the complexities of contemporary conditions. So, too, his grammatical metaphor, with its comparable insistence on accord in number, gender and case, never quite engages with the material realities it purports to address.

One may observe this conflict between grammatical discourse and contemporary realities already in Langland's earlier use of grammatical terminology in B 13. Such a conflict emerges clearly in the Doctor of Divinity's response to the speech which Patience makes using the Latin grammatical tag *Ex vi transicionis*. The Doctor views Patience's language from, as it were, the perspective of the *Visio*, with its 'topical' debate. He thus heaps

---

[57] Galloway (1995; 98).
[58] Galloway (2006; 289) rightly describes it as 'one of the poem's most daring and stylistically risky efforts to import inkhorn materials into sharply satiric and topical allegory'.

scorn on Patience's ideas about contemporary politics (B.13.172–76). From his point of view, Patience's language appears hopelessly out of touch with the realities of contemporary life. Slightly later in the poem, Haukin offers a similar perspective on Patience's language. As most commentators on this figure notice, Haukin is very much a *Visio* character, positioning himself as the hard-working avatar of Piers Plowman before he tore the pardon.[59] In B 13–14, of course, the poem discovers in Haukin the world of the *Visio* from a less than ideal perspective. Haukin represents an altogether grubbier version of the ideals with which Piers was first identified in the poem. He stands for the 'winning' that Langland originally presented as the opposite of morally offensive 'wasting', but which Piers redefined as over-worldly 'busyness' when he tore the pardon. Yet in the dialogic mode of this poem, even as Haukin seems now a compromised figure, standing for ideas the poem has already rejected, nevertheless he serves also to qualify and critique the ideals put forward originally by the post-pardon-tearing Piers and now by Patience.[60] Haukin thus vocalises what might be regarded as practical, commonsense objections to the language of Patience's and Piers's 'patient poverty'. He does so from the point of view of the poem's earlier, positive valuation of socially responsible labour. From this perspective, the claim to be able to feed the world with a piece of the paternoster looks a little ridiculous: 'laughed haukyn a litel and lightly gan swerye' (B.14.34). Haukin has experienced enough of the effects of actual famine to find sustenance by merely metaphorical bread a difficult proposition:

> 'There was a careful commune whan no cart com to towne
> Wiþ bake breed fro Stratford; þo gonnen beggeris wepe
> And werkmen were agast a lite; þis wole be þou3t longe:
> In þe date of oure dri3te, in a drye Aprill,
> A thousand and þre hundred, twies þritty and ten,
> My wafres were gesene whan Chichestre was Maire.'

(B.13.265–70)

Haukin's *Visio*-eye view of Patience's language of patient poverty provides a useful perspective from which to examine Conscience's use of grammatical language within the *Visio* in the C text. I believe Langland intended the grammatical metaphor in C 3, whatever its difficulties for modern readers, to be as exhilarating as Patience's rapturous praise of poverty in B 14. Nevertheless, he seems to have been acutely aware in both

---

[59] Cf. Maguire (1969); Stokes (1984; 245–52); and Harwood (1992; 99). On Haukin and Patience as Piers's avatars, see also Watson (2007; 99).
[60] Cf. the recent reading of Watson (2007; 84), in which Patience and Haukin are equally under scrutiny, and Aers (2004; 123–33, 148).

cases of the difficulties he faced in introducing these materials into the frame he had originally created for the work as a 'topical' debate. Thus one finds that both Patience in B 14 and Conscience in C 3 encounter difficulties in the presentation of their materials to a somewhat sceptical audience:

> 'What is Pouerte, pacience', quod he, 'properly to mene?'
> '*Paupertas,*' quod Pacience, '*est odibile bonum, Remocio curarum, possessio sine calumpnia, donum dei, sanitatis mater, absque sollicitudine semita, sapiencie temperatrix, negocium sine dampno, Incerta fortuna, absque sollicitudine felicitas.*'
> 'I kan no3t construe', quod haukyn; 'ye moste kenne me þis on englissh.'
> 'Al þis in englissh', quod Pacience, 'it is wel hard to expounen.'
>
> (B.14.275–78)

*

> Quod the kyng to Consience, 'knowen y wolde
> What is relacion rect and indirect aftur,
> Thenne adiectyf and sustantyf, for englisch was it neuere.'
>
> (C.3.341–43)[61]

Langland's references to 'construing' in English always suggest more than simply the literal distinction between English- and Latin-language materials. They seem also to imply an awareness of differences or conflicts between *discourses* and the modes of reading required by them. Haukin and the king experience difficulties not simply because they lack Latin knowledge, but because Patience's and Conscience's materials represent unfamiliar uses of language. From Haukin's *Visio*-eye view, the paradoxical language of patient poverty—poverty as possession—turns on its head all the assumptions about socially productive labour that he brings from the pre-pardon *Visio* world (although one might note that just as Piers does not quit labour altogether, but only resolves not to work so hard, so too Patience really preaches 'mesure'; cf. B.14.71–81). Similarly, the king's bafflement at Conscience's grammatical metaphor implies that his Latinate language brings with it something of the academic setting of the banquet in B 13, where grammatical analogies were deployed in the previous version of the poem. The king's bemusement suggests that when Conscience uses the grammatical mode of B 13 within the C *Visio*, it comes into conflict with the 'topical' debate mode within which Langland originally composed this part of the poem. Rather like Patience's language, Conscience's grammatical metaphor tends to gloss over rather than engage with the contemporary realities it purports to address.

---

[61] For a slightly different comparison of these two moments in the poem, see Galloway (2006; 344).

It is easy to give a specific example which locates Conscience's grammatical analogy within contemporary political/economic conditions even as it shows his evasion or elision of such a context. The 'ryhtful custume' (C.3.374) to which Conscience compares 'relacioun rect' looks to the past to legitimate social relationships. Like the excised B-text formula 'mesurable hire' (B.3.256), the phrase is reminiscent of the parliamentary discourse of the mid-century. As Conscience does, this discourse seeks to regulate social relationships, particularly those involving reward or remuneration, in accordance with a vanished past.[62] The 1349 Statute of Labourers attempts to restore wages to the levels that were customarily given in previous years ('consueta sunt prestari'),[63] a formula reminiscent of Conscience's 'ryhtful custume'.[64] Both the Statute and Conscience would do away with the contemporary situation that Meed fosters: the *temporary* (not customary) accord agreed between master and servant in the immediate conditions of the market ('Seruantes for here seruyse… Taken mede of here maistres as þei mowen acorde', C.3.273–74).

But Conscience's grammatical analogy, even more than the Statute (which is after all an Ordinance/Act), eschews instrumentality, and avoids any direct engagement with the material facts it would change. Instead, Conscience transposes Meed's arguments into the terms of a new discourse. In this mode, Meed's temporary 'accord' of market value becomes the eternal accord of grammar as a manifestation of God's law and God's own practice of reward. Within the terms of Conscience's grammatical discourse, that which Meed presents as an 'acordaunce' between master and servant would become an example of 'indirect' relation—discord—because it promiscuously attaches itself to all without regard for 'customary', loyal relationships. Meed's description implies that master and servant are bound *only* by the 'accord' of an agreed wage and thus seems to leave open the possibility that the servant might make an accord with another master, should he find one willing to agree more favourable terms. For Conscience, conversely, wages only qualify as legitimate, like grammatical 'acordaunce' (C.3.337), if they are paid within the context of a *pre-existing*, stable relationship. Such a relationship does

---

[62] For other connections between the grammatical metaphor and the labour laws, see Galloway (2006; 346) and Robertson, K. (2006; 48).

[63] *Statutes of the Realm*, I, 23 Edward III, c. I, p. 307.

[64] The emphasis on 'custume' and antecedents throughout the handling of reward in C 3 might suggest that this revision predates the 1388 Statute of Labourers, a statute which may underwrite the 'autobiographical' passage in C 5. The mid-century labour legislation to which I have just referred looks to restore customary, pre-'pestilence tyme', relationships between labourers and employers. On the contrary, as Middleton (1997; 225–6) points out, the 1388 Statute acknowledges that hitherto there has been no customary standard.

not in fact depend upon strict performance of the terms of the contract (cf. C.3.348–51).

Conscience's substitution of one discourse for another, however, is only analogous to the actual work of reform. Langland draws attention to this sleight of hand by marking out Conscience's grammatical analogy precisely as discourse—a specific use of language invested in particular social practices—not Truth.[65] Certainly, the grammatical metaphor posits a more socially accessible use of grammatical language, reoriented towards the 'applied' context of the government of the realm.[66] But the king's bemused response suggests that although Conscience uses the vernacular in his speech, it is not a variety of the vernacular comprehensible to its audience.

Even in the B text, Langland marks out Conscience's language in this section as a particular Latinate form of discourse. In B, this particular discourse is not grammar, but 'bible-talk' in the form of a commentary on the fourteenth psalm, *'Domine, quis habitabit in tabernaculo tuo'* (B.3.234a). One should see this sequence not as merely regular Langlandian quotation, but marked as Conscience's own particular linguistic practice. This is the only biblical quotation to have appeared in B 3 since, toward the beginning of the passus, the narrator cited Matthew on the proper way to practice charitable giving and Job on the vengeance that will (he hopes) fall upon those who accept bribes (B.3.72a and 96).[67] Conscience's bible commentary, that is, stands out as a discourse different from its immediate context, the presentation of the contemporary ills fostered by Meed. Moreover, the psalm Conscience quotes itself connects him with Holy Church, who cited the same text at B.2.39, and who earlier rejected Caesar's earthly economy by making it the ground of a metaphor for the divine: 'Whan alle tresors arn tried treuþe is þe beste' (B.1.85).

Conscience's mode of biblical citation works along similar lines. He distinguishes, in B, between God's reward in the hereafter for 'hem þat werchen wel while þei ben here' (B.3.233) and the 'Mede on þis molde'

---

[65] In Aers's well-known account of the poem (1980; 8–9), Langland consistently draws attention to such lacunae in the narrative, moments at which Langland is tempted to substitute 'consoling fantasies' for the more troubling insights of his imagination as it engages with contemporary realities. Aers also finds the B-text version of Conscience's speech on reward uncompelling, a 'bland statement' that 'simply ignores' contemporary labour struggles.

[66] Compare Galloway's characterization of the audience of riddles—'a large and diverse clerical audience whose uses of learning would extend less into the higher reaches of logical, philosophical, and theological discourses than into a variety of more vocational, administrative, legal, and bureaucratic purposes' (Galloway 1995; 71–72)—and Middleton's characterization (1982b; 104) of the audience of *Piers Plowman*.

[67] See Alford (1992; 38).

(B.3.254) that constitutes all the reward wrongdoers—*In quorum manibus iniquitates sunt* (B.3.249)—will ever receive. It amounts to a rejection of any legitimate reward here on earth.

Nevertheless, the absolute binarism of Conscience's mode of thought, if not the basic conclusion, does not go unchallenged within the poem. Piers queries this binary mode most dramatically when he rips up the pardon. And Langland denies Conscience's practice of biblical citation, as a particularly Latinate or 'clerical' mode of discourse, absolute authority within its immediate context as well.

In the B text, the challenge to Conscience's discursive mode comes via the dispute over Latin literacy that closes passus 3 in both B and C (B.3.332–53; C.3.485–500). Meed here denies to Conscience's mode of biblical citation any claim to absolute truth, countering his text with one of her own (B.3.336). Conscience appears to win the immediate argument by pointing out Meed's dependence on arguments taken out of context. Nevertheless, Meed's intervention makes her point: the king's testy interruption at the head of passus 4 seems to acknowledge that the process of argument and counter-argument could go on indefinitely. Conscience's own argument, indeed, demonstrates how, in his citational poetic, a text can deconstruct the very argument it is presented to support. In the C text, precisely this happens with Conscience's own quotation from Matthew, '*Amen, Amen . . . Mercedem suam receperunt*' (C.3.312). The text tends to unsettle his new categories of (bad) meed and (good) mercede.[68]

In the B text, then, Conscience's foray into the language of clerkly misogyny ('yow failed a konnynge clerk þat kouþe þe leef han torned', B.3.347) draws attention to the imbrication of his discourse within a particular social practice. Meed's attempt to claim Latin literacy for herself points up Conscience's biblical mode as an alienating Latinity, one socially invested. It recalls the moment in passus 1 when Holy Church rebuked Will for his inattentiveness at school and implied that moral understanding meant the same thing as Latin literacy (B.1.140–41).

In the C text, the king's more neutral intervention for clarification of Conscience's terms, 'for englisch was it neuere' (C.3.343), marks what Conscience does in this version of passus 3 as a similarly off-putting

---

[68] Cf. Overstreet (1984; 276). The lines have caused confusion for Conscience's readers: Overstreet as well as Amassian and Sadowsky construes this as an example of a bad mercede, despite the fact that, as Adams points out, the example is clearly labelled in English as a meed. See Amassian and Sadowsky (1971; 460) and Adams (1988; 227).

Latinity. The king is unable to recognize Conscience's heavily Latinate (and French)[69] vernacular as his own language. This moment of what Fiona Somerset has recently called linguistic 'dissonance'[70] configures Conscience and the king in roles rather like those of the Lord and the Clerk in Trevisa's *Dialogus* with his employer, Lord Berkeley. Trevisa's Lord here sees Latin as, potentially, a universal language, one which might be acquired by native speakers of all other languages to allow mutual comprehension. Nevertheless, he argues for English translation on the basis of Latin's social inaccessibility to those without sufficient leisure from more practical business, or without sufficient wealth for extensive education.[71] Similarly, the king's interruption in *Piers Plowman* draws attention to the social context of language use. By signalling the difficulties of Conscience's language for a vernacular audience, it explodes the idea that Latin grammar might ever function as a universal language, able to describe social practices because standing outside them.[72] The king's interruption, highlighting the difficulties of Conscience's speech for a non-academic audience, serves as a reminder of the embeddedness of language within a particular social situation. Grammatical language, even as it aspires towards eternal truth, the reflection in human institutions of God's own law, must necessarily be grounded, like all language, in social practice, and thus in the historical and contingent.

Although Conscience receives no reply, his grammatical analogy does not, therefore, represent Langland's last word on the subject of reward. Rather, it stands in C passus 3 as a virtuoso performance in an idiom that remains imperfectly reconciled with its surrounding context.[73] Conscience's grammatical metaphor boldly experiments with the possibilities of vernacular poetry by imitating the style of sermons *ad clerum*. Yet the lingering 'clerkly' tenor to the grammatical metaphor only exaggerates and highlights the conflict of discourses present in all versions of the debate—the collision between Meed's language of aristocratic 'gift' and

---

[69] For which, see *Middle English Grammatical Texts*, p. xvi. The English vocabulary for Latin instruction was drawn from Latin, often by way of French, reflecting the status of the latter as the language of grammatical instruction until the middle of the fourteenth century.

[70] Somerset (2005; 111).

[71] Waldron, 'Trevisa's Original Prefaces on Translation: a Critical Edition', p. 291, ll. 65–90.

[72] As Robertson, K. (2006; 49) observes, 'the king's question raises the possibility that these unchanging grammatical structures are themselves open to question, potential misinterpretation, or mistranslation'.

[73] As Galloway notes (2006; 333), 'The section as a whole is no longer a closely argued attack against Lady Meed's points but a rhetorical tour-de-force of its own; no answer to Conscience's claims is offered or seems expected'.

what Ralph Hanna calls Conscience's 'sober biblicism'.[74] The grammatical discourse that Langland intrudes into the original debate mode of passus 3 can only ever be, in this restlessly dialogic poem, one discourse among many. Conscience's expanding role in the first vision of C as corrector and counsellor of the court calls forth the new mode of vernacular grammatical counsel. But the implicit limitations of grammatical discourse—the failure, perhaps, of any existing mode adequately to describe the contemporary crisis that Conscience's verbal battle with Meed signals—points towards the potentially endless remaking of the poem in new, alternative modes.

[74] Hanna (2005; 258).

6
Conscience in the Versions of *Piers Plowman*

The series of discourses I have been describing in the first five chapters of this book represent, as I argued in the Introduction, a series of stages in the compositional and argumentative process of the poem, a process in which Conscience appears to 'develop' as he is transformed within the different discourses used to develop the themes of *Piers Plowman* during its composition as a reiterative series of episodes—as one discourse gives way to another in the course of the poem's developing argument. But of course, as my examination in the previous chapter of the new discourses introduced in the C text has already indicated, this compositional process is not confined to the (re)iterative structure of the single version, but continues through successive iterations of the whole poem. Conscience changes not only through Langland's composition of the B text as a series of episodes in various modes, but also during Langland's composition of the poem as a series of versions. The serial versions of *Piers Plowman* form, as I argued in the Introduction, a single continuous composition, in which each version is in dialogue with the previous version. In this ongoing dialogue, Conscience appears to 'develop' within the progression of an argument through the course of the versions as well as within the single version; the narrative of B forms a cumulative set of 'experiences' upon which Conscience's subsequent appearances in C are predicated.

A full appreciation of the revisions and expansions to Conscience's role in the C text therefore requires that we examine Conscience's appearances in C not only in terms of their 'intertextual' relationships with other contemporary texts or discourses (such as those explored in the previous chapter) but also in terms of their *internal* intertextuality:[1] their relationship to Conscience's compositionally earlier appearances in the B version. In this chapter, then, I consider the major revisions to Conscience's role in the C version. These revisions are the Latin lines on kingship that are

[1] A phrase I borrow from Middleton (1997; 208).

spoken by the Angel in the B text but reassigned to Conscience in C.Prol.152–59, and three new passages that are interpolated into existing B-text materials: Conscience's speech on clerical abuses in C.Prol.95–127, his grammatical metaphor in C 3, and the 'autobiographical' encounter with Will at the beginning of C 5. I will examine each of these passages in relation to Conscience's previous appearances in various episodes in the B version. I shall argue that many aspects of Conscience's changed appearance in the C text are intelligible not so much in terms of changes to Langland's understanding of the concept of 'conscience' (as Whitworth, for example, supposes)[2] but in terms of the compositional 'history' of the poem. The changes to Conscience in the course of the versions are intelligible if we read the versions of *Piers Plowman* attentively in sequence, from end to end, rather than, as more typically is done, reading Langland's revisions only in relation to the immediately parallel passages in the earlier versions.

CONSCIENCE AND CLERGY: C.PROL. 95–127

Conscience's first appearance in the C text, his newly-inserted speech on Hophni and Phineas,[3] follows on, in my view, from his final appearance at the end of the B version. The discussions of other scholars have already implied that Langland's presentation of Conscience in the C Prologue might contain echoes of, and have been written in the light of, the conclusion of the first long version of the poem. Andrew Galloway has suggested that the C Prologue, echoing the conclusion of the poem, has a more apocalyptic tone than earlier versions. As he also points out, Conscience speaks in his newly-inserted first appearance at C.Prol.95 with the same 'lone and unlocatable voice' as he had in the final lines of the B text where he called out for grace.[4] I have already suggested in the previous chapter, too, that this passage develops the associations already made in B 20 between the 'suffraunce' of sin and the practice of maintenance.

But there is also another sense in which Conscience's role in this new passage in the C Prologue implicitly develops his presentation in B 20. One might notice that the exemplum of Hophni and Phineas in Conscience's speech expands a suggestion originally spoken by Clergy in the B

---

[2] See Whitworth (1972).
[3] C.Prol.95–127. Lines 125–27 correspond to B.Prol.97–99, there spoken by the Dreamer; lines 95–124 are a new interpolation, inserted after B.Prol.96 and expanding materials originally from B passus 10.
[4] Galloway (2006; 104).

text (B.10.285–88; it is probably no accident that much of Clergy's speech is transferred to Conscience's partner Reason in C 5). No previous explanation for Langland's reassignment of these lines to Conscience in the C text has seemed wholly adequate. It is true, as Galloway argues, that the passage 'on the sins of parsons and parish priests [perhaps] seemed out of place in Clergy's mouth', and, as Ralph Hanna points out, this is one of several C revisions addressing 'the need for a pious and corrective clergy, not a clergy of lords' servants'.[5] One might also, following Wendy Scase, see Conscience's appropriation of Clergy's lines in the C Prologue as part of a more general trend of fourteenth- and fifteenth-century history, the 'usurpation of the spiritual power of the clergy', the empowering of the individual conscience, for which Scase finds evidence in the increasingly direct availability to the laity of pastoral literature originally intended for the clergy (a trend I discussed in Chapter 2 in connection with the role Conscience plays in B 13–14).[6] But this particular revision is most intelligible in the context of the poem's *own* history as a single serial composition. The reassignment of Clergy's lines to Conscience in the C Prologue implicitly continues a dialogue between the two figures that has been developing since B passus 13, when they parted ways with Clergy's prediction that Conscience would in future have need for his counsel.

As I argued in Chapter 2, the parting between Conscience and Clergy in B 13 implies a reorientation of 'clergy' itself away from theoretical, academic knowledge and towards more pragmatic forms of learning, directed at pastoral practice. Clergy, predicting that Conscience will in future have need of his aid (B.13.203–4), announces that he will remain behind to do humble pastoral work, rather than continuing with the high-flying biblical exegesis he had earlier wished to display (B.13.185–86). Instead, he promises to 'confermen fauntekyns ooþer folk ylered' (B.13.213).

But in B passus 20 when, as Clergy predicted, Conscience indeed calls for his aid (B.20.228, 375), we are merely made the more forcibly aware that Conscience now lacks anyone willing to perform precisely the kind of non-lucrative, unglamorous pastoral work that 'confirming fauntekyns' suggests. No-one seems ready at this point in *Piers Plowman* to take on the similar task of administering the sacrament of penance as a properly non-profit-making exercise. As I suggested in Chapter 2, the poem ultimately exposes the limits of Conscience's and Patience's vernacular project in B 13–14, for as a layman Conscience may counsel penance, but he relies on 'Clergy' for the actual administration of the sacrament. Friars, of

---

[5] Hanna (1996; 243); Galloway (2006; 101).
[6] Scase (1989; 40–6, section headed ' "Clergie" and Conscience').

course, as the antimendicant polemic I discussed in Chapter 4 insists, are only in it for the money. Will rebukes the friars in passus 11 for being interested only in the more lucrative forms of pastoral work (B.11.75–83). They prefer burial to baptism, because although the latter is more spiritually necessary ('a barn wiþouten bapteme may noȝt be saued', B.11.82), they can profit financially from the former.[7] Will's criticisms certainly seem justified by the action of B 20, in which the friars show themselves quite content to let their penitents remain in sin so long as they can benefit from their 'privy payments'.

However, Langland shows, both in B 20 and in the C Prologue, that the secular clergy are equally culpable. The proliferation of friars at the poem's end merely signals the absence of a properly active and engaged parish clergy, one that will rebuke sin rather than, as the friars do, exploiting uncorrected citizens (properly the concern of a parish priest) to line their own pockets:

> For persons and parissh preestes þat sholde þe peple shryue
> Ben Curatours called to knowe and to hele,
> Alle þat ben hir parisshens penaunce enioigne,
> And be ashamed in hir shrift; ac shame makeþ hem wende
> And fleen to þe freres, as fals folk to westmynstre.
>
> (B.20.281–85)

Conscience's cry for Clergy's aid in B 20 signals the contemporary absence of the pastoral ideal projected at their parting in B 13.

Conscience's speech in the C Prologue represents a third variation on this same theme, a sequel to his call for Clergy in B 20 and the continuation of the conversation between the two figures begun in B 13.[8] For in the C Prologue, Conscience once again feels the absence of a clergy properly oriented toward good pastoral practice, one which will set about rebuking sinners rather than securing their own material advantage. Like the friars, the secular clergy refrain from providing correction for the sake of 'privy payments', here the offerings made at shrines (C.Prol.96–104). Where in B 20 Conscience called for Clergy's aid, in the C Prologue he implicitly rebukes him for his failure to appear at the end of the B text, for the failure of the contemporary clergy to embody the idealized version of 'Clergy' imagined in B 13. In reassigning what had originally been Clergy's

---

[7] FitzRalph also criticized the friars for bullying people into agreements over burial; see Trevisa, *Defensio curatorum,* p. 42, ll. 14–17, and Scase (1989; 33).

[8] Conscience speaks in the C Prologue specifically to 'Bischopes and bachelers' (C.Prol.85), but he also addresses 'Clergy' more generally, and that figure actually appears, momentarily (C.Prol.152), to listen to his Latin lines on the responsibilities of the king.

lines in B 10 to Conscience, the new speech in the C Prologue attacking the contemporary clergy implicitly continues a dialogue between Conscience and Clergy begun in the previous version of the poem about a pastoral ideal and its contemporary failure. Understanding why Langland may have reassigned this passage from Clergy to Conscience in the C Prologue requires a mode of reading that attends to the versions as a single intelligible compositional sequence; a reading practice which assumes that, while Langland must necessarily have revised with the parallel passages of the previous version in front of him (in the manuscript into which he presumably inserted his revisions),[9] as he revised he also had in mind *all* that he had previously composed on related topics. As Conscience 'develops' within the composition of the single version through his representation within a variety of different discourses, so he also 'develops' with the continued development of the poem's themes in successive versions. His dialogue with Clergy in the course of B sees him become increasingly the interrogator of the failings of the clergy in C.

CONSCIENCE AND KINGSHIP IN B 19 AND THE C PROLOGUE[10]

A second example in which Langland reassigns to Conscience in the C text lines previously spoken by other figures in B is the passage discussing the virtues of a king that was spoken by the Angel in the B Prologue (B.Prol.132–38), but which is reassigned to Conscience in C.Prol.153–59. The probable reasons for this reassignment have again been overlooked. Galloway discusses the change in terms of an increasing tendency on Langland's part towards the 'abstract', which Talbot Donaldson also suggested was a feature of the C Prologue. Anna Baldwin takes the revision as further evidence for what she calls the 'triumph of absolutism' in the C text, in which the only restraints placed on the king are his own moral faculties.[11] But the revision makes best sense if it is read not only against the immediately parallel passage in the B Prologue, but also in the light of developments to Conscience's role

---

[9] In this particular instance, however, Russell and Kane have argued that the Hophni and Phineas passage—also defective in alliteration and perhaps unfinished 'draft' material—was in fact misplaced in its present position by a 'literary executor' after the poet's death (*C Version*, pp. 87–8). My own argument for how well this passage develops the conclusion of B will indicate that I do not share Russell and Kane's view that the passage does not belong here.

[10] This section of the chapter appeared in an earlier form in my essay, 'Ecce Rex' (Wood, 2007). It is reproduced in revised form with kind permission from Brepols Publishers.

[11] Donaldson (1949; 89–90); Baldwin (1981; 16); and Galloway (2006; 115).

elsewhere in the course of the B version, specifically his 'sermon' on Christ as knight, king, and conqueror in B 19.

As I discussed in Chapter 3, the preoccupations of the Angel's speech in the B Prologue closely coincide with those of Conscience's speech in B 19. Both are passages which discuss the kingly virtues of justice and mercy; both are passages which draw, as I have argued, on homiletic commonplaces about kingship and about Christ as an ideal king. In the C Prologue, Conscience warns the king that he must temper justice with piety or pity: '*Nudum ius a te vestiri vult pietate*' (C.Prol.156). He reminds him, too, that he administers the laws of a higher king, Christ: '*O qui iura regis christi specialia regis*' (C.Prol.154). In B 19, Conscience had described the kingly Christ in very similar terms, discussing the gifts of the Magi as symbols of Christ's own regal qualities of *ius* and *pietas* or, in Conscience's vernacular terms, 'Reson and Rightwisnesse and Ruþe' (B.19.83). In reassigning to Conscience the material in the Prologue on the duties of kingship, Langland configures the C Prologue as the continuation of the narrative of B passus 19. Conscience engages in an ongoing conversation with himself, a discussion he initiated in B passus 19[12] and one that now extends across the versions of the poem. If the versions are read in sequence, from end to end, the reassignment of the lines in the Prologue to Conscience in the C text follows quite naturally from his sermon on Christ as knight, king, and conqueror in the previous version of the poem. In setting out, in the C Prologue, the virtues that a king ought to display, Langland surely recalled the very similar passage in which Conscience appeared in B 19.[13]

CONSCIENCE AND PATIENCE: GRAMMATICAL METAPHOR AND REWARD IN B 13–14 AND C 3

As Langland revised Conscience in the C text, then, he recalled the character's earlier appearances throughout the course of the B version. And he did so in such a way that Conscience, too, appears to recollect the scenes

---

[12] Or rather a discussion Conscience *continues* in B passus 19: I have already argued in Chapter 3 that his arguments here take up issues raised by Meed in B passus 3.

[13] Warner (2002, 2007) has recently claimed that an early draft of C is in part attested by National Library of Wales MS 733B (sigil N of A, N² of C), and that the last two passus of B in fact originate in the C-text tradition. I am sceptical about these claims. But even if correct, Warner's argument does not significantly affect my own argument about Conscience's two new speeches in the C Prologue, which insists that Langland revised with all that he had previously composed—and not just the immediately parallel passages in earlier versions—in mind. From the point of view of this argument, it makes little difference whether we view 'B 19–20' as part of Langland's 'B'- or 'C'-text revision; what is important is that this section seems to have been connected in his mind to the related passages in the C Prologue and to the revisions he made there.

in which he appeared in the previous version of the poem. While I do not think that Langland writes characters who 'develop' or learn in the same way as characters in a novel, nevertheless the way Langland composes characters to highlight the development of particular ideas within the poem requires that certain themes cluster around individual characters in a way that produces effects that we read as character 'development'. As these themes are developed in successive versions of the poem, characters such as Conscience appear to 'develop' through the course of the versions, as well as within the single version. In his grammatical metaphor in C 3, Conscience appears to have learned from his 'experiences' in B 13–14. This is not real biographical development or education, but an effect which is produced because Conscience is engaged in reiterating and developing topics that were previously discussed in his presence in the earlier version of the poem.

Conscience's grammatical metaphor, as I have shown in the previous chapter, has been extensively discussed in terms of medieval grammatical theory. Other readers have also shown how the passage develops Langland's existing discussion of reward in passus 3 of the B text. But there has been no previous effort to relate the passage in C 3 to Langland's earlier uses of 'grammatical metaphor' in the previous long version of the poem: the 'two Infinites' in Clergy's reference to Piers's definition of the three Do's in B passus 13 (B.13.128–30), and Patience's use, in the same passage, of the Latin grammatical tag *Ex vi transicionis* (B.13.151). Both of these grammatical passages are performed in Conscience's presence and form part of his cumulative textual 'experience' in the B version of *Piers Plowman*. The grammatical discussions in B 13 and C 3 may, then, most profitably be considered together.

Indeed, Langland's major development in the revised discussion of reward in passus 3 of the C text, the introduction of a temporal distinction (good reward is not received in advance),[14] derives chiefly from a proximate locale in the earlier version of his own poem. During his pilgrimage with Conscience in B passus 14, Patience also elaborates a temporal distinction. As Conscience, Will, and Haukin listen, Patience argues that to have a reward here (in the form of wealth) is to disqualify oneself from the reward of the hereafter:

> Hewen þat han hir hire afore arn eueremoore nedy,
> And selden deyeþ he out of dette þat dyneþ er he deserue it,
> And til he haue doon his deuoir and his dayes iournee.

---

[14] See Smith (2001; 158): 'In revising his discussion of the relation between labor and reward, Langland's significant innovation is to introduce a temporal distinction'.

> For whan a werkman haþ wroȝt, þan may men se þe soþe,
> What he were worþi for his werk and what he haþ deserued,
> And noȝt to fonge bifore for drede of disalowyng.
> So I seye by yow riche, it semeþ noȝt þat ye shulle
> Haue heuene in youre herberwyng and heuene þerafter
> Riȝt as a seruaunt takeþ his salarie bifore, & siþþe wolde clayme moore.
>
> (B.14.134–42)

The argument about reward that Conscience makes in C is based on exactly this same idea of the proper temporal sequence of reward. In B 3, Conscience had defined the moral quality of reward according to its innate quality as 'measurable' or otherwise. In the reformulated version in the C text, following the temporal distinction put forward by Patience in B 13, Conscience defines meed, improper reward, as that which is given before it has been earned. Proper reward or 'mercede', on the other hand, is only given when the working day is done:

> Y halde hym ouer hardy or elles nat trewe
> That *pre manibus* is paied or his pay asketh.
> Harlotes and hoores and also fals leches,
> They asken here huyre ar thei hit haue deserued
> And Gylours gyuen byfore and goode men at þe ende
> When þe dede is ydo and þe day endit.
> And þat is no mede but a mercede, a manere dewe dette,
> And but hit prestly be ypayed þe payere is to blame,
> As by the book þat byt nobody withholde
> The huyre of his hewe ouer eue til amorwe:
> *Non morabitur opus mersenarii &c.*
>
> (C.3.299–308a)

The use here of the same temporal distinction that Patience had made in B 14 replicates Patience's example of the labourer as well as his underlying argument (compare C.3.348–51).[15] Conscience's example of the king's conditional gift, which like God's grace may subsequently be withdrawn (C.3.320, 'May *desauowe* that thei dede and douwe þerwith another'), also expands upon the logic of Patience's 'noȝt to fonge bifore for drede of *disalowyng*' (B.14.139) (my emphasis).[16]

---

[15] Conscience does give an example involving labour in AB 3, but there the legitimacy of waged labour rests on its basis in a just exchange, 'mesurable hire' (B.3.256), rather than on the condition of its receipt *after* performance. The new category of 'mercede' seems to subsume this earlier argument of commensurate exchange while adding a temporal aspect.

[16] Manuscripts XQSF of C substitute Patience's term, 'disalowyng' ('May desalowe') for the majority reading 'desauowe' in Conscience's C-text version.

The relationship between the passages in C 3 and B 14 is further indicated by revisions to Patience's original formulation in the C text. The argument about the proper temporal sequence of reward having been advanced to C 3, Patience's original full presentation of the idea has now become redundant. Consequently, while B.14.134–41 remains intact in the C-text revision of this sequence, the subsequent elaboration of the argument in B.14.142–57 is omitted in C (cf. C.16.1–10). An analogous process of 'frontloading' into earlier parts of the poem with subsequent streamlining of later passus sees Haukin's 'confession' dispersed among the seven deadly sins in the C text. Most significantly, though, the material that was originally presented by Patience in the B text is reassigned in C to one of the characters who witnessed that original presentation. Having heard Patience's argument about reward in B 14, Conscience repeats it as part of his own analysis of reward in C 3.

I do not mean to suggest that Conscience *actually* learns from Patience, or that he is educated in any real sense in the course of the poem. Rather, Langland's mode of composing the serial versions produces the *effect* of development, of a consistent character who has 'experiences' in one version that are reflected in how he appears in the next. Just as within the single version Langland composes reiterative 'type scenes' in which the character is repeatedly associated with certain topics, so during the course of the composition of the serial versions, Conscience is repeatedly linked with particular themes, including the theme of reward discussed in B 14 and C 3. The development of the same theme in connection with the same character in the later version of the poem produces the effect of development, because Conscience appears to assent in C 3 to the argument about reward earlier made in his presence in B 14.

Of course, the language of reward in both C 3 and B 14 is ultimately that of Piers Plowman's half-acre. Patience's application of the truisms of labour relations to the divine economy, 'selden deyeþ he out of dette þat dyneþ er he deserue it' (B.14.135), is an expansion of Hunger's terse advice, 'he shal soupe swetter whan he it haþ deserued' (B.6.217). Conscience's ideal employer in C passus 3 also recalls the poem's originary recourse to the field of labour, the description Piers gives of his employer Truth, who 'wiþhalt noon hewe his hire þat he ne haþ it at euen' (B.5.551–52), in keeping with Conscience's appeal to bible lore/law, 'the book þat byt nobody withholde/The huyre of his hewe ouer eue til amorwe' (C.3.307–08, alluding to Lev. 19:13, quoted in the following line).

Nevertheless, one may infer that, in C 3, Conscience recalls specifically the discussion of these ideas by Patience in B passus 14. Indeed, he couches his version of Patience's temporal distinction in the language of B passus 13, Piers's/Clergy's and Patience's grammatical metaphor (also all but eliminated in its original locale by the C text).[17] Conscience replicates not only Patience's underlying argument about the proper sequence of labour and reward, but also his earlier grammatical language.

In that portion of Conscience's speech on grammar that follows the king's interruption at C.3.341–43, Conscience's language strongly implies that he has in mind Patience's earlier grammatical passage. The king interrupts to ask for clarification of two concepts: 'relacion rect' (where the relative agrees in case as well as in gender, person, and number with its antecedent) and 'adiectyf and sustantyf'. In replying, Conscience describes 'relacioun rect', but in a way that suggests that he is here implicitly comparing this concept, which he has already compared with the accord between adjective and substantive (C.3.333–38), with a third grammatical category:

> 'Relacioun rect,' quod Consience, 'is a record of treuthe –
> *Quia antelate rei recordatiuum est* –
> Folowynge and fyndynge out þe fundement of a strenghe,
> And styfliche stande forth to strenghe þe fundement,
> In kynde and in case and in cours of nombre.
>
> (C.3.344–47)

As Vance Smith shows, the Latin tag *Quia antelate rei recordatiuum est* occurs frequently in medieval discussions of relation and derives ultimately from Priscian's *Institutiones,* where it is used to describe the relationship between a pronoun and its antecedent. 'Fundement' too, as Smith also argues, seems to be a rendering of the term 'fundamentum' established in discussions of relation.[18] But the word 'strenghe' seems out of place in this discussion because in its most obvious grammatical sense it refers not to relation but to a different grammatical category.

In his gloss of these lines, Derek Pearsall mistranslates 'strenghe' by implying that it means simply 'concord', the 'Acordaunce' referred to several lines earlier (C.3.337).[19] But as Priscilla Martin shows, 'strenghe'

---

[17] C cuts Patience's grammatical tag, *Ex vi transicionis,* and arguably the adaptation of Clergy's/Piers's 'two Infinites' would be recognizable as specifically grammatical discourse only to readers familiar with the earlier B version; cf. C.15.135–35a, 'And preueth by puyre skile inparfyt alle thynges-/*Nemo bonus*'. For discussion of the revision, see also Middleton (1972; 173, 182).

[18] Smith (2001; 159, 169).

[19] *The C-text,* p. 94, n. 344–7: 'Direct relation is a record and witness to truth, corresponding to and revealing in its nature the firm foundation of concord, and acting to strengthen that foundation'.

is in fact a translation of the Latin grammatical term 'vis'.[20] By using the word 'strenghe', Langland seems to be conflating relation with another grammatical category: government or regimen. Regimen is the term that in medieval grammars describes the various grammatical 'powers' by which one word determines the case of another.[21] Patience had alluded to the same grammatical category at Conscience's banquet in B 13 when he quoted the Latin tag '*Ex vi transicionis*'. As R. E. Kaske shows, Patience here refers to the 'power' by which the verb rules its direct object in the accusative case.[22]

Conscience's use of the term 'strenghe' in C 3, then, recalls the earlier reference to regimen in Patience's phrase *Ex vi transicionis*. It implies that the composition of C passus 3 registers interference from Langland's— and Conscience's—recollection of the earlier grammatical discussion in B passus 13. Just as Conscience elaborates an argument on reward like the one developed by Patience in B 14, so too he repeats the grammatical terminology he heard used by Patience at the banquet in his own house in the earlier version of the poem.

That the discussion of grammar in C 3 recalls similar discussions in B 13 is also suggested by the metaphor of pilgrimage with which Langland presents both the 'relacioun rect' of C passus 3 and another grammatical category in B passus 13: Clergy's/Piers's 'two Infinites'. In B passus 13, Clergy says that Piers has described Dowel and Dobet as 'two Infinites', 'Whiche Infinites wiþ a feiþ *fynden out* dobest,/Which shal saue mannes soule' (B.13.128–30, my emphasis). Similarly, according to Conscience,

---

[20] Martin (1993 ; 174). The Middle English grammatical text in Cambridge, Trinity College, MS O. 5. 4., for example, uses both the English 'strengthe' and the Latin 'vis' interchangeably: 'In how many maners schal the nominatyf case be gouernyd of a verbe? In on, by strengthe of person, as *Ego sum homo*: *ego* is gouernyd of *sum* ex vi persone'. See Text EE, in *Middle English Grammatical Texts*, p. 182. See also *MED*, s.v. 'strength', 6 (d): 'The ability to govern or require a certain construction, grammatical force'. No Middle English grammatical texts survive from the fourteenth century, and the *MED* therefore has no citations for this sense of 'strength' until the fifteenth century. But given the consistency of usage in these later texts, it seems likely that by the time Langland wrote the C text the term was already established in technical usage.

[21] As the grammarian Peter Helias explained, '[M]etaphorically it is said that one word governs another, and this is a very apt metaphor. For as a general rules an army, so the verb rules the nominative placed in the construction' ('[M]ethaphorice dictum est quod regat dictio dictionem, et est metaphora satis congrua. Sicut enim dux regit exercitum sic verbum regit nominativum in constructione positum'). See Helias, *The Summa of Petrus Helias on Priscianus Minor*, I, 153, ll. 16–19.

[22] Kaske (1969; 236). Cf. the discussion in Cambridge, Trinity College MS O. 5. 4, Text EE in *Middle English Grammatical Texts*, pp. 183–84. This text contains references to numerous other 'powers'. For example, the author explains that the genitive case is ruled 'ex vi possessoris' and 'ex vi particionis'. These various 'powers' were developed by Johannes Balbus (of Genoa), *Catholicon* (Lyons: Perrinus Lathomi, Bonifacius Johannis, and Johannes de Villa Veteri, 1496), fol. f iiij'. For this edition, see Coates and others, *Catalogue*, II, B-018. See also Thomson, *Catalogue*, p. 35, for discussion.

'relacioun rect' is 'a record of treuthe...Folowynge and *fyndynge out* þe fundement of a strenghe' (C.3.344–45, my emphasis). Langland is again alluding to different grammatical categories in these two passages. As Anne Middleton shows, Dowel and Dobest as 'two Infinites' refers to two distinct grammatical classes that were both described by Priscian as 'infinite': the uninflected form of the verb, and the 'infinite' or interrogative pronoun.[23] But the verbal resemblance between these two passages, which both employ the same miniature personification allegory, again implies that Conscience has the grammatical discussions of B passus 13 in mind during his own exposition of grammar in C passus 3.

The reappearance in C passus 3 of the concept of regimen (vis/strenghe) and of the metaphor of pilgrimage ('fyndynge out') suggests that Conscience's discussion of grammar should not be viewed as composition *ex nihilo*, nor only in comparison with the A and B versions of the first vision, but as a further meditation on the possibilities of grammatical metaphor first explored in B 13. In some senses, C 3 can be seen as a rewriting of the grammatical metaphor of B 13, translating similar underlying ideas into a different grammatical category. Langland, as I have noted, refers to different grammatical concepts in these two passages: relation in C 3 and regimen/infinites in B 13. But the mode in which he expresses these different concepts suggests that for his poetic purposes they were related to similar preoccupations. Like the 'two Infinites' of B 13, the concept of relation stages in grammatical terms the basic form of the poem: a quest.[24] But appropriately for a passage that depends upon previous poetic labours (both the AB versions of passus 3, and passus 13–14 of the B text), the substitution of the idea of relation for the concept of 'infinites' transforms the nature of the search. It is no longer staged as an outward journey, but as a return, an act of memory, the recollection of what went before ('*Quia antelate rei recordatiuum est*', C.3.344a).[25] That Langland had his earlier grammatical efforts in mind when composing C 3 suggests that Conscience's grammatical analogy might ultimately be taken as a useful metaphor for the development of the poem itself. As I have argued, to read Conscience's grammatical metaphor in its fullest context is to read it as the development of its 'antecedents' in the earlier version of the poem, as a reiteration and recasting of Patience's/Clergy's grammatical language and discussion of reward in B 13–14. As Langland revised C 3, he not only had

---

[23] See Middleton (1972; 175–77).
[24] See Middleton (1972; 171): the three lives 'order the progressive form of the search for perfection'.
[25] On relation as implying an act of memory and 'recordatio' as a technical term of memory, see Smith (2001; 162–64).

the immediately parallel passages in AB passus 3 in mind, but recollected *all* that he had previously composed on related topics.

However, as I have been suggesting, not only Langland, but also Conscience, remembers (or appears to) the earlier grammatical passages of B 13 when elaborating his own grammatical analogies in C 3. Having heard Patience's arguments about reward in B 14 and the grammatical analogies at his own banquet in B 13, Conscience repeats and develops them in C 3. Thus, Conscience appears to 'learn' or develop through the development of Langland's themes in the course of the versions, as well as within the single version.

Of course, Langland is not writing a novel, and there can be no sense in which Conscience can really be said to 'learn' or develop during the course of the versions of *Piers Plowman*. Nevertheless, the compositional process of the poem as a series of reiterations and transformations of particular themes—as both a series of episodes and a series of versions—produces effects that we read as character 'development'. Roland Barthes's discussion of literary character may be useful here:

> When identical semes traverse the same proper name several times and appear to settle upon it, a character is created...The proper name acts as a magnetic field for the semes; referring in fact to a body, it draws the semic configuration into an evolving (biographical) tense.[26]

As the same 'semes' or units of meaning are linked with the same 'proper name', as the same character is repeatedly associated with the same themes during the composition of the versions of *Piers Plowman*, the versions come to resemble a single continuous narrative, like 'biographical' time. A character such as Conscience appears to exist in a 'biographical' time extending through the versions, in which his 'experiences' in the B text (the themes within which he was presented) are reflected in the way he appears in the C text. Conscience appears to have changed or learned as he reiterates in C the same arguments that were previously made in his presence in B.

CONSCIENCE IN C 5: PATIENT POVERTY AND A 'FYNDYNG' FOR WILL

One can see how Langland's development of particular themes in connection with particular characters during the course of the versions produces the effect of 'biographical' time or character 'development' in the final

---

[26] Barthes (1974; 67–8); the passage is cited by Griffiths (1985; 5), although she is not concerned, as I am, with the versions and revision of the poem.

major revision to Conscience's role in the C text: the 'autobiographical' encounter with Will at the beginning of C passus 5. Middleton has comprehensively discussed this passage in terms of its intertextual relations to one controversial contemporary discourse: labour legislation (and in particular the 1388 Statute of Labourers). But as Middleton argues, the passage also has a 'complex *internal* intertextuality'.[27] My own contribution to the discussion of this much-analysed part of the poem, then, will be a reflection upon one aspect of this 'internal intertextuality': the way this part of C 5 implicitly recalls two of Conscience's earlier appearances in the B text, namely his pilgrimage with Patience in B 14 and his run-in with the friars at the end of the poem.

As all commentators on the 'autobiographical' passage notice, the interrogation of Will by Reason and Conscience focuses on the apparent irregularity of Will's mode of life: his failure to provide for himself or the community through productive labour. The new passage thus implicates the poetic persona and the project of writing *Piers Plowman* itself in the poem's examination of the themes of labour, reward, poverty, and mendicancy. However, previous discussions have failed to notice exactly why Conscience is here. Partly, he is present in this scene because he has earlier discussed reward in C 3, and because he has been promoted by the king at the end of C 4 to a judicial role consistent with his attempt to enforce the secular law on vagrancy at the beginning of C 5. But Conscience is also an appropriate interlocutor in this scene because he participated in one of the poem's central discussions of poverty in its previous version: the elaboration of 'patient poverty' by Patience in B 14.

Will certainly recalls this scene when he appeals to Conscience in a passage which echoes Patience's language in the earlier version of the poem:

> 'Forthy rebuke me ryhte nauhte, resoun, y ʒow praye,
> For in my Consience y knowe what Crist wolde y wrouhte.
> Preeyeres of a parfit man and penaunce discrete
> Is the leuest labour þat oure lord pleseth.
> *Non de solo*', y sayde, 'for sothe *viuit homo,*
> *Nec in pane nec in pabulo;* the paternoster wittenesseth
> *Fiat voluntas dei* fynt vs alle thynges.'
> Quod Consience, 'by Crist, y can nat se this lyeth;
> Ac it semeth no sad parfitnesse in Citees to begge
> But he be obediencer to prior or to mynistre.'
>
> (C.5.82–91)

---

[27] Middleton (1997; 208).

One should remember that it was Conscience, to whom Will specifically appeals, who listened with Will in B 14 as Patience used the very same language that Will echoes here:

> And seide, 'lo! here liflode ynogh, if oure bileue be trewe.
> For lent neuere was lif but liflode were shapen,
> Wherof or wherfore or wherby to libbe:
> ...
> *Quodcumque pecieritis a patre in nomine meo &c; Et alibi, Non in solo pane viuit homo set in omni verbo quod procedit de ore dei.'*
> But I listnede and lokede what liflode it was
> That pacience so preisede, and of his poke hente
> A pece of þe Paternoster and profrede vs alle;
> And þanne was it *fiat voluntas tua* sholde fynde vs alle.
>
> (B.14.38–40, 46a–50)

In drawing Conscience into the conversation with the same language about the 'fyndyng' that God will provide to those who throw themselves upon his mercy, Will recollects the earlier scene in which he and Conscience heard Patience describe 'patient poverty'.

Will is also recalling another scene in which Conscience appeared in the previous version of the poem that is also relevant to his own situation. In B 20, Conscience argued that the friars should be provided with an adequate 'fyndyng' to alleviate their institutional neediness. Such a provision would prevent the abuses of the system of penance which that neediness causes. Will seems implicitly to acknowledge that the friars' failing at the end of the poem is also his own, for the verbal form of the key noun Conscience uses there, 'fyndyng', appears five times in his speech (C.5.36, 40 (in a different sense), 49, 76, and 88). The immediate trigger is Reason's use of the same verb (C.5.21, 27), but Will surely also hears in Reason's remarks an echo of Conscience's speech in B 20: 'And þat freres hadde a fyndyng þat for nede flateren' (B.20.383). He must be aware that, in accordance with this statement, Conscience will here find him wanting a legitimate 'fyndyng' in precisely the same way as the friars. In C 5, in Conscience's presence, Will returns persistently to the theme of one of Conscience's final speeches in the B text.

This passage in C 5 appears, then, to be another example of the way that Langland's development of particular themes in connection with certain characters (his use of reiterative 'type scenes') produces the effect of 'biographical time' or character development—and 'development' not only through the narrative of one version, but through the course of the serial versions. Will seems to remember that Conscience had, in the compositionally earlier scene in B 20, attacked others for lacking a stable 'fyndyng', and he repeatedly invokes Conscience's key word throughout his self-defence. At the same time, Will apparently also recalls that Conscience had also listened in B 14 as Patience expounded the virtues of poverty. In repeating Patience's language of patient poverty in C 5, Will seems to assume that Conscience might, like the poet, remember this earlier scene in B 14. He appeals to Conscience with an argument that Conscience had himself heard in the previous version of the poem, thus eliciting his sympathy. Like the other revisions to Conscience's role in the early parts of the C text, then, Conscience's appearance in C 5 implicitly develops his previous appearances elsewhere in the B text. Changes to Conscience's role in the C version need to be read in the light of the figure's development through the whole course of the B version.

CONSCIENCE AND THE VERSIONS OF *PIERS PLOWMAN*

The way Conscience's appearances in C recall in various ways his earlier roles in the B text suggests that the revisions Langland made to this particular figure in the early parts of C can be explained not so much in terms of any change in Langland's understanding of the concept of 'conscience', or in terms of his increasingly authoritarian view of government, or a general tendency to write in more 'abstract' terms in C, but rather in the context of developments to the presentation of Conscience within the whole of the previous versions. This relationship between Conscience's appearances in C and his previous appearances elsewhere in B also has wider implications for the poem as a whole.

As I have suggested, the changes to Conscience's role in the C text imply that while Langland must have revised with the parallel passages in B into which he inserted his revisions in front of him, he nevertheless had in mind not only the immediately parallel passages from the earlier version, but *all* that he had previously composed on related subjects (and with the same characters). Of course, as will become clear below, this argument about Langland's process of composition and revision does not only apply to Conscience, but also has implications for how we read other figures within the poem, and for how we might investigate the relationship between the versions of *Piers Plowman* in future. Our thinking about the versions and their relationship, I suggest, has been conditioned by the ways in which the text of *Piers Plowman* has typically been presented in editions—ways which obscure continuities in compositional process and argumentative logic between the versions such as those I have identified in my discussion of Conscience.

As Middleton has pointed out, textual presentation is a 'complex form of representation of authorial process in the product';[28] assumptions about Langland's compositional process—the relationship between the versions of the poem—have thus inevitably been shaped by the form in which the versions have usually been presented. Since Walter Skeat first presented the versions in his parallel-text edition (the edition in which most readers until recently first encountered the versions of the poem), the representations of the 'authorial process' implicit in the parallel-text edition have conditioned responses to the status of the poem as a series of versions. Carl Schmidt's edition of the versions follows Skeat in adopting parallel-text presentation and, as I shall argue, the recent magisterial *Penn Commentary on Piers Plowman*,[29] although keyed to the Athlone *Piers Plowman*, which is not of course a parallel-text edition, nevertheless treats the versions of the poem similarly.

Such a presentation brings with it certain assumptions about the relationship between the versions, facilitating investigation into some kinds of relationship but tending to close off others. It was reading the poem for the first time in single volumes rather than in Skeat's parallel-text edition, for instance, that first led J. M. Manly to perceive such radical discontinuities between the versions as he felt could only be explained by multiple authorship. While I would not seek a revival of the authorship controversy, the case of Manly illustrates that factors that have nothing to do with the text per se can nevertheless influence perceptions of it.[30] Any decision about textual presentation is not a neutral one, but carries with it an implicit *interpretation* of the textual evidence. The parallel-text edition implies, obviously, that the state of any given passage is best viewed in comparison with the immediately parallel passages in the other versions. In the case of the *Penn Commentary*, 'keyed first of all to the C Version of the poem, then in reverse chronology to the B and A versions',[31] the assumption is that a given passage in C should be examined by comparison with its parallels in the two previous versions of the poem as, presumably, the underlying 'causes' of the C material. Galloway says in the preface to his volume of the *Commentary* that the poem is thus viewed 'in archaeological terms', a metaphor also used by Hanna, another member of the commentary team.[32]

---

[28] Middleton (1990; 183).
[29] Two volumes of this commentary have been published to date: see Barney (2006) and Galloway (2006).
[30] See Brewer (1996; 186).
[31] Galloway (2006; vii).
[32] Galloway (2006; xii); cf. Hanna (1994; 159): 'The existence of our work in three distinct versions necessitates a perpetual *excavation* of the work's life in its maker's' (my emphasis).

But as I have argued, there is a linear or 'horizontal' continuity between the versions, conceived as a single discussion or dialogue to be read from *end to end*, that is obscured by the metaphor of the versions as geological strata explicable by vertical 'excavation' of the compositional layers or sediments presented in cross-section on the pages of the parallel-text edition/commentary. The 'reverse chronology' of the *Commentary*'s presentation potentially occludes connections that are most visible if the versions of the poem are read forwards in sequence, rather than backwards in parallel.[33]

The potential difficulties with the *Commentary*'s presentation of the poem in 'reverse chronology' from the C version become apparent, for instance, in Stephen Barney's remarks on the final lines of the poem. For Barney, Conscience's final words at the end of the C version, in which he expresses his wish that the friars might have a 'fyndyng' to relieve their need, are the culmination of the earlier narrative of C and its B equivalent:

> Conscience wishes that the friars had a stable provision, of precisely the kind he had promised, conditionally, in [C.22] 248–50...that is, 'property and ecclesiastical livings like the rest of the church' [quoting Szittya (1986)], and the kind that Piers promised to friars who did not flatter (C.8.147–48). He wishes, indeed, what Reason prophesied in C.5.173–74: 'Freres in here fraytour shal fynde þat tyme / Bred withouten beggynge to lyue by euere aftur,' and what Clergie prophesied in B.10.328–29: 'And þanne Freres in hir fraytour shul fynden a keye / Of Costantyns cofres þer þe catel is Inne'.[34]

One might query the way in which Barney handles these passages from the B and C versions of the poem here. Of course, for a reader of C as a single, discrete text, it is true that in C passus 22 Conscience wishes for the friars what Piers had promised them in C passus 8. But in the sequence of composition, *Piers*, not Conscience, is the respondent here. As Barney observes elsewhere, Piers's promise to provide a 'fyndyng' to friars who do not flatter is present only in the C version and 'surely reflects the earlier composition of B passus 20', where Conscience's closing remarks on a 'fyndyng' for the friars are already in place.[35]

---

[33] My critique of the *Commentary*'s mode of presentation shares with David C. Fowler's assessment a feeling that 'the presentation is backwards, in that it focuses on the C-version and then works its way back to B...and eventually back to A' (Fowler, 1997; 154). I do not share with Fowler, however, the view that the B and C versions are the work of a 'conservative reviser' other than the author of A.
[34] Barney (2006; 247–48).
[35] Barney (2006; 194).

This is only a very minor quibble, since Barney does notice elsewhere that Piers in fact develops in C passus 8 materials from B passus 20.[36] But Barney's handling of the relevant passages from Clergy's 'prophecy' in B passus 10 and its rewriting as part of Reason's sermon in C passus 5 is potentially more problematic, for these passages are used to support an interpretation of the notorious 'fyndyng' for the friars that I would think unlikely if one attends to the sequence in which the passages were composed.

Barney presents the two speeches of Reason and Clergy as if both were 'prophecies' of the poem's C-text conclusion and as if both said the same thing. But while Clergy's speech in B 10 might be taken—as Hanna has argued—as the 'prophecy' of the poem's conclusion in B 20,[37] Reason's version of the speech in C passus 5 must surely be read as a revision of B 10 *in the light of* B 20. And it seems to be revised in such a way as to exclude the possibility that the 'fyndyng' to which Conscience refers at the end of the poem might be understood as 'property and ecclesiastical livings like the rest of the church'. Clergy had said in B that friars would find 'a keye/Of Costantyns cofres' (B.10.328–29), which could be interpreted as meaning that the friars would receive endowments (although, as I noted in Chapter 4, the passage implies that the endowments have been removed from the church and the 'coffers' are therefore empty). But if Clergy's prophecy is at least potentially susceptible to the reading that the friars shall have 'property and ecclesiastical livings like the rest of the church', Reason's revised version of the prophecy surely excludes such a possibility; in the corresponding lines, Reason specifies that the friars shall have (only) 'Bred withouten beggynge' (the conventional sense of 'fyndyng', provision of food). Constantine shall provide only food and shelter, 'shal be here cook and couerour of here churches' (C.5.175). Reason takes up, in fact, Conscience's own implicit definition of the 'fyndyng' for the friars in B 20 as 'necessaries ynowe', 'breed and cloþes' (B.20.248–49).

Reason's speech, then, should not be conflated with Clergy's as being fulfilled in Conscience's final words in the poem, but viewed as a further separate stage of development, a revision of Clergy's speech that takes up

---

[36] Barney (2006; 102) also provides a comprehensive list in his 'Headnote' to C 21 (B 19) of instances, including this one, in which materials early in B and C seem to 'reflect materials composed in the last two passus of B'. Since I discuss here only my reservations about the assumptions implicit in its mode of presentation, I should also record my deep admiration for the scholarship of the *Penn Commentary*. My own discussion in Chapter 3 of the connections between B 19 and the B Prologue is indebted, especially, to Barney's discussion.

[37] Hanna (1998; 153–57).

Conscience's final words in B 20. Reason in C passus 5—and he is here accompanied by Conscience—takes up the project of reform of the friars that his partner articulated at the end of the previous version of the poem.[38] And as I have already suggested above, there are other echoes of Conscience's final words in B passus 20 in C passus 5, too. When confronted by Reason and Conscience in C 5, Will's self-defence returns repeatedly to the question of a 'fyndyng': as I have shown, some form of the verb 'fynden' occurs five times in his speech.

In his remarks on the poem's conclusion, in keeping with the *Commentary's* presentation of the poem in 'reverse chronology', Barney sees the 'fyndyng' mentioned by Conscience at the end of the poem as already defined by earlier sequences. But at the end of B passus 20, where the idea emerges merely as a pious hope, the 'fyndyng' remains something to be worried out in further revisions in C that take up the challenge of Conscience's final words in B. The *Commentary's* presentation of the poem in 'reverse chronology' tends, in Barney's comments on the relationship between Conscience's speech and the relevant speeches of Piers, Clergy, and Reason in B and C, to segue into what Míċeál Vaughan has elsewhere called the fallacy of the 'Platonic idea' of *Piers Plowman*. Vaughan's term draws attention to a widely-held feeling that there is a work that somehow transcends its textual form as a series of versions, a kind of conflation of the 'best bits' of all versions. Barney sees Conscience's final words as the culmination of all the speeches on this topic in all versions.[39] Most readers of the poem have probably succumbed to this temptation at one time or another, and it perhaps does not inevitably follow from the choice of the 'reverse chronology' presentation of the *Penn Commentary*. But even where the commentators recognize how materials at the end of one version initiate revisions in the next, the 'reverse chronology' presentation cannot easily represent the necessarily *forward* chronology of the poem's composition and revision as a series of versions.

The difficulties inherent in the *Penn Commentary*'s presentation of the poem in 'reverse chronology' from C become apparent again if one considers, for instance, the treatment of Conscience's first appearance in the C-text Prologue, which I also discussed above.[40] Here the commentators inevitably face a dilemma, for as Galloway points out, 'Although Conscience first

---

[38] As Barney (2006; 162–63) notices elsewhere, Reason's speech in C passus 5 contains another echo of Conscience's words in B 19–20: his instruction 'Holde ȝow in vnite' (C.5.189) is an echo of Conscience's similar words at B.19.355–56 and B.20.74–75.

[39] Vaughan (2002; 123). Medieval as well as modern readers, of course, believed in the 'Platonic idea' of *Piers Plowman*, as the conflated text in Huntington Library MS HM 114 indicates.

[40] Galloway (2006; 100–14).

appears here in C, he is of course a developed figure in later parts of earlier versions, starting with passus 3 and reappearing throughout the poem'. The difficulty this situation presents can be observed in Galloway's comments on the way this speech reallocates to Conscience materials originally assigned to Clergy in B. Galloway argues that such a move is justified by the fact that 'arguably...Conscience carries more authority than that figure'.[41] But, of course, such an assessment can only be made within the context of Galloway's own prior knowledge of the relationship between these two figures in an earlier version of the poem (I assume his sense of Conscience's greater 'authority' is based upon the exchange between the two figures in B passus 13). Here again one can see the difficulties inherent in the *Commentary*'s representation of the versions in 'reverse chronology': a true 'reverse chronology' would arguably need to bring the whole narrative of B to bear on this 'first' appearance of Conscience in the poem. The presentation of the poem in 'reverse chronology' from C tends inevitably to elide what a 'parallel-text' mode has no real way of representing: the development in earlier parts of the narrative of one version of materials that come later in a previous version, a feature endemic to C.

One further example, this time not related directly to Conscience, should illustrate my argument about the possible limitations of the reading of the versions implicit in the presentation of the poem in 'reverse chronology' or parallel-text form. This example is 'Lewte', the personification and the concept. Like Conscience, Lewte's development in the first vision of B and C cannot be fully understood apart from the later narrative of B. It does not yield, that is, to a straightforward comparison of parallel passages in ABC Prologue to passus 4, such as the basic format of the *Penn Commentary* provides.

Commenting on the first appearance of 'Lewte' in the C Prologue, Galloway observes that 'The entity Lewte...elsewhere develops into a principle of publicly speaking the truth, like Sothness'.[42] As Galloway's cross-references here to C.2.20–21, 2.24, and 2.51–52 (B.2.21–22, 24, 48–49) indicate, Lewte's first appearance in such a connection in the first vision of the poem is in Holy Church's speech at the beginning of passus 2 in the B version, where she complains that Meed has slandered ('ylakked') Lewte (B.2.21) and urges Will to bear witness against Meed and her followers at some future date when Lewte will be a justice:

> And lakke hem no3t but lat hem worþe til leaute be Iustice
> And haue power to punysshe hem; þanne put forþ þi reson.
>
> (B.2.48–49)

---

[41] Galloway (2006; 101).
[42] Galloway (2006; 125).

Commenting on the addition of Lewte in these passages in the B version, Galloway observes:

> B introduces the personage Leaute into this passage as it has also at B. Prol.122 and 125–7... Holy Church here licenses the dreamer, at some utopian future moment, to denounce Meed's followers... In the present age, Leaute has been the recipient of Meed's abuse at a lord's court... but elsewhere Leaute urges the narrator and all laymen to denounce 'Falsnesse' and 'fayterye'.[43]

The 'elsewhere' to which Galloway here refers is, of course, the dialogue between the Dreamer and Lewte in B passus 11 (C passus 12). But while there is nothing wrong with saying that Lewte 'elsewhere' urges the narrator to denounce wrongdoing, it presents B passus 11 as simply an analogous spatial locale without offering any comment on the *temporal* process implied by the comment that Lewte 'elsewhere *develops*' into a principle of public truth-telling. In fact, it seems likely that the presentation of Lewte as a figure of public truth-telling in this and one further addition to the first vision of B (B.4.161, where Love and Lewte—Love only in A—denounce Meed before the court) are additions to the first vision of B made *after*, and dependent upon, the more lengthy and explicit discussion of the responsibilities of truth-telling in B passus 11.[44] Comparison of the B version of these early passages with their equivalents in A does not fully explain the development of Lewte as a figure here, which is predicated on developments that may occur later in the narrative of B, but were probably actually earlier in Langland's process of composition.

The same is probably also true of other developments to Lewte's role in the first vision of B. In additions to the B Prologue, 'lewte' is particularly associated with the king, who must 'lede [his] lond so leaute [him] louye' (B.Prol.126; cf. 121–22). These passages may also develop the presentation of 'lewte' in previously composed materials later in the narrative of the B text, particularly the suggestion in Conscience's speech in B passus 19 that 'lewte' is a particularly 'kingly' quality, symbolically conferred upon Christ by one of the three kings under the guise of gold (B.19.89). As I discussed in Chapter 3, the B Prologue seems to reflect the prior composition of B passus 19 in other ways as well. One may feel, then,

---

[43] Galloway (2006; 233, 246).

[44] Of course, it is possible that (rejecting Gwynn's and Hanna's chronology) B passus 11 could be developing more explicitly a topic broached obliquely in B passus 2, but it seems to me more likely that Holy Church's assumption that Lewte stands for truth-telling responds to the explicit characterization of Lewte in these terms in B passus 11. Cf. Lawler (1996; 163–4), for the development in the successive versions of the themes of 'lakkyng' and 'lewte'.

that the significant developments to 'Lewte' in the first vision of B, his evolving association with both the qualities of a good king and with the principle of public truth-telling, grow out of two developments later in the narrative of B but earlier in the process of composition, the discussions of these two themes in B passus 19 and B passus 11 respectively.

If one returns to Galloway's comment on C.2.20–21, however, one finds that he simply groups together the B-text additions to Lewte's role in the first vision: 'B introduces [Lewte] into this passage [in B passus 2] as it has also at B.Prol.122 and 125–7'. But one might properly distinguish two separate strands of development, each dependent upon a different passage earlier in the sequence of composition: B passus 11 and B passus 19. These developments are obscured if one simply groups together all the new passages on 'lewte' in the first vision of B as if Langland composed this sequence with *only* its parallel passage in A in mind.

Galloway does, in fact, elsewhere attempt to disentangle the development of the triad 'lawe, loue and lewete' in terms of the 'sequence of composition' of the poem.[45] And the *Commentary*'s exhaustive system of cross-referencing provides an invaluable tool for reconstructing narratives about the development of the poem's ideas through the sequence of versions, such as my example of Lewte, even where these do not form part of the *Commentary*'s own explicit interpretations. The *Commentary* thus provides an invaluable stimulus to and aid for future research into the poem's development in the three versions presented in the Athlone editions (in particular, Barney's collation of passages early in the B and C texts that apparently respond to materials in B 19–20 offers a suggestive basis for future elaboration). Nevertheless, the presentation of the *Commentary* in the parallel-text format of other editions of the poem tends inevitably to privilege some kinds of investigation into the phenomenon of versions over others. The 'archaeological terms' in which it views the poem means the *Commentary* has no consistent way of representing the temporal relationships between horizontally dispersed 'dig-sites': it prioritizes the relationships between 'vertical' layers/parallel passages (between Lewte's appearances in the first vision of A, B, and C for instance) only by obscuring those between parts of the poem viewed 'horizontally' from end to end (the fact that Lewte's development may have to be read, for instance, from A passus 2 through B passus 11 to B passus 2). In his review of Galloway's *Commentary* volume, Thorlac Turville-Petre rightly says that the format of the *Commentary* 'provides an opportunity to discuss the evolution of Langland's thought over three versions'. But the

---

[45] Galloway (2006; 357–8, 364).

format also has inherent limitations in the kinds of relationship between the three versions it can easily represent. Turville-Petre's first example, the king's increased hostility towards Meed at the beginning of passus 3 in the C as compared with the AB versions, perhaps lends itself well to exclusive comparison of parallel passages in all three texts; his second example, Conscience's grammatical metaphor, as I hope to have demonstrated above, does not.[46]

Yet it is not only the *Penn Commentary* that is committed to reading the versions in parallel. More importantly, the very editions upon which it predicates its presentation—the Athlone editions—are based on parallel-text reading, even though they are not presented in parallel-text format. 'For about a third of the poem', Kane and Donaldson note in their introduction to the B text,

> there are many single lines, as well as passages of various length, where the three versions recognizably correspond and can be minutely compared at the textual level with respect to local expression and to technical form, without distraction by larger considerations of meaning and structure.[47]

The Kane and Donaldson text of B was thus established by a sustained parallel-text reading of the versions, in which corruption in the B archetype was identified by comparison with the parallel readings in AC.[48] The implications of this method have been criticized elsewhere, for instance by Robert Adams, who questions the resulting displacement of 'many strongly attested B manuscript readings'.[49] And Russell and Kane claimed that they had repressed this technique in their text of C, noting that agreement of any C variant with B was a 'confirming rather decisive factor' in their decisions to emend their copy-text of C.[50] Nevertheless, the presumption in the Athlone editions of B and C is that the original reading of any line can be determined by examination of its own variants and of its parallels in other versions, '*without distraction by larger considerations of meaning and structure*' (my emphasis). Ironically, although not presented in parallel-text format, the Athlone edition is perhaps the presentation of the versions of *Piers Plowman* most thoroughly invested in parallel-text reading.

Of course, none of this is intended to suggest that parallel-text editions and comparison of parallel passages in the different versions of the poem are

---

[46] Turville-Petre (2006; 232–33).
[47] *The B Version*, p. 74.
[48] See *The B Version*, pp. 74–97 for discussion.
[49] Adams (1992; 31).
[50] *The C Version*, p. 106. As Adams shows (1992, 38–39), Kane's A text restricted the use of the evidence of variants from other versions.

not useful, or indeed essential. As I have already observed above, Langland himself presumably revised precisely by marking additions, alterations, and deletions into the parallel passages in the manuscript of the previous version that he used in making his new version. Indeed, it may well be, as has often been suggested, that scribal corruption in the copy of the previous version from which he worked may have been the inspiration for many of Langland's revisions. Here, as Middleton has argued, parallel-text presentation accompanied by full textual apparatus has a particularly important place in offering the opportunity to investigate such processes.[51]

Neither do I wish to suggest that the versions cannot be read as autonomous productions, or that any single version cannot be understood independently of reference to Langland's earlier work. What I do claim, however, is that if we wish to understand why Langland revised as he did, we need to beware of reading (and this is what parallel-text presentation tempts us to assume) as if Langland would have written with *only* the immediately parallel passages in the previous version in mind.[52] A clearer sense of *Piers Plowman*'s development as a series of versions might emerge if we read those versions seriously *as* a sequence, from end to end. The example of Conscience suggests to me that many interpretative cruces in the poem might yield as much to sustained attentiveness to the continuities between the serial versions as to investigation of 'sources' outside the text (which is not, of course, to deny the poem's very real embeddedness in contemporary discourses). It is also my sense that our perception of these relationships between the versions tends to be obscured by the assumptions about the versions that are ingrained in and replicated by the ways in which the serial versions are presented in editions and commentaries. Schmidt's stimulating essay on Langland's revisions, for instance, draws attention to a number of interesting examples in which Langland draws upon related materials in previous versions of the poem, but like most other readers Schmidt remains bound to the parallel-text mode of investigation into versions.[53]

---

[51] Middleton (1990; 183).

[52] I stress that I am attempting to describe how the poem might have unfolded in *Langland*'s mind, and how it might profitably be approached by students of the poem interested in its composition and revision as it so unfolded—not how it might have been read by medieval readers. There are, of course, no manuscripts which contain all three versions one after the other, and little evidence that the existence of, and distinctions between, the various versions were widely recognized by medieval readers (although the absence of surviving manuscript witnesses cannot in itself be an objection: Lawrence Warner has recently put forward a claim about the composition of the versions—that 'B 19–20' were not originally part of the B text—which has absolutely no support among the surviving manuscripts but which cannot be dismissed on those grounds alone).

[53] See Schmidt (2000; 5–27). Schmidt speculates that Langland may have thought of the poem in 'parallel-text' terms, and he is additionally, of course, the editor of the latest parallel-text edition of the poem.

Nevertheless, even the oldest parallel-text edition may yet offer productive cues for future editions of *Piers Plowman*. For as well as presenting the three versions where they run in parallel with each other, Skeat also offered cross-references in his text to related materials from elsewhere in the poem, and often printed these related portions of text rather than leave blank pages where no direct parallel appears in the other versions. So alongside the exemplum of Hophni and Phineas in the C Prologue, for instance (his passus 1), Skeat prints on the facing page 'Compare B.X.280–83', directing his reader to the original position of this passage in Clergy's speech in B passus 10.[54] Similarly in C passus 5 (his passus 6), Skeat prints in parallel to his C.6.147–80 (that part of Reason's speech dealing with a 'fyndyng' for the friars quoted above) his B.10.292–329, the section of Clergy's speech that forms the basis of this part of Reason's sermon in C.[55] Again, in his C passus 7–8 (Russell-Kane passus 6–7), Skeat prints on facing pages the materials from Haukin's confession interpolated into this part of C from B 13.

Schmidt follows Skeat's example in his parallel-text edition, and future editions of *Piers Plowman* might well develop such a mode of presentation in order to provide a fuller representation of Langland's processes of composition. A hypertext edition of all the versions, if combined with a computerized version of the concordance already published by Joseph Wittig, might offer the possibility, for instance, of viewing side by side not only groups of lines that run directly parallel in ABC, but also related passages remote in the narrative, but potentially connected in the sequence of composition. The digital age might well open up avenues of investigation into the development of the poem through its serial versions; avenues that have been obscured by more conventional modes of textual presentation. Of course, the act of interpretation would remain paramount (an electronic concordance or search facility might have difficulty, for instance, with the connection for which I have argued in this chapter between the English 'sermon' on Christ as knight, king, and conqueror preached by Conscience in B 19 and his Latin verses on the theme of kingship in the C Prologue, or with other passages which are thematically related but not lexically identical). Ultimately, to develop our understanding of the relationship between the versions of *Piers Plowman* may require no technology other than those we already possess: we must simply begin to read the poem—as I have suggested we read Conscience's appearances within it—in sequence, in each of its versions, from beginning to end.

---

[54] *Parallel Text*, I, C.1.95–124.
[55] *Parallel Text*, I, C.6.147–80.

Conclusion

Conscience and the Composition of *Piers Plowman*

The preceding chapters should have signalled the difficulty of attempting to align Conscience with a single concept, or even a series of concepts, in his various appearances during the course of the serial versions of *Piers Plowman*, and hence the difficulty of arriving at any straightforward summary of his role and representation in the poem. As I have argued, Conscience never exists simply as an allegorical idea nor quite as a 'character' such as one might find in a novel. As Larry Scanlon has recently observed,[1] Langland's personifications are capable of being both fully allegorical and fully mimetic at once, and the allegorical and mimetic or literal levels of *Piers Plowman* frequently interact in complex ways. In B 13 and B 20, for instance, Conscience represents, allegorically, the consciousness of guilt that is the precondition of penance. But he figures simultaneously, as I have argued, as a lay penitent and a secular lord respectively. In B 20, the literal level of Conscience's presentation as a knightly 'character' threatens the allegorical level of the poem altogether. In this part of *Piers Plowman*, as Priscilla Jenkins shows, personifications such as Conscience and Contrition cease to behave like allegorizations and start behaving as fully mimetic—and therefore fallible—creations. In Jenkins's terms, Conscience stops behaving like an allegorical and starts behaving like a literal example of conscience.[2] Similarly, Meed attacks Conscience in B 3 at the literal level of his representation as a king's knight, calling into question his allegorical identity as 'conscience' in a way that recalls, as I argued in Chapter 1, other literary debates such as *Wynnere and Wastoure*.

Conscience, therefore, is never simply one thing or another—neither pure allegoresis nor mimesis—at any single point in the poem. Furthermore,

[1] Scanlon (2007; 24).
[2] Jenkins (1969; 140).

like Will in David Lawton's account of the 'subject' of the poem, he also appears differently, as I have shown, within diverse discourses at various points of the poem: as a witness or accuser of Meed in the first vision, with its modes of complaint and invective; as an example of the virtuous (lay) penitent put forward in contemporary vernacular texts in B 13; as one of those lords who patronize friars within a particular strand of antimendicant polemic in B 20. These transformations, as I have argued, occur as the result of a process of composition: Conscience changes as Langland accretively expands in a series of different discourses—representing new argumentative departures—a poem which he perhaps originally conceived as a more limited project, a single-vision debate in the manner of *Wynnere and Wastoure*. And as I have shown, Conscience is further transformed through the process of composition in the C text, as Langland continues to rework the themes he had earlier associated with the figure in B.

The multiple discourses upon which Langland draws in his presentation of Conscience constitute, then, as I have been suggesting, a series of stages in the compositional and argumentative process of the poem: they represent the means by which Langland heightens or 'spiritualizes' Conscience's significance during the course of *Piers Plowman* B, and subsequently develops his role further in C. But the composition of the poem from this *particular* selection of contemporary discourses also involves an attempt to render the poem legible within a specific social and historical context. The composition of Conscience from multiple contemporary discourses also points to the composition of the public towards which Langland directed his poem.[3]

In his presentation within the debate mode of passus 3 and the penitential discourse of passus 13, Conscience straddles the poem's interests in secular government and penitence, the secular and the divine law. As 'con-scientia', 'knowledge-with', he appears as both legal and penitential accuser. He perhaps speaks particularly strongly, then, to the composite or 'heterogeneous' readership of *Piers Plowman* discussed by Anne Middleton:

> Whether laymen or ecclesiastics, their customary activities involve them in counsel, policy, education, administration, pastoral care—in those tasks and offices where spiritual and temporal governance meet.[4]

The various modes I discussed in Chapter 1—debate, petition, and complaint—would certainly address the interests of one kind of 'administrative' audience, an audience connected with the practice of law and the production of documents. The textual form of the lines in passus 3

---

[3] Cf. the discussion in Middleton (1982b; 102).
[4] Middleton (1982b; 104).

that I have called (in Chapter 1) Conscience's 'petition' against Meed would undoubtedly have been recognizable to one possible audience that has been suggested for *Piers Plowman*: a London legal audience. The way the poem 'enrols' or incorporates 'documents' such as Conscience's petition might have struck a chord, for example, with chancery clerks. These clerks seem to have been responsible for the accounts of parliaments that were incorporated into the historical narratives of the *Anonimalle Chronicle* and the chronicles of the Monk of Eynsham and Adam Usk, and they have been proposed before as possible members of Langland's original 'coterie'.[5] A legal audience would also have recognized the debate mode of passus 3. As Thomas Reed discusses, instruction in the Inns of Court took the form of disputation, and mock debates may have been used as recreation for lawyers.[6] Ralph Hanna has argued for an early coterie audience for the poem located around 'Temple Bar and Westminster',[7] and the evidence for ownership of *Piers Plowman* manuscripts supports such associations. Two copies of the poem are associated with Lincoln's Inn and another was owned by Sir Thomas Charleton, Speaker of the House of Commons.[8]

Secular lords and their servants would also, of course, have found themselves regularly involved in legal affairs and in business in London. One can readily imagine the appeal for an early reader like Walter Brugge, receiver-general of the great Mortimer estates, of the debate between Conscience and Meed. Brugge might well have enjoyed such a passage as a literary recreation after long days 'filled with [real] petitions... from the plowmen and peasants... of the Mortimer estates', or during stays in London 'near to the exchequer and law courts'.[9] The legal diction (discussed in the Introduction) that connects Conscience, 'goddes clerk and his Notarie' (B.15.31–32), with those very 'Bisshopes and Bachelers' who serve the king and 'In Cheker and in Chauncelrie chalangen hise dettes' (B.Prol.87–93) is perhaps something of an embarrassment to those modern scholars of *Piers Plowman* who would see Conscience as an 'unerring' figure immune from criticism. But for somebody like Brugge, it might have served as a reassuring reminder of the moral complexities of contemporary life. Brugge had himself received clerical training, but he spent his life in the service of earls and the king, including appointments in the Irish Exchequer and as a 'king's

---

[5] See Kerby-Fulton and Justice (1997; 79).
[6] Reed (1990; 70–1, 78–9).
[7] Hanna (1993; 23).
[8] Middleton (1982b; 103); Hanna (1996; 237).
[9] Davies (1999; 60, 58).

clerk'.[10] A conscientious administrator like Brugge might well have identified with God's/the king's clerk Conscience. The conjunction of legal and penitential modes in Langland's representation of Conscience would have possessed a particular resonance for a man whose work was embedded in secular administration, but whose clerical training and interest in his spiritual welfare is indicated by his ownership, together with *Piers Plowman*, of a copy of William of Pagula's pastoral manual *Oculus sacerdotis*.[11] The exchange between Conscience and Meed in passus 3 may well have appealed to Brugge, one imagines, as a debate that invested with a spiritual import and urgency the legal procedure with which he frequently engaged.

The composite mode of address of the poem that Middleton identifies can be detected not only in the conjunction of debate in B 3 with penitence in B 13, but also in Conscience's appearances elsewhere in the poem. As I have shown, B 20 draws on a particular kind of antimendicant satire that highlights specifically the friars' relationship with secular lords. It therefore implicitly forms part of the poem's address to 'Ye lordes and ladies and legates of holy chirche' (B.13.421)—people who patronize flatterers rather than those who would offer them spiritual correction and edification. Langland addresses secular lords directly at several points in the poem, notably the famous 'disendowment' passage in B.15.564, 'Takeþ hire landes, ye lordes, and leteþ hem lyue by dymes'. Yet more frequently, *Piers Plowman* addresses secular and religious authorities simultaneously. In B.13.421, the poem speaks both to 'lordes and ladies' *and* 'legates of holy chirche'. Similarly in B 20, Langland implicitly addresses lords like Sire leef-to-lyue-in-lecherie, but Conscience explicitly addresses Clergy, too, since the friars' abuses are shown to be only the symptom, as I have argued, of the failings of the secular clergy.

But the 'heterogeneous' nature of the poem's mode of address perhaps emerges most clearly in those passages in which Conscience explicitly analyses contemporary social institutions in terms of divine, eternal laws or 'measure', or where his discursive mode incorporates both 'secular' and 'spiritual' forms of reference. Such passages include the speech to the king in the C Prologue, the complaint about 'numberless' friars at the end of the poem, and the grammatical metaphor in C 3. Conscience's speech on Christ as knight, king, and conqueror in B 19 is another example. The homiletic discourse of B 19 (like the homiletic style of the grammatical metaphor in C 3) would doubtless have been recognizable to those readers

---

[10] Davies (1999; 52).
[11] For Brugge's library, which also included bibles, missals, and works of canon law, see Davies (1999; 50 n. 7).

whose occupations included the composition of sermons. Such readers may have used the poem, as Andrew Galloway has suggested, in part as a source of sermon materials.[12] But Conscience's 'sermon' in B 19 adopts as its controlling idea, one must notice, an analogy from secular government. This fact might serve as a reminder that sermons could be as much about policy as they were about pastoral care. Thomas Brinton's sermon preached during the Good Parliament (which has been frequently linked with *Piers Plowman*, including by me in Chapter 5) would indicate as much.

Of course, as Middleton argues, no literary work simply fulfils its readers' generic expectations in offering them exactly what they already recognize.[13] The originality of *Piers Plowman* lies in Langland's re-combination and re-invention of existing modes. In passages like B 13–14 or the grammatical metaphor of C 3, where he stretches the capacities of vernacular poetry to accommodate new materials, Langland's presentation of Conscience is at its most compelling. In B 13, Langland responds to, but also shapes himself, a new vernacular audience for religious materials of greater spiritual scope than official statements of doctrine for the laity. In C 3, he ambitiously tries to accommodate grammatical obscurities within 'topical' vernacular verse. Such passages offer perhaps the strongest case against reading Conscience in the Latinate terms of scholastic discourse about moral faculties, for in passages like these, Langland is most conspicuously opening up new possibilities for vernacular verse and its audiences. Such literary experiments, of course, challenge and therefore always risk over-stretching their readers' abilities to accommodate new modes and reformulations of existing discourse. As I discussed in Chapter 5, Langland himself inscribes into the poem one negative reader response, the king's doubtful questioning of Conscience's grammatical analogies in C 3 (a response from which many modern readers, as well as doubtless some medieval ones, have taken their cue).

Taken as a whole, the range of discourses within which Langland presents Conscience in the versions of *Piers Plowman* points to a sophisticated audience. It was not one necessarily versed in scholastic moral psychology: there is no sense of 'conscience' used in the poem that Langland could not have found in vernacular texts like *The Prick of Conscience* or *The Cleansing of Man's Soul*, or derived from his own evident interest in Latin etymologies.[14] But it was an audience familiar with the procedures of the legal and literary

---

[12] Galloway (2004; 251–52).
[13] Middleton (1982b; 102).
[14] Cf. Hanna's discussion (2002; 91) of Ymaginatif, who, he argues, 'does very little which is not fully explained by the most pedestrian Middle English uses of his name'. See also Middleton (1982b; 109): 'Nothing...associates [the poem] with speculative theology, or with an academic readership before the mid-sixteenth century'.

debate of passus 3, and with the satirical conventions employed in B 20. This was an audience interested in its spiritual welfare, and indeed in more than the bare minimum of pastoral instruction that the laity was officially believed to require; interested, too, in seeing 'learned' materials like Latin grammar applied to vernacular and practical, 'real-world' situations. Conscience's name, 'con-scientia', perhaps signals, in another of its senses, the kind of knowledge possessed or aspired to by the audience which his presentation in the poem seems to address: practical knowledge, knowledge applied to deeds—to both penitential practice and 'secular' government and administration.[15] Such an audience, I suspect, may well have read Conscience in more sophisticated ways—and more ambivalently—than he has sometimes been read in modern scholarship, rooted though that scholarship is in an academic theology probably more sophisticated than anything possessed by many of the poem's earliest readers. As Rees Davies has wisely suggested, for a reader like Walter Brugge, a marriage between Conscience and Meed may well have seemed a practical necessity.[16] Yet such a man as Brugge would doubtless also have admired Conscience's idealism, expressed in passages like his penitential pilgrimage with Patience in B 13. Though Brugge's ecclesiastical appointments were 'largely non-residentiary', he nevertheless found time for a pilgrimage of his own (at his own expense) during his work tours of Mortimer properties in south-west Wales.[17] Conscience does not have all the answers in *Piers Plowman*—indeed, he often serves as the site upon which Langland's ideals come up against troubling contemporary realities. Nevertheless, the question Langland poses through the proposed marriage of Conscience and Meed is one that, as Middleton indicates,[18] must have possessed a compelling urgency for Langland's readers. Conscience continues to struggle with this question in all versions of the poem, from his wish that the 'numberless' friars could be accommodated to God's principle of order, to his grammatical metaphor in the C text. How are world and spirit to be reconciled; how is moral principle to be accommodated to social and institutional practice?

In considering the variety of discourses upon which Langland draws in his presentation of Conscience, I finally turn to Davies's closing observations on Walter Brugge:

> [A]s we ponder the paradoxes and incongruities of Walter's life – the well-trained and well-read cleric who spent his life in the service of earls and of

---

[15] For further discussion of this possible sense of 'conscience', see Chapter 2.
[16] Davies (1999; 62).
[17] Davies (1999; 61, 55).
[18] Cf. Middleton (1982b; 104). Middleton suggests that the interests of Langland's readership are encapsulated in Will's first two questions to Holy Church: 'the ownership and use of all "this tresor" of the earthly field, and the salvation of the soul'.

Mammon (or Waster) but who also thumbed the pages of *Piers* of an evening – we may be reminded that the readers of the fourteenth century were complex, multi-faceted and contradictory characters, as are all audiences.[19]

This remark suggests to me the importance of a reading that is receptive to the similar 'paradoxes and incongruities' of the character Conscience: God's clerk but simultaneously a failed Winner/king's knight; the legal witness and preacher to the court who nevertheless presides with fatal lordly politeness over the catastrophe of Unity; a figure who can speak in a range of registers and modes, from the Latin verses of the C Prologue and the grammatical hair-splitting of C 3, to the invective of the debate with Meed, the pastoral mnemonics of B 13, and the 'sermon' on Christ as chivalric hero in B 19. The complex and contradictory character who emerges from attentiveness to the many facets of Conscience's composition in the three versions of *Piers Plowman* may, perhaps, bring us closer to an appreciation of the complexity of his contemporary milieu, as well as to the generous imagination of his creator.

[19] Davies (1999; 62).

Bibliography

MANUSCRIPTS

Dublin, Trinity College, MS 244.
Oxford, Bodleian Library, MS Bodley 448.
Oxford, Bodleian Library, MS Bodley 923.
Oxford, Bodleian Library, MS Lat. th. e. 7.
San Marino, Huntington Library, MS HM 114.

CATALOGUES AND HANDBOOKS ON BOOKS AND MANUSCRIPTS

Catalogue of Books Printed in the XVth Century now in the British Museum, 12 vols. London: British Museum, 1908–85.

Coates, Alan, Kristian Jensen, Cristina Dondi, Bettina Wagner, and Helen Dixon, with others. *A Catalogue of Books Printed in the Fifteenth Century now in the Bodleian Library,* 6 vols. Oxford: Oxford University Press, 2005.

Jolliffe, P.S. *A Check-list of Middle English Prose Writings of Spiritual Guidance,* Subsidia Mediaevalia, II. Toronto: Pontifical Institute of Mediaeval Studies, 1974.

Schneyer, Johannes Baptist, *Repertorium der lateinischen Sermones des Mittelalters für die Zeit von 1150–1350,* 11 vols, Beiträge zur Geschichte der Philosophie und Theologie des Mittelalters, 43. Münster: Aschendorffsche Verlagsbuchhandlung, 1969–90.

Sharpe, Richard, *A Handlist of the Latin Writers of Great Britain and Ireland before 1540*, Publications of the Journal of Medieval Latin, 1. Turnhout: Brepols, 1997.

Thomson, David, *A Descriptive Catalogue of Middle English Grammatical Texts.* New York and London: Garland, 1979.

Wells, J. Edwin, J. Burke Severs, Albert E. Hartung, and Peter G. Beidler, *A Manual of the Writings in Middle English 1050–1500,* 11 vols. New Haven: Connecticut Academy of Arts and Sciences, 1967–2005.

EDITIONS OF *PIERS PLOWMAN*

Kane, George, ed., *Piers Plowman: The A Version.* London: Athlone Press, 1960.

Kane, George and E. Talbot Donaldson, eds., *Piers Plowman: The B Version.* London: Athlone Press, 1975.

Pearsall, Derek, ed., *Piers Plowman: A New Annotated Edition of the C-text.* 1978; rev. edn. Exeter: Exeter University Press, 2008.

Rigg, A.G. and Charlotte Brewer, eds., *Piers Plowman: The Z Version*, Pontifical Institute of Mediaeval Studies, Studies and Texts, 59. Toronto: Pontifical Institute of Mediaeval Studies, 1983.

Russell, George and George Kane, eds., *Piers Plowman: The C Version.* London: Athlone Press; Berkeley: University of California Press, 1997.

Schmidt, A.V.C., *Piers Plowman: A Parallel-Text Edition of the A, B, C and Z versions*, Vol. I: Text. London and New York: Longman, 1995.
——, ed., *The Vision of Piers Plowman: A Critical Edition of the B-Text.* 2nd edn. London: Dent/Everyman, 1995.
Skeat, Walter W., ed., *The Vision of William Concerning Piers the Plowman: In Three Parallel Texts*, 2 vols. 1886; repr. London: Oxford University Press, 1965.

OTHER PRIMARY TEXTS AND SOURCES

Alliterative Poetry of the Later Middle Ages: An Anthology, ed. Thorlac Turville-Petre, Routledge Medieval English Texts. London: Routledge, 1989.
Aquavilla, Nicholas de, *Sermones dominicales moralissimi*. Paris: Jean Bonhomme, 1486 x 1490.
Artes praedicandi: Contribution a l'histoire de la rhétorique au moyen âge, ed. Th.-M. Charland, Publications de l'Institut d'Études Médiévales d'Ottowa, 7. Paris: Vrin, 1936.
Augustine, *In Iohannis evangelium tractatus CXXIV*, ed. Radbodus Willems, CCSL, 36. Turnhout: Brepols, 1954.
Balbus, Johannes (of Genoa), *Catholicon*. Lyons: Perrinus Lathomi, Bonifacius Johannis, and Johannes de Villa Veteri, 1496.
Basevorn, Robert of, *Forma praedicandi*, in *Artes praedicandi*, pp. 231–323.
Bede, *Opera exegetica*, ed. M.L.W. Laistner and David Hurst, CCSL, 121. Turnhout: Brepols, 1983.
Biblia sacra vulgata, ed. Robert Weber, B. Fischer, I. Gribomont, H. I. Frede, H. F.D. Sparks, W. Thiele, and Roger Gryson, 4th edn. 1969; repr. Stuttgart: Deutsche Bibelgesellschaft, 1994.
The Bible: Douay Rheims Version, revised Bishop Richard Challoner. Rockford, IL: Tan Books, 1989.
Bonaventure, *S. Bonaventurae: Opera omnia,* 10 vols. Quaracchi: Ex typographia Collegi S. Bonaventurae, 1882–1902.
The Book of Vices and Virtues, ed. W. Nelson Francis, EETS o.s. 217. 1942; repr. London: Oxford University Press, 1998.
Brinton, Thomas, *The Sermons of Thomas Brinton, Bishop of Rochester (1373–1389)*, ed. Mary A. Devlin, 2 vols, Camden 3rd ser., vols 85–86. London: Royal Historical Society, 1954.
Bromyard, Johannes, *Summa praedicantium*. Nuremberg: Koberger, 1485.
The Chastising of God's Children and The Treatise of Perfection of the Sons of God, ed. Joyce Bazire and Eric Colledge. Oxford: Blackwell, 1957.
Chaucer, Geoffrey, *The Riverside Chaucer*, ed. Larry D. Benson et al. 3rd edn. Boston: Houghton Mifflin, 1987.
Cursor Mundi, ed. Richard Morris, 7 vols, EETS o.s. 57, 59, 62, 66, 68, 99, 101. 1874–93; repr. Oxford: Oxford University Press, 1966.
The English Text of the Ancrene Riwle: Magdalene College, Cambridge MS Pepys 2498, ed. A. Zettersten, EETS o.s. 274. London: Oxford University Press, 1976.

English Wycliffite Sermons, ed. Pamela Gradon and Anne Hudson, 5 vols. Oxford: Clarendon, 1983–96.
Eulogium historiarum sive temporis, ed. Frank Scott Haydon, 3 vols, Rolls Series. London: Longman, 1858–63.
Fasciculi zizaniorum, ed. Walter Waddington Shirley, Rolls Series. London: Longman, 1858.
Fasciculus morum: A Fourteenth-Century Preacher's Handbook, ed. and trans. Siegfried Wenzel. University Park: Pennsylvania State University Press, 1989.
Helias, Peter, *The Summa of Petrus Helias on Priscianus Minor*, ed. James E. Tolson with an introduction by Margaret Gibson, 2 vols, *Cahiers de l'Institut du Moyen Âge Grec et Latin*, 27–8 (1978).
Jacob's Well: An English Treatise on the Cleansing of Man's Conscience, ed. Arthur Brandeis, Part I (all published), EETS o.s. 115. London: Kegan Paul, 1900.
John of Gaunt's Register, 1372–1376, ed. Sydney Armitage-Smith, 2 vols, Camden 3rd ser., vols 20–21. London: Royal Historical Society, 1911.
Meech, Sanford Brown, 'An Early Treatise in English Concerning Latin Grammar', in *Essays and Studies in English and Comparative Literature*, University of Michigan Publications, Language and Literature, 13. Ann Arbor, MI: University of Michigan Press, pp. 81–125, 1935.
Memoriale credencium: A late Middle English Manual of Theology for Lay People, ed. J.H.L. Kengen. Doctoral dissertation, Nijmegen, 1979.
An Edition of the Middle English Grammatical Texts, ed. David Thomson, Garland Medieval Texts, 8. New York and London: Garland, 1984.
Middle English Sermons, ed. Woodburn O. Ross, EETS o.s. 209. London: Milford, 1940.
Minot, Laurence, *The Poems of Laurence Minot 1333–1352*, ed. Thomas Beaumont James and John Simons, Exeter Medieval English Texts and Studies. Exeter: University of Exeter Press, 1989.
Mirk, John, *Mirk's Festial*, ed. Theodor Erbe, EETS e.s. 96. London: Kegan Paul, 1905.
The N-Town Play, ed. Stephen Spector, 2 vols, EETS s.s. 11–12. Oxford: Oxford University Press, 1991.
The Northern Homily Cycle: The Expanded Version in MSS Harley 4196 and Cotton Tiberius E vii, ed. Saara Nevanlinna, 3 vols, Mémoires de la Société Néophilologique de Helsinki, 38, 41, and 43. Helsinki: Société Néophilologique, 1972–84.
The Owl and the Nightingale: Text and Translation, ed. Neil Cartlidge, Exeter Medieval English Texts and Studies. Exeter: Exeter University Press, 2001.
Peniafort, Raymund de, *Summa de poenitentia et matrimonio cum glossis Ioannis de Friburgo*. Rome: Ioannis Tallini, 1603.
The Pricke of Conscience (Stimulus conscientiae): A Northumbrian Poem by Richard Rolle de Hampole, ed. Richard Morris, Philological Society. Berlin: A. Asher and Co., 1863.
Priscian, *Institutiones grammaticae*, ed. Henrich Keil, Grammatici Latini, vols II and III. Leipzig, 1855–58.

The Prymer or Lay Folks' Prayer Book, ed. Henry Littlehales, 2 vols, EETS o.s. 105, 109. London: Kegan Paul, 1895–97.
The Register of John de Grandisson, Bishop of Exeter, ed. F.C. Hingeston-Randolph, 3 vols. London: Bell, 1894–99.
Religious Lyrics of the XVth Century, ed. Carleton Brown. 1939; repr. Oxford: Clarendon, 1952.
Rolle, Richard, *English Writings of Richard Rolle*, ed. Hope Emily Allen. Oxford: Clarendon, 1931.
——, *Richard Rolle: Prose and Verse*, ed. S.J. Ogilvie-Thomson, EETS o.s. 293. Oxford: Oxford University Press, 1988.
The Middle English Translation of the Rosarium Theologie: A Selection ed. from Cbr., Gonville and Caius Coll. MS 354/581, ed. Christina von Nolcken. Heidelberg: Middle English Texts, 1979.
Selections from English Wycliffite Writings, ed. Anne Hudson. Cambridge: Cambridge University Press, 1978.
Speculum sacerdotale, ed. Edward H. Weatherly, EETS o.s. 200. London: Milford, 1936.
Statutes of the Realm, 9 vols. London: Eyre and Strahan, 1810–22.
Stow, John, *Stow's Survey of London*, introduction by Henry B. Wheatley. 1912; repr. London: Dent/Everyman, 1956.
The Three Kings of Cologne, ed. C. Horstmann, EETS o.s. 85. London: Trübner, 1886.
Three Medieval Rhetorical Arts, ed. James J. Murphy. Berkeley and Los Angeles: University of California Press, 1971.
The Towneley Plays, ed. Martin Stevens and A.C. Cawley, 2 vols, EETS s.s. 13–14. Oxford: Oxford University Press, 1994.
Trevisa, John, *Dialogus inter militem et clericum, Richard FitzRalph's Sermon: 'Defensio curatorum', and Methodius: 'Þe Begynnyng of þe World and þe Ende of Worldes'*, ed. Aaron Jenkins Perry, EETS o.s. 167. London: Milford, 1925.
——, *Prefaces on Translation*. See Waldron, Ronald, 'Trevisa's Original Prefaces on Translation: a Critical Edition'.
Voragine, Jacobus de, *Sermones de tempore et de sanctis et quadragesimales*, ed. Nicolaus Campanus and Hieronymus de Cherio, 3 vols. Pavia: Jacobus de Paucis Drapis, 1499–1500.
Waldron, Ronald, 'Trevisa's Original Prefaces on Translation: a Critical Edition', in Kennedy, Waldron, and Wittig (1988; pp. 285–99).
Waleys, Thomas, *De modo componendi sermones*, in *Artes praedicandi*, pp. 325–403.
Walsingham, Thomas, *The St Albans Chronicle: The Chronica maiora of Thomas Walsingham*, Vol. I: 1376–1394, ed. and trans. John Taylor, Wendy R. Childs and Leslie Watkiss, Oxford Medieval Texts. Oxford: Clarendon, 2003.
[Walwayn, John], *Vita Edwardi Secvndi: The Life of Edward the Second*, ed. and trans. Wendy R. Childs, Oxford Medieval Texts. Oxford: Clarendon, 2005.
The Westminster Chronicle 1381–1394, ed. and trans. L.C. Hector and Barbara F. Harvey, Oxford Medieval Texts. Oxford: Clarendon, 1982.

Wyclif, John, *Opera minora*, ed. Johann Loserth. London: C.K. Paul/Wyclif Society, 1913.
——, *Polemical Works*, ed. Rudolf Buddensieg, 2 vols. London: Trübner/Wyclif Society, 1883.
——, *Sermones*, ed. Johann Loserth, 4 vols. London: Trübner/Wyclif Society, 1887–90.

SECONDARY SOURCES

Adams, Robert (1978) 'The Nature of Need in *Piers Plowman* XX', *Traditio*, 34, 273–301.
——, (1988) 'Mede and Mercede: The Evolution of the Economics of Grace in the *Piers Plowman* B and C Versions', in Kennedy, Waldron, and Wittig (1988; pp. 217–32).
——, (1992) 'Editing *Piers Plowman* B: The Imperative of an Intermittently Critical Edition', *SB*, 45, 31–68.
Aers, David (1975) *Piers Plowman and Christian Allegory*. London: Arnold.
——, (1980) *Chaucer, Langland and the Creative Imagination*. London: Routledge.
——, (2004) *Sanctifying Signs: Making Christian Tradition in Late Medieval England*. Notre Dame, IN: University of Notre Dame Press.
Alford, John A. (1977) 'The Role of the Quotations in *Piers Plowman*', *Speculum*, 52, 80–99.
——, (1982) 'The Grammatical Metaphor: A Survey of Its Use in the Middle Ages', *Speculum*, 57, 728–60.
——, (1988a) *Piers Plowman: A Glossary of Legal Diction*, Piers Plowman Studies, 5. Cambridge: Brewer.
——, (1988b) 'The Idea of Reason in *Piers Plowman*', in Kennedy, Waldron, and Wittig (1988; pp. 199–215).
——, (1992) *Piers Plowman: A Guide to the Quotations*, Medieval and Renaissance Texts and Studies, 77. Binghamton, NY: Medieval and Renaissance Texts and Studies.
——, (1993) 'The Figure of Repentance in *Piers Plowman*', in Vaughan (1993; 3–28).
Amassian, Margaret and James Sadowsky (1971) 'Mede and Mercede: A Study of the Grammatical Metaphor in *Piers Plowman* C: IV: 335–409', *NM*, 72, 457–76.
Armitage-Smith, Sydney (1904) *John of Gaunt*; repr. London: Constable, 1964.
Avery, Margaret E. (1969) 'The History of the Equitable Jurisdiction of Chancery before 1460'. *BIHR*, 42, 129–44.
Baldwin, Anna P. (1981) *The Theme of Government in Piers Plowman*, Piers Plowman Studies, 1. Cambridge: Brewer.
Barney, Stephen A. (2006) *The Penn Commentary on Piers Plowman, V: C Passūs 20–22; B Passūs 18–20*. Philadelphia: University of Pennsylvania Press, 2006.

Barthes, Roland (1974) *S/Z*, trans. Richard Miller; repr. London: Jonathan Cape, 1975.
Bennett, J.A.W. (1943a) 'The Date of the A-Text of *Piers Plowman*', *PMLA*, 58, 566–72.
——, (1943b) 'The Date of the B-Text of *Piers Plowman*', *Medium Ævum*, 12, 55–64.
Benson, Larry D. (1976) *Malory's Morte Darthur*. Cambridge, MA: Harvard University Press.
Blanch, Robert J., ed. (1969) *Style and Symbolism in* Piers Plowman: *A Modern Critical Anthology.* Knoxville: University of Tennessee Press.
Bland, Cynthia Renée (1988) 'Langland's Use of the Term *Ex vi transicionis*', *YLS*, 2, 125–35.
Bloomfield, Morton W. (1952) *The Seven Deadly Sins: An Introduction to the History of a Religious Concept, with Special Reference to Medieval English Literature*. East Lansing, MI: Michigan State College Press.
——, (1962) *Piers Plowman as a Fourteenth-century Apocalypse*. New Brunswick, NJ: Rutgers University Press.
Bowers, John M. (1986) *The Crisis of Will in Piers Plowman*. Washington, DC: Catholic University of America Press.
Brady, Mary Teresa (1980) 'Rolle's *Form of Living* and *The Pore Caitif*'. *Traditio*, 36, 426–35.
Brewer, Charlotte (1996) *Editing Piers Plowman: The Evolution of the Text*. Cambridge Studies in Medieval Literature, 28. Cambridge: Cambridge University Press.
Burrow, John (1969) 'The Action of Langland's Second Vision', in Blanch (1969; 209–27).
——, (1993) *Langland's Fictions*. Oxford: Clarendon.
——, (2009) 'Conscience on Knights, Kings, and Conquerors: *Piers Plowman* B.19.26–198', *YLS* 23, 85–95.
Cargill, Oscar (1932) 'The Date of the A-Text of *Piers Ploughman*', *PMLA*, 47, 354–62.
Clopper, Lawrence M. (1997) *'Songes of Rechelesnesse': Langland and the Franciscans*, Studies in Medieval and Early Modern Civilization. Ann Arbor, MI: University of Michigan Press.
Cole, Andrew (2008) *Literature and Heresy in the Age of Chaucer*, Cambridge Studies in Medieval Literature. Cambridge: Cambridge University Press.
Constable, Giles (1969) 'Twelfth-Century Spirituality and the Late Middle Ages', in *Medieval and Renaissance Studies: Proceedings of the Southeastern Institute of Medieval and Renaissance Studies, Summer 1969*, ed. O.B. Hardison, Jr. Chapel Hill, NC: University of North Carolina Press, pp. 27–60.
Craun, Edwin D. (1997) *Lies, Slander, and Obscenity in Medieval English Literature: Pastoral Rhetoric and the Deviant Speaker*, Cambridge Studies in Medieval Literature, 31. Cambridge: Cambridge University Press.
Crook, David (2004) 'The Disgrace of Sir Richard de Willoughby, Chief Justice of King's Bench', *Nottingham Medieval Studies*, 48, 15–36.
Davies, Rees (1995) *The Revolt of Owain Glyn Dŵr*. Oxford: Oxford University Press.

———, (1999) 'The Life, Travels, and Library of an Early Reader of *Piers Plowman*', *YLS*, 13, 49–64.
Dobson, R.B. (1983) *The Peasants' Revolt of 1381*, 2nd edn; repr. Hampshire: Macmillan, 1993.
Donaldson, E. Talbot (1949) *Piers Plowman: The C-Text and Its Poet*, Yale Studies in English, 113. New Haven, CT: Yale University Press.
Doyle, A.I. (1958) 'Books Connected with the Vere Family and Barking Abbey', *Transactions of the Essex Archaeological Society*, n.s. 25, 222–43.
Dunham, William Huse, Jr (1955) 'Lord Hastings' Indentured Retainers, 1461–1483', *Transactions of the Connecticut Academy of Arts and Sciences,* 39, 1–175.
Dunning, T.P. (1980) *Piers Plowman: An Interpretation of the A Text*, 2nd edn rev. and ed. T.P. Dolan. Oxford: Clarendon.
Fletcher, Alan J. (1998) *Preaching, Politics and Poetry in Late-Medieval England*. Dublin: Four Courts.
———, (2001) 'The Essential (Ephemeral) William Langland: Textual Revision as Ethical Process in *Piers Plowman*', *YLS*, 15, 61–84.
Forrest, Ian (2009) 'Defamation, Heresy and Late Medieval Social Life', in *Image, Text, and Church, 1380–1600: Essays for Margaret Aston,* ed. Linda Clark, Maureen Jurkowski, and Colin Richmond, Papers in Medieval Studies 20. Toronto: Pontifical Institute for Medieval Studies, pp. 142–61.
Fowler, David C. (1997) 'Annotating *Piers Plowman*: The Athlone Project', *Text*, 10, 151–60.
Frank, Robert Worth, Jr (1953) 'The Art of Reading Medieval Personification-Allegory', *ELH,* 20, 237–50.
———, (1957) *Piers Plowman and the Scheme of Salvation*, Yale Studies in English, 136. New Haven, CT: Yale University Press.
Friedman, John B. (1994) 'The Friar Portrait in Bodleian Library MS. Douce 104: Contemporary Satire?', *YLS*, 8, 177–85.
Galloway, Andrew (1995) 'The Rhetoric of Riddling in Late-Medieval England: The "Oxford" Riddles, the *Secretum philosophorum*, and the Riddles in *Piers Plowman*', *Speculum,* 70, 68–105.
———, (2004) 'Reading *Piers Plowman* in the Fifteenth and Twenty-First Centuries: Notes on Manuscripts F and W in the *Piers Plowman Electronic Archive*', *JEGP,* 14, 232–52.
———, (2006) *The Penn Commentary on Piers Plowman, I: C Prologue-Passus 4; B Prologue-Passus 4; A Prologue-Passus 4.* Philadelphia: University of Pennsylvania Press.
Ganshof, F.L. (1952) *Feudalism*, trans. Philip Grierson; repr. London: Longman, 1959.
Giancarlo, Matthew (2003) '*Piers Plowman,* Parliament, and the Public Voice', *YLS,* 17, 135–74.
———, (2007) *Parliament and Literature in Late Medieval England*, Cambridge Studies in Medieval Literature. Cambridge: Cambridge University Press.
Gillespie, Vincent Anthony (1981) 'The Literary Form of the Middle English Pastoral Manual with Particular Reference to the *Speculum Christiani* and Some Related Texts'. Unpublished D.Phil. thesis, University of Oxford.

Gillespie, Vincent Anthony (1989) 'Vernacular books of religion', in *Book Production and Publishing in Britain 1375–1475*, ed. Jeremy Griffiths and Derek Pearsall, Cambridge Studies in Publishing and Printing History; repr. Cambridge: University Press, 2007, pp. 317–44.

Ginsberg, Warren (1983) *The Cast of Character: The Representation of Personality in Ancient and Medieval Literature*. Toronto: University of Toronto Press.

Given-Wilson, Chris (1986) *The Royal Household and the King's Affinity: Service, Politics and Finance in England 1360–1413*. New Haven, CT: Yale University Press.

Goodman, Anthony (1992) *John of Gaunt: The Exercise of Princely Power in Fourteenth-Century Europe*. Harlow: Longman.

Green, Richard Firth (1997) 'Friar William Appleton and the Date of Langland's B Text', *YLS*, 11, 87–96.

Griffiths, Lavinia (1985) *Personification in Piers Plowman*, Piers Plowman Studies, 3. Cambridge: Brewer.

Gwynn, Aubery (1940) *The English Austin Friars in the Time of Wyclif*. London: Oxford University Press.

——, (1943) 'The Date of the B-Text of *Piers Plowman*', *RES*, 19, 1–24.

Hanna, Ralph (1993) *William Langland*, Authors of the Middle Ages, 3. Aldershot: Variorum.

——, (1994) 'Annotating *Piers Plowman*', *Text*, 6, 153–63.

——, (1995) 'Robert the Ruyflare and His Companions', in *Literature and Religion in the Later Middle Ages: Philological Studies in Honor of Siegfried Wenzel*, ed. Richard G. Newhauser and John A. Alford, Medieval and Renaissance Texts and Studies, 118. Binghamton, NY: State University of New York at Binghamton, pp. 81–96.

——, (1996) *Pursuing History: Middle English Manuscripts and Their Texts*, Figurae: Reading Medieval Culture. Stanford, CA: Stanford University Press.

——, (1998) 'Reading Prophecy/Reading Piers', *YLS*, 12, 153–7.

——, (2002) 'Langland's Ymaginatif: Images and the Limits of Poetry', in *Images, Idolatry and Iconoclasm in Late Medieval England: Textuality and the Visual Image*, ed. Jeremy Dimmick, James Simpson, and Nicolette Zeeman. Oxford: Oxford University Press, pp. 81–94.

——, (2005) *London Literature, 1300–1380*, Cambridge Studies in Medieval Literature. Cambridge: Cambridge University Press.

Hanna, Ralph and Sarah Wood (2010) 'Mendicants and the Economies of *Piers Plowman*', in *The Friars in Medieval Britain: Proceedings of the 2007 Harlaxton Symposium*, ed. Nicholas Rogers. Donington: Shaun Tyas, pp. 218–38.

Harding, Alan (1975) 'Plaints and Bills in the History of English Law, mainly in the period 1250–1330', in *Legal History Studies 1972: Papers Presented to the Legal History Conference Aberystwyth, 18–21 July 1972*, ed. Dafydd Jenkins. Cardiff: University of Wales Press, pp. 65–86.

Harwood, Britton J. (1990) 'Dame Study and the Place of Orality in *Piers Plowman*', *ELH*, 57, 1–17.

——, (1992) *Piers Plowman and the Problem of Belief*. Toronto: University of Toronto Press.

——, (2004) 'The Displacement of Labor in *Winner and Waster*', in *The Middle Ages at Work: Practicing Labor in Late Medieval England*, ed. Kellie Robertson and Michael Uebel. New York and Basingstoke: Macmillan, pp. 157–77.

——, (2006) 'Anxious over Peasants: Textual Disorder in *Winner and Waster*', *Journal of Medieval and Early Modern Studies*, 36, 291–319.

Hewitt, H.J. (1966) *The Organization of War under Edward III, 1338–62*. Manchester: Manchester University Press.

Higgs, Elton D. (1993) 'Conscience, Piers, and the Dreamer in the Structure of *Piers Plowman* B', in Vaughan (1993; 123–46).

Holmes, George (1975) *The Good Parliament*. Oxford: Clarendon.

Hopkins, Andrea (1990) *The Sinful Knights: A Study of Middle English Penitential Romance*. Oxford: Clarendon.

Hort, Greta (1938) *Piers Plowman and Contemporary Religious Thought*. London: SPCK; New York: Macmillan.

Hudson, Anne (1988) *The Premature Reformation: Wycliffite Texts and Lollard History*; repr. Oxford: Clarendon, 2002.

Huppé, Bernard F. (1939) 'The A-Text of *Piers Plowman* and the Norman Wars', *PMLA*, 54, 37–64.

Jenkins, Priscilla (1969) 'Conscience: the Frustration of Allegory', in *Piers Plowman: Critical Approaches*, ed. S.S. Hussey. London: Methuen, pp. 125–42.

[——, see also Martin, Priscilla.]

Justice, Steven (1996) *Writing and Rebellion: England in 1381*. Berkeley and Los Angeles: University of California Press.

Kane, George (1985) 'The "Z Version" of *Piers Plowman*', *Speculum*, 60, 910–30.

——, (2005) *Piers Plowman Glossary: A Glossary of the English Vocabulary of the A, B, and C Versions as presented in the Athlone editions*. London and New York: Continuum.

Kaske, R.E. (1969) '"*Ex vi transicionis*" and Its Passage in *Piers Plowman*', in Blanch (1969; 228–63).

Kennedy, Edward Donald, Ronald Waldron, and Joseph S. Wittig, eds. (1988) *Medieval English Studies presented to George Kane*. Woodbridge: Brewer.

Kennedy, Kathleen E. (2003) 'Retaining a Court of Chancery in *Piers Plowman*', *YLS*, 17, 175–89.

——, (2006) 'Retaining Men (and a Retaining Woman) in *Piers Plowman*', *YLS*, 20, 191–214.

——, (2009) *Maintenance, Meed, and Marriage in Medieval English Literature*, The New Middle Ages. New York and Basingstoke: Macmillan.

Kerby-Fulton, Kathryn and Steven Justice (1997) 'Langlandian Reading Circles and the Civil Service in London and Dublin, 1380–1427', *New Medieval Literatures*, 1, 59–83.

Kipling, Gordon (1998) *Enter the King: Theatre, Liturgy, and Ritual in the Medieval Civic Triumph*. Oxford: Clarendon.

Kirk, Elizabeth D. (1972) *The Dream Thought of Piers Plowman*, Yale Studies in English, 178. New Haven, CT: Yale University Press.

Lambert, M.D. (1961) *Franciscan Poverty: the Doctrine of the Absolute Poverty of Christ and the Apostles in the Franciscan Order, 1210–1323*. London: SPCK.

Lawler, Traugott (1995) 'Conscience's Dinner', in *The Endless Knot: Essays on Old and Middle English in Honor of Marie Borroff*, ed. M. Teresa Tavormina and R.F. Yeager. Cambridge: Brewer, pp. 87–103.

——, (1996) 'A Reply to Jill Mann, Reaffirming the Traditional Relation between the A and B Versions of *Piers Plowman*', *YLS*, 10, 145–80.

——, (2002) 'The Secular Clergy in *Piers Plowman*', *YLS*, 16, 85–117.

——, (2006) 'Harlots' Holiness: The System of Absolution for Miswinning in the C Version of *Piers Plowman*', *YLS*, 20, 141–89.

Lawton, David (1987) 'The Subject of *Piers Plowman*', *YLS*, 1, 1–30.

Lees, Clare A. (1994) 'Gender and Exchange in *Piers Plowman*', in *Class and Gender in Early English Literature*, ed. Britton J. Harwood and Gillian R. Overing. Bloomington and Indianapolis: Indiana University Press, pp. 112–30.

Lewis, N.B. (1945) 'The Organisation of Indentured Retinues in Fourteenth-Century England', *TRHS*, 4th ser., 27, 29–39.

Little, A.G. (1934) 'The Franciscans and the Statute of Mortmain', *EHR*, 49, 673–6.

McFarlane, K.B. (1981) 'Bastard Feudalism', in *England in the Fifteenth Century: Collected Essays*. London: Hambledon Press, 23–43.

McNiven, Peter (1987) *Heresy and Politics in the Reign of Henry IV: The Burning of John Badby*. Woodbridge: Boydell.

Maguire, Stella (1969) 'The Significance of Haukyn, *Activa Vita*, in *Piers Plowman*', in Blanch (1969; 194–208).

Mander, M.N.K. (1979) 'Grammatical Analogy in Langland and Alan of Lille', *NQ*, 26 (224), 501–4.

Mann, Jill (1994) 'Allegorical Buildings in Medieval Literature', *Medium Ævum*, 63, 191–210.

Marcett, Mildred Elizabeth (1938) *Uhtred de Boldon, Friar William Jordan and Piers Plowman*. New York: published by the author.

Martin, Priscilla (1993) '*Piers Plowman*: Indirect Relations and the Record of Truth', in Vaughan (1993; 169–90).

[——, see also Jenkins, Priscilla.]

Mayer, Cornelius, with others (1986–2006) *Augustinus-Lexikon*, 3 vols. Basel: Verlag/Schwabe.

Middleton, Anne (1972) 'Two Infinites: Grammatical Metaphor in *Piers Plowman*', *ELH*, 39, 169–88.

——, (1982a) 'Narration and the Invention of Experience: Episodic Form in *Piers Plowman*', in *The Wisdom of Poetry: Essays in Early English Literature in honor of Morton W. Bloomfield*, ed. Larry D. Benson and Siegfried Wenzel. Kalamazoo, MI: Medieval Institute, pp. 91–122.

——, (1982b) 'The Audience and Public of *Piers Plowman*', in *Middle English Alliterative Poetry and its Literary Background: Seven Essays*, ed. David Lawton. Cambridge: Brewer, pp. 101–23, 147–54 (notes).

——, (1990) 'Life in the Margins, or, What's an Annotator to Do?', *The Library Chronicle of the University of Texas at Austin*, 20, 167–83.

——, (1997) 'Acts of Vagrancy: The C Version "Autobiography" and the Statute of 1388', in *Written Work: Langland, Labor, and Authorship,* ed. Steven Justice and Kathryn Kerby-Fulton. Philadelphia, University of Pennsylvania Press, pp. 208–317.

Millett, Bella (1999) '*Ancrene Wisse* and the Conditions of Confession', *ES*, 80, 193–215.

Mitchell, A.G. (1969) 'Lady Meed and the Art of *Piers Plowman*', in Blanch (1969; 174–93).

Morgan, Gerald (1987) 'The Meaning of Kind Wit, Conscience, and Reason in the first Vision of *Piers Plowman*', *MP*, 84, 351–8.

Musson, Anthony and W.M. Ormrod (1999) *The Evolution of English Justice: Law, Politics and Society in the Fourteenth Century*, British Studies Series. Basingstoke: Macmillan.

Myers, A.R. (1937) 'Parliamentary Petitions in the Fifteenth Century', *EHR*, 52, 385–404, 590–613.

Ormrod, W.M. (1989) 'The Personal Religion of Edward III', *Speculum,* 64, 849–77.

Overstreet, Samuel A. (1984) '*Grammaticus ludens*: Theological Aspects of Langland's Grammatical Allegory', *Traditio*, 40, 251–96.

Owst, G.R. (1926) *Preaching in Medieval England: An Introduction to Sermon Manuscripts of the period c. 1350–1450*, Cambridge Studies in Medieval Life and Thought. Cambridge: Cambridge University Press.

——, (1961) *Literature and Pulpit in Medieval England: A Neglected Chapter in the History of English Letters and of the English People*, 2nd rev. edn. Oxford: Blackwell.

Pantin, W.A. (1955) *The English Church in the Fourteenth Century.* Cambridge: Cambridge University Press; repr. Notre Dame, IN: University of Notre Dame Press, 1962.

Patterson, Lee W. (1978) 'The *Parson's Tale* and the Quitting of the *Canterbury Tales*', *Traditio*, 34, 331–80.

Paxson, James J. (1994) *The Poetics of Personification*, Literature, Culture, Theory, 6. Cambridge: Cambridge University Press.

Plucknett, T.F.T. (1942) 'The Origin of Impeachment', *TRHS*, 4th ser., 24, 47–71.

Potts, Timothy C. (1980) *Conscience in Medieval Philosophy.* repr. Cambridge: Cambridge University Press, 2002.

Reed, Thomas L., Jr (1990) *Middle English Debate Poetry and the Aesthetics of Irresolution*. Columbia, MO: University of Missouri Press.

Robertson, D.W., Jr (1946) 'A Note on the Classical Origin of "Circumstances" in the Medieval Confessional', *SP*, 43, 6–14.

——, (1947) 'The Cultural Tradition of *Handlyng Synne*', *Speculum*, 22, 162–85.

Robertson, Kellie (2006) *The Laborer's Two Bodies: Literary and Legal Productions in Britain, 1350–1550*, The New Middle Ages. New York: Palgrave Macmillan, 2006.

St Jacques, Raymond (1977) 'Langland's Bells of the Resurrection and the Easter Liturgy', *English Studies in Canada*, 3, 129–35.
Salter, Elizabeth (1963) *Piers Plowman: An Introduction*. Oxford: Blackwell.
Sandler, Lucy Freeman (2004) *The Lichtenthal Psalter and the Manuscript Patronage of the Bohun Family*. London and Turnhout: Brepols/Harvey Miller.
Saul, Nigel (1997) *Richard II*, Yale English Monarchs; repr. New Haven: Yale University Press, 1999.
Scanlon, Larry (2007) 'Personification and Penance', *YLS*, 21, 1–29.
Scase, Wendy (1989) *Piers Plowman and the New Anticlericalism*, Cambridge Studies in Medieval Literature, 4; repr. Cambridge: Cambridge University Press, 2007.
——, (1998) '"Strange and Wonderful Bills": Bill-Casting and Political Discourse in Late Medieval England', *New Medieval Literatures*, 2, 225–47.
——, (2007) *Literature and Complaint in England, 1272–1553*. Oxford: Oxford University Press.
Schmidt, A.V.C. (1982) 'Langland's "Book of Conscience" and Alanus de Insulis', *NQ*, 29 (227), 482–4.
——, (2000) 'Langland's Visions and Revisions', *YLS*, 14, 5–27.
Schroeder, Mary C. (1970) 'The Character of Conscience in *Piers Plowman*', *SP*, 67, 13–30.
Selzer, John L. (1980) 'Topical Allegory in *Piers Plowman*: Lady Meed's B-Text Debate with Conscience', *PQ*, 59, 257–67.
Simpson, James (1985) 'Spiritual and Earthly Nobility in *Piers Plowman*', *NM*, 86, 467–81.
——, (1986a) 'From Reason to Affective Knowledge: Modes of Thought and Poetic Form in *Piers Plowman*', *Medium Ævum*, 55, 1–23.
——, (1986b) 'The Role of *Scientia* in *Piers Plowman*', in *Medieval English Religious and Ethical Literature: Essays in Honour of G. H. Russell*, ed. Gregory Kratzmann and James Simpson. Cambridge: Brewer, pp. 49–65.
——, (1986c) 'The Transformation of Meaning: A Figure of Thought in *Piers Plowman*, *RES* n.s. 37, 161–83.
——, (2007) *Piers Plowman: An Introduction*, 2nd rev. edn, Exeter Medieval Texts and Studies. Exeter: University of Exeter Press.
Smith, D. Vance (1994) 'The Labors of Reward: Meed, Mercede, and the Beginning of Salvation', *YLS*, 8, 127–54.
——, (2001) *The Book of the Incipit: Beginnings in the Fourteenth Century*, Medieval Cultures, 28. Minneapolis: University of Minnesota Press.
Somerset, Fiona (1998) *Clerical Discourse and Lay Audience in Late Medieval England*, Cambridge Studies in Medieval Literature. Cambridge: Cambridge University Press.
——, (2005) '"Al þe comonys with o voys atonys": Multilingual Latin and Vernacular Voice in *Piers Plowman*', *YLS*, 19, 107–36.
Spearing, A.C. (1972) 'The Art of Preaching and *Piers Plowman*', in *Criticism and Medieval Poetry*, 2nd edn. London: Arnold, pp. 107–34.
——, (2005) *Textual Subjectivity: The Encoding of Subjectivity in Medieval Narratives and Lyrics*. Oxford: Oxford University Press.

Spencer, H. Leith (1993) *English Preaching in the Late Middle Ages*. Oxford: Clarendon.
Staley, Lynn (2006) 'The Penitential Psalms and Vernacular Theology', *ELN*, 44, 113–20.
Steiner, Emily (2003) *Documentary Culture and the Making of Medieval English Literature*, Cambridge Studies in Medieval Literature. Cambridge: Cambridge University Press.
Stokes, Myra (1984) *Justice and Mercy in Piers Plowman: A Reading of the B Text Visio*. London and Canberra: Croom Helm.
Sutherland, Annie (2005) '*The Chastising of God's Children*: A Neglected Text', in *Text and Controversy from Wyclif to Bale: Essays in Honour of Anne Hudson*, ed. Helen Barr and Ann M. Hutchison, Medieval Church Studies, 4. Turnhout: Brepols, pp. 353–73.
Szittya, Penn R. (1986) *The Antifraternal Tradition in Medieval Literature*. Princeton, NJ: Princeton University Press.
Thurot, Charles (1869) *Extraits de divers manuscrits latins pour servir à l'histoire des doctrines grammaticales au moyen âge*; repr. Frankfurt: Minerva, 1964.
Tolmie, Sarah (2006) 'Langland, Wittgenstein, and the End of Language'. *YLS*, 20, 115–39.
Trigg, Stephanie (1998) 'The Traffic in Medieval Women: Alice Perrers, Feminist Criticism and *Piers Plowman*', *YLS*, 12, 5–29.
Turville-Petre, Thorlac (1977) Review of *Piers Plowman: The B Version*, ed. George Kane and E. Talbot Donaldson, *Studia Neophilologica*, 49, 153–5.
——, (2006) Review of *The Penn Commentary on Piers Plowman, I*, by Andrew Galloway, *YLS*, 20, 231–4.
Vaughan, Míċeál F., ed. (1993) *Suche Werkis to Werche: Essays on Piers Plowman In Honor of David C. Fowler*. East Lansing, MI: Colleagues Press, 1993.
——, (2002) Response to Traugott Lawler, 'The Secular Clergy in *Piers Plowman*', *YLS*, 16, 118–29.
Wagner, Anthony Richard (1939) *Heralds and Heraldry in the Middle Ages: An Inquiry into the Growth of the Armorial Function of Heralds*. London: Oxford University Press.
Walsh, Katherine (1981) *A Fourteenth-Century Scholar and Primate: Richard FitzRalph in Oxford, Avignon, and Armagh*. Oxford: Clarendon.
Warner, Lawrence (2002) 'The Ur-B *Piers Plowman* and the Earliest Production of C and B', *YLS*, 16, 3–39.
——, (2007) 'The Ending, and End, of *Piers Plowman* B: The C-version origins of the final two passus', *Medium Ævum*, 76, 225–50.
Watson, Nicholas (2007) '*Piers Plowman*, Pastoral Theology, and Spiritual Perfectionism: Hawkyn's Cloak and Patience's *Pater Noster*', *YLS*, 21, 83–118.
Weldon, James F.G. (1989) 'Gesture of Perception: the Pattern of Kneeling in *Piers Plowman* B.18–19', *YLS*, 3, 49–66.
Wenzel, Siegfried (1967) *The Sin of Sloth: Acedia in Medieval Thought and Literature*. Chapel Hill, NC: University of North Carolina Press.
——, (1986) *Preachers, Poets, and the Early English Lyric*. Princeton, NJ: Princeton University Press.

Wenzel, Siegfried (1988) 'Medieval Sermons', in *A Companion to Piers Plowman*, ed. John A. Alford. Berkeley and Los Angeles: University of California Press, pp. 155–72.

Whitworth, Charles W., Jr. (1972) 'Changes in the Roles of Reason and Conscience in the Revisions of *Piers Plowman*', *NQ*, 19 (217), 4–7.

Williams, Arnold (1960) 'Relations Between the Mendicant Friars and the Regular Clergy in England in the later Fourteenth Century', *Annuale Mediaevale*, 1, 22–95.

Wilson, Edward (1983) 'Langland's "Book of Conscience": Two Middle English Analogues and Another Possible Latin Source', *NQ*, 30 (228), 387–9.

Wittig, Joseph S. (1972) '*Piers Plowman* B, passus IX-XII: Elements in the Design of the Inward Journey', *Traditio*, 28, 211–80.

——, (2001) *Piers Plowman: Concordance*. London and New York: Athlone Press.

Wittig, Susan (1978) *Stylistic and narrative structures in the Middle English romances*. Austin: University of Texas Press.

Wood, Sarah (2007) 'Ecce Rex: *Piers Plowman* B.19.1–212 and Its Contexts', *YLS*, 21, 31–56.

Woolf, Rosemary (1962) 'The Theme of Christ the Lover-Knight in Medieval English Literature', *RES*, n.s. 13, 1–16.

Workman, Herbert B. (1926), *John Wyclif: A Study of the English Medieval Church*, 2 vols. Oxford: Clarendon.

Wright, Nicholas (1998) *Knights and Peasants: The Hundred Years War in the French Countryside*. Woodbridge: Boydell.

Wylie, James Hamilton (1884–94) *History of England under Henry the Fourth*, 2 vols. London: Longman.

Yunck, John A. (1963) *The Lineage of Lady Meed: The Development of Mediaeval Venality Satire*, University of Notre Dame Publications in Mediaeval Studies, 17. Notre Dame, IN: University of Notre Dame Press.

Zeeman, Nicolette (2006) *Piers Plowman and the Medieval Discourse of Desire*, Cambridge Studies in Medieval Literature. Cambridge: Cambridge University Press.

——, (2008) 'Tales of Piers and Perceval: *Piers Plowman* and the Grail Romances', *YLS*, 22, 199–236.

Index

Abelard, Peter 57
Abraham, *see* Faith
academic knowledge 46–8, 56–9, 64–5; *see also* Clergy
Accedence 115–16
accord (grammatical) 115–16, 126, 129
Adams, Robert xi, 114, 117, 157
adultery 29–30, 94; *see also* lechery
Aers, David 3, 5, 12, 105
affective knowledge 46–8
affinity, *see* retinues
Alford, John 3, 17, 109–10, 118, 124–5
allegory, *see* personification
alliterative poetry, diction of 71–2
Amends/amends 25, 42, 71, 118
Ancrene Riwle 50
Anima 4
Anonimalle Chronicle 162
Antichrist 103
antimendicant satire 87, 97; *see also* friars
Appleton, William 96, 103
Aquinas, Thomas 2–4
Augustine, *In Iohannis evangelium tractatus* 120
Augustinian order, of friars 92; *see also* friars

Bache, Alexander 92, 98
Baddby, William 103
Baldwin, Anna 22, 84–5, 138
Bannockburn, battle of (1314) 29
banquet, *see* feasting
Barking Abbey 52 n.23, 53
Barney, Stephen 77, 81–2, 84, 90, 151–3, 156
Barthes, Roland, *S/Z* 146
Bede, *In epistolas septem catholicas* 120
Bennett, J. A. W. 21, 82
Berkeley, Thomas, *see* Trevisa, John
Bernard of Clairvaux 57
Beverley, John 33
biblical narrative 70, 72, 85
bills 35, 37
Bloomfield, Morton 3 n.7, 80
Bohun family 92
Bonaventure 2, 58
The Book of Vices and Virtues 52 n.22
Brewer, Charlotte 88
Brinton, Thomas 83, 85, 94, 123–4, 164

Bromyard, John, *Summa praedicantium* 49, 85, 125
Brugge, Walter 162–3, 165–6
Bury, Adam 37
Buxhill, Alan 34

Cargill, Oscar 20, 32
Carmelite order:
  anti-Wycliffitism of 97
  patronage of 92
Chancery:
  clerks 162
  court of 5, 26
character, *see* personification
Charleton, Thomas 162
The Chastising of God's Children 47, 52, 54–5
Chaucer, Geoffrey:
  The Parson's Tale 52 n.22
  'Truth' 33–4
Christ:
  as knight, king and conqueror 42, 71–4, 76, 77 n.31, 80–3, 85, 139
  as leader of retinue 42, 71, 79, 103
  names of 76–9
  see also crucifixion; harrowing of hell; knights, knighthood; kings, kingship
Clanvowe, John, *The Two Ways* 50
The Cleansing of Man's Soul 47, 53–8, 61, 63, 65–7, 164
Clergy/clergy:
  as academic knowledge 46–8, 50–1, 58, 64–5
  and administration of the sacraments 68–9, 136
  called upon by Conscience 68, 136–7
  inadequacy of 38 n.60, 55, 61, 67–8, 108, 110–11, 136–8, 163
  parting from Conscience 67–8, 136, 154
  as pastoral practice 67–8, 136
  'prophecy' of 152–3
  reform of 67–8, 136
  see also pastoral literature
Clopper, Lawrence 3 n.10, 62, 103–5
Cole, Andrew 50
Commons, the 37, 40, 162; *see also* parliament

confession 16–17, 45, 46 n.4, 54, 62;
        see also Contrition/contrition;
        friars; penance
Conscience/conscience:
    as distinct from *scientia* 58
    Dominican view of 2–4
    fallibility of 3, 104 n.78, 165
    Franciscan view of 2
    in legal discourse 4, 26–7
    monastic conception of 3 n.7
    in *Piers Plowman* [in order of
        chronology within the poem]:
        disappearances of 9, 45, 70
        'education' of 2, 8–9, 146
        idealism of 165
        memory of 139–40, 144, 146
        misogyny of 28, 131
        as member of court faction 32,
            90, 95
        as king's knight 18, 20, 24–5, 27–8,
            43, 71, 79, 102
        as legal witness 4 n.18, 26, 35, 39,
            71, 107, 111–12
        as king's justice 9, 40, 111, 147
        as preacher 15–16, 18–19, 43, 72,
            112, 119, 125
        as teacher and disciple of Piers
            46, 64
        as accuser of sins 43, 62 n.58,
            69, 88, 104
        as virtuous layman 47, 51,
            59, 61
        as practical or applied knowledge
            58, 165
        as penitential knight 43, 61
        as pilgrim 9, 50, 61
        as herald 43, 71
        as God's clerk 4–5
        as lord 43, 59, 88, 104
        as constable of Unity 69, 88
    in scholastic discourse 2–3, 20, 51
    in vernacular literature 26, 57, 164
    see also self-knowledge; synderesis
Constantine, donation of 105, 152
contemporary conditions, satire on 70;
        see also Piers Plowman, as 'topical'
        poem
Contrition/contrition 43, 46 n.4,
        62 n.58, 63 n.61, 68, 88, 104
correction, *see* counsel
counsel 50, 52–4, 61–4, 68, 82, 107–8,
        119, 133
court 33, 45, 94; *see also* slander
creed, commentaries on 120–2
crucifixion, the 17, 70, 73
Cursor Mundi 52, 78

Dagworth, Nicholas 33
Daniel, Henry 96
Davies, Rees 165–6
debate mode 23–9, 34, 39–41, 45, 107,
        126, 128, 162; *see also* invective;
        slander
defamation 38–40
Disse, Walter 103
Doctor of Divinity 49, 58–61, 67,
        96, 126–7
Dominican order:
    patronage of 92
    satire against 96
    see also friars; Jordan, William;
        Daniel, Henry
Donaldson, E. Talbot 83, 138; *see also*
        Piers Plowman, editions of
Donatus, *Ars minor* 115
Dowel 48, 63, 66–7, 74–5, 144–5; *see also*
        grammar; Piers Plowman
Dread 27
Dunning, T. P. 2

Easter 17
Edmund of Abingdon, *Speculum ecclesie*
        56
Edward II 32; *see also* Gaveston, Piers
Edward III 20, 29, 31, 92, 95, 97, 103
Edward, the Black Prince 20, 31
etymologies, Latin 84–5, 164; *see also*
        grammar
Eulogium historiarum sive temporis 98

Faith 71
Fasciculi zizaniorum 97; *see also* Carmelite
        order
Fasciculus morum 78 n.33
feasting 59–61
Felton, John, *Sermones dominicales* 80–1
Felton, Sibyl 53
'Fifty Heresies and Errors of Friars'
        92–3
FitzRalph, Richard 92, 97, 100
The Fyve Wittes 50
Fletcher, Alan 77
flytyng, *see* invective
Floretum, the 77 n.32, 123
'founding of the commonwealth' 7,
        82–6, 118; *see also* kings,
        kingship
Four Daughters of God 81
Fourth Lateran Council (1215) 50, 61
Franciscan order 98; *see also* friars
Franciscan Rule, Wycliffite
        commentary on 93
Frank, Robert Worth 6–7

Index

Friar Flatterer 87–8, 90, 93, 96–8, 103, 105, 119
friars:
  as confessors 91–3, 103
  copes 103–4
  failure to insist upon restitution 60–1, 89 n.10, 94, 111
  'fyndyng' for 88, 90, 100, 104–5, 148–9, 151–3
  and flattery 59, 93
  as go–betweens 94
  influence of 98
  licensing of 91
  as magicians 95–6, 98
  'numberless' proliferation of 101–2
  and pastoral work 62, 68, 136–7
  and poverty 87, 103
  as physicians 96–7
  in retinues of the great 43, 88, 90–4, 103
  royal patronage of 92, 103
  and women 94, 97
  in Wycliffite writings 92–4, 97, 105–6
  see also retinues; penance
Friedman, John 96

Galloway, Andrew 1, 3–4, 7, 10, 25, 27, 31, 49, 85, 107, 109, 111, 119, 121, 125–6, 135–6, 138, 150, 153–6, 164
Gaveston, Piers 36
Giancarlo, Matthew 22
Gillespie, Vincent 51
Ginsberg, Warren 8, 10–11
Given–Wilson, Chris 98
Good Parliament (1376) 20–1, 35, 94, 95, 102, 123, 164
government 71, 124, 130, 161; *see also* law
Grace/grace 68
grammar:
  in *Piers Plowman* B text 112, 126, 128, 140, 142–6
  in *Piers Plowman* C text 113–18, 140, 142–6
  in sermons 124–5
  as universal language 126, 132
  see also infinite; regimen; relation; accord
Grandisson, John, Bishop of Exeter 91
Green, Richard Firth 94, 96
Greyfriars church 92
Griffiths, Lavinia 8

handbooks for priests, *see* pastoral literature
Hanna, Ralph 23–4, 27, 50, 82, 104, 133, 136, 150, 162
harrowing of hell 17, 70, 73
Harwood, Britton 3, 25, 71, 88
Haukin 9–10, 62, 65–6, 70, 125, 127–8, 140, 142
Helias, Peter, *Summa on Priscianus Minor* 144
Hende Speche 99, 104; *see also* lords
Henry IV 98
Henry V 98
Hewitt, H. J. 102
Higgs, Elton 8–9, 12, 14, 44
Holy Church 116, 122, 130–1, 154
homiletic discourse, *see* sermons
Hophni and Phineas, exemplum concerning 107–12, 119, 135–6; *see also* mercy; Clergy; counsel
Hopkins, Andrea 61
Hort, Greta 2–3
household 42, 59–60, 104; *see also* retinues
'How Religious Men Should Keep Certain Articles' 94, 97
Hugh of St Victor 57
Hundred Years' War, *see* war
Hunger 45, 142
Huppé, Bernard 20–1

idolatry 108
illegitimacy 30
Ymaginatif 47, 60, 68, 164 n.14
impeachment 37–8; *see also* notoriety
infinite, grammatical term 48, 66, 144–5; *see also* Dowel
invective 28–9, 41; *see also* slander
Isidore of Seville, *Etymologies* 4

Jacob's Well 52 n.22
Jacobus de Voragine, *Sermones* 78–9, 81
Jenkins, Priscilla, *see* Martin, Priscilla
Jerome, *Commentary on Ezekiel* 2
Johannes Balbus, *Catholicon* 122, 144 n.22
John of Gaunt, Duke of Lancaster 21, 29–31, 33–4, 38, 92, 95–8, 103
Jordan, William 96; *see also* Doctor of Divinity
justice 42, 45, 81–3, 110, 139; *see also* law
Justice, Stephen 5

Kane, George 28, 88; *see also Piers Plowman*, editions of
Kaske, R. E. 144

Kennedy, Kathleen 21
Kentwood, John 96
Kynde Wit 46–7
kings, kingship 12, 26, 70–1, 79, 82–6, 118–19, 138–9, 155–6
Kipling, Gordon 84
Kirk, Elizabeth 19
Kirkby, Margaret 52
knights, knighthood 12, 45, 59, 70–1, 79

labour 45–6, 66, 127, 142, 147; *see also* Statute of Labourers
Langland, William:
  ideals of 165
  knowledge of scholastic theology 5 n.21, 164
  memory, used when revising 16, 19, 138–9, 145–6, 149
  political views of 138
  semi–Pelagianism of 113 n.16, 117
  see also Piers Plowman
Latimer, John 94–5
Latimer, William 29, 37–8
Latin 116, 131–2; *see also* etymologies; grammar
law 3, 5, 26, 34, 41, 46, 71–2, 74, 89, 161–2
Lawler, Traugott 8, 48, 58, 61, 67, 99, 104, 111
Lawton, David 2, 5, 7, 12, 161
lay readers 47, 50–8, 66–7, 125–6, 136
'Of the Leaven of Pharisees' 92, 94, 97
lechery 30, 33, 91, 93–4; *see also* friars
Sire leef–to–lyue–in–lecherie 90, 92, 94, 97, 119, 163
Lees, Clare 21
Lewte 154–6
libels 30, 38; *see also* petitions
Liber de spiritu et anima 4
liveries 101, 103–4; *see also* retinues; household
London, city of 30
lords 42, 60, 88, 90–1, 94, 162, 163; *see also* retinues
Love/love 48–9, 55, 57, 122, 155
Lyons, Richard 33

Magi, gifts of 79–82, 139
Maidstone, Richard 61 n.54
maintenance 21–2, 26–7, 90, 100, 105, 107, 109, 111
Manly, J. M. 150
Marcett, Mildred 96
de la Mare, John 96
de la Mare, Peter 21

Martin, Priscilla 143–4, 160
Meed/meed:
  and Alice Perrers 20–2, 95
  attack on Conscience 24–5, 27–8, 30–1, 88
  charges against 35–7
  and corruption of law 20, 37, 40–1, 71, 89, 108, 111
  and friar–confessor 32–3, 89–91, 93–5, 104–5
  parentage of 22, 25, 30, 118
  promiscuity of 24, 28, 30, 40, 101, 117, 129
  proposed marriage to Conscience 117, 165
  as reader 28, 131
  and regicide 30–1
  and her retinue 22, 25, 27, 60–1, 68, 71–2, 87–8, 90, 99, 154
  self–defence of 38–9
  two kinds of 25–6, 111–12
  utility of 23–4, 41–2
  see also amends; maintenance; mercy; reward
Memoriale credencium 47, 51–2, 54, 56
mercy 41–3, 45, 61, 68, 81–3, 87, 119, 139
Middleton, Anne 9, 11, 145, 147, 150, 158, 163–5
Minot, Laurence 28–9
minstrels, minstrelsy 59–60, 70, 79; *see also* feasting
Mirk, John, *Festial* 75, 80 n.40
Morgan, Gerald 2–3
Mortimers, Earls of March:
  Edmund, third Earl 21
  Mortimer estates 162, 165

Need 103; *see also* friars
Neville, John 102
Nicholas de Aquavilla 76
Nine Worthies 72
The Northern Homily Cycle 72 n.12, 78 n.33
notoriety 37–8; *see also* bills
The N–Town Play 80 n.40, n.42

Ordinance of the Justices (1346) 26–7, 99, 109–10
Overstreet, Samuel 116, 121–2
The Owl and the Nightingale 24, 28–9, 39
Owst, G. R. 73

Pantin, W. A. 91
parataxis 7, 10–11

Index

pardons 71, 74, 81; *see also* Piers Plowman
The Parlement of the Thre Ages 72
parliament 22, 36; *see also* Good Parliament; Rolls of Parliament; petitions
pastoral literature 52, 55, 62
   mnemonic devices in 63–4
   and sins of the tongue 34 n.48
   see also lay readers; penance
Patience 8–9, 47–9, 58, 61–2, 64–5, 70, 87, 125–8, 140–4
'patient poverty' 65, 70, 87, 127–8, 146–9
Patrington, Stephen 98
patronage, *see* friars
Peace 7, 27, 35, 42, 99
Pearsall, Derek 78, 120, 143
Peasants' Revolt (1381) 96–7
Pecham, John, Archbishop of Canterbury 50, 56, 67 n.68
penance:
   corruption of 68, 89, 111
   as first stage in pursuit of perfection 55–6, 65–6
   friars as practitioners of 87
   as merriment 60
   self-imposed 62
   three parts of 44, 46 n.4, 62–3, 66
   in vernacular texts 47, 51–8, 61, 67
   see also Dowel; lay readers; 'patient poverty'
Sire *Penetrans domos* 87, 91, 96–7
penitential psalms 59–61
Perrers, Alice 20–2, 32–4, 95–7; *see also* Meed
personification 1–2, 5–14, 22, 25, 27, 140, 142, 146, 160; *see also* subjectivity
Peter Lombard, *Sententiarum* 120–2
petitions 35–6, 38–9; *see also* bills
Piers Plowman:
   on Dowel 48, 66, 140, 144
   entrance into poem of 7
   as focus for development of *Piers Plowman* 12
   and pardon from Christ 42, 71, 74
   and ploughing of the half-acre 45, 142
   in seventh vision 16
   'spiritualisation' of 9
   as student of Conscience 46, 49, 64
   and tearing of the pardon 9, 41–2, 46, 60–2, 65–6, 127–8, 131
   as vernacular teacher 46–8, 50–1, 62, 64, 68–9
   see also 'patient poverty'

Piers Plowman:
   audience of 5, 13, 130 n.66, 161–5
   authorship of xii, 150, 151 n.33
   biographical time in 146, 148
   B-text archetype of xi–xii
   composition of 7, 11, 13–14, 18, 134–5, 161
   dating of 20–1, 96–7
   digressions in 73
   discontinuity of 2, 10
   editions of:
      Kane, A text xi, 157
      Kane and Donaldson, B text xi–xii, 157
      Russell and Kane, C text 157
      parallel-text presentation in 150–1, 154, 156–9
      as representations of compositional process 149–51
      Schmidt, Parallel-text 150, 159
      Skeat, Parallel-text 150, 159
   episodic form of 10–11, 13, 146
   manuscripts of:
      Oxford, Bodleian Library, MS Bodley 851 88–9, 104
      Oxford, Bodleian Library, MS Douce 104 96
      San Marino, Huntington Library MS HM 114 153
      scribal corruption in as stimulus to revision 158
   multiple discourses of 12–14
   narrative form of 10–12
   narrator of, *see* Will
   Penn Commentary on 150–7
   'Platonic idea' of 153
   as quest 15, 145
   reiterations in 11–12, 69, 146
   retrospective reading of 7, 10–11
   and romance narrative 11
   sequential reading of 19, 135, 139, 151, 158–9
   and Shakespearean drama 11
   as 'topical' poem 15, 20–1, 70
   type scenes 11–12, 43, 142, 148
   and typology 11
   versions of xii, 5 n.21, 13–14, 18–19, 107, 134, 138, 140, 142, 146, 148–59
   vocabulary of 4–5
   see also alliterative poetry, diction of; biblical narrative; romance, penitential

Index

pilgrimage 9, 50, 61–2, 69, 144–5, 147, 165; *see also Piers Plowman*, as quest
Pleshey Castle, *see* Bohun family
ploughing 11, 45, 86; *see also* Piers Plowman
The Prick of Conscience 26, 164
priest, office of 54, 64; *see also* Clergy; pastoral literature
The Prymer or Lay Folks' Prayer Book 61 n.54
Priscian, *Institutiones grammaticae* 143, 145
provisors 35–6

Radulphus Brito 116
Raymund de Peniafort, *Summa de poenitentia et matrimonio* 54, 63–4
Reason/reason 3–4, 16, 18, 40–2, 56, 109, 136, 147–8, 152–3; *see also* law
Reed, Thomas 23, 25, 28, 34, 39, 162
regicide 31–2
regimen, in grammar 49, 143–5; *see also* government
relation, grammatical 113, 115–17, 120, 143–5
Repentance 16–17, 77
restitution, *see* friars
retinues 42–3, 45, 60, 71, 79, 87–8, 99–1, 103–6; *see also* maintenance
reward:
    in *Piers Plowman* B text 24–6, 41, 43, 66, 112–13, 130–1, 140–2
    in *Piers Plowman* C text 113–18, 124, 131, 140–2
    see also grammar
Richard II 31–2, 82–5, 92, 95, 98, 100
Richard of St Victor 57
riddles 48–9, 125–6; *see also* grammar
Rigg, George 88
Robert of Basevorn, *Forma praedicandi* 74–5, 77, 84–5, 124
Robert the Robber 17
Rolle, Richard, *The Form of Living* 47, 52–6, 61
Rolls of Parliament 32–7, 110
romance, penitential 61
Rosarium theologie 78 n.33
Ross, Woodburn 76–7
royal entries 84–5
royal virtues, *see* kings, kingship
Rushook, Thomas 92

Salter, Elizabeth 73
Samuel and Saul, exemplum of 119; *see also* mercy

satisfaction 46 n.4, 54–5, 62; *see also* penance
Scanlon, Larry 6 n.27, 160
Scase, Wendy 38, 105, 136
Schmidt, Carl 158; *see also Piers Plowman*, editions of
Schroeder, Mary 2 n.2
Scripture 46
Skeat, Walter 4 n.14, 20, 109, 113, 126; *see also Piers Plowman*, editions of
self-knowledge 57–8
Selzer, John 21
sermons:
    for Advent 72, 74–5, 79–81, 84–5
    comparatives in 75, 124
    concluding prayers in 76
    guides to composition of 72, 74
    'modern' or 'scholastic' type 74, 77
    in *Piers Plowman* 15–17, 45, 72–3, 77, 119–20, 122–6
    questions in 76–7
    subjects of 77–82
    'theme' of 74
    triadic structure of 73–5
    see also grammar; Robert of Basevorn
'On the Seven Deadly Sins' 94
sins, seven deadly 3, 15, 52–3, 142
Simpson, James 57
Siward, William 103
slander 28–30, 33–4, 39, 41, 95; *see also* defamation; libels; notoriety
Smith, Vance 143
Somerset, Fiona 50–1, 55–6, 132
Sothness 33–4, 154
Spearing, A. C. 10, 73
Speculum sacerdotale 74–5, 80
Statute of Labourers:
    of 1349 129
    of 1388 129 n.64, 147
Stokes, Myra 32, 39, 89
Stow, John, *Survey of London* 92 n.24
Study 7, 46, 59, 67–8, 93
Stury, Richard 29, 31–2
subjectivity, in medieval texts 10, 12
Super cathedram (papal bull, 1300) 91
supersedeas, writ of 110
synderesis 2–3
Szittya, Penn 87, 97

ten commandments 62
Theology 25, 30, 118
Thought 46
The Three Kings of Cologne 80
The Towneley Plays 80 n.40

Index

Trevisa, John, *Dialogus inter militem et clericum* 132
Trigg, Stephanie 21
Truth 41, 81, 142
truth–telling, *see* Lewte
Turville–Petre, Thorlac xi–xii, 156–7

Unity 43, 68, 86–7, 92, 153 n.38
Usk, Adam 162

la Vache, Philip 33
vagrancy 105; *see also* Statute of Labourers
Vaughan, Míčeál 153

Walsingham, Thomas:
　Chronicon Angliae 20
　St Alban's Chronicle 22–3, 29–32, 83–4, 95–8
Waleys, Thomas, *De modo componendi sermones* 74
Walwayn, John, *Vita Edwardi Secundi* 36–7
Wales 98, 165
war:
　organisation of 100–1
　pillaging in 28, 101–3
Waster (in *Piers Plowman*) 86
Westminster 21, 89, 162
Westminster Chronicle 32 n.44, 92
Whitworth, Charles 5 n.21, 135

Will/will:
　academic pretensions of 77
　apologia of, in *Piers Plowman* C text 18, 147–9
　and despair 46
　as grammatical subject 12
　instructed by Conscience 16–18, 71
　and Patience 58, 140, 147
　and 'patient poverty' 65, 70, 147–9
　reform of 56
　as tournament spectator 71
　as *voluntas* 2, 6
William of Pagula, *Oculus sacerdotis* 52, 163
William of St Amour 87
Williams, Arnold 91
Willoughby, Richard, Chief Justice of King's Bench 37
Windsor, William 33
Wynnere and Wastoure 13, 15, 23–5, 28–9, 70
Wit 46
Wittig, Joseph 4, 159
Wrong 27, 41, 61, 68, 71, 87, 99
Wyclif, John 97, 98 n.52
　Expositio textus Matthei xxiii, 93
　De Ordinacione Fratrum 95
　Sermones 92–3
Wycliffite bible 125

Zeeman, Nicolette 6–7